An A–Z of type designers

Yale University Press

Neil Macmillan

AN A–Z OF TYPE DESIGNERS

ESSAYS

Designers

INTRODUCTION

This book succeeds *Rookledge's International Handbook of Type Designers*, published in 1991. Its aim, as before, is to provide those interested in type and type design with illustrated biographies of type designers of influence, from the era of Gutenberg to the present day. Those featured have, through commitment, creativity and evolving means of production, enhanced this most basic element of communication. The original biographies from the handbook have been updated where necessary and abridged to allow space for illustrations. It has been my pleasure to fill in some gaps and to introduce many of the outstanding type designers who have come to the fore since the early 1990s.

As a result of the rapid development of digital technology since the early 1990s, typefaces now play a greater and much less anonymous role in everyday communication. Whilst previously the domain of designers and printers, typefaces as fonts have now become an essential part of working life. As new versions of operating systems are released, font menus expand accordingly, giving users greater options for typographic expression. On offer is a variety of letter forms that reflects the history of type development. Fonts inspired by Roman inscriptions, revered printing types of the eighteenth century, familiar twentieth-century classics, formal and casual scripts, as well as an abundance of novel contemporary designs are all simply accessed through a keyboard or mouse.

The computer technology which has enabled the type user also empowers today's type designers with manufacturing independence and unprecedented ease and speed of production. This technology is no substitute for the creative skills required to craft the dynamics that enable letter forms to combine with harmony into words and text. However, it is no surprise that we are witnessing a proliferation in the availability of display, and, to a lesser extent text, typefaces. The increasing prospect of market saturation may reduce the incentive to produce, threatening the quality of type development. The introduction, however, of more sophisticated, and more demanding, font formats may help to stem this threat.

It is obvious that the digital age offers both advantage and disadvantage. Long gone are the days when large and prosperous manufacturers of typesetting equipment supported type designers as vital suppliers of their proprietary fonts. These manufacturers of yesterday have become the major font distributors of today. To capitalize on their historical legacy, their marketing strategies result in discounted volume selling to purchasers and increased licensing to software manufacturers for inclusive distribution of fonts with products. The latter instance may, with cost effectiveness a dominant issue in the business world, lead to end users becoming reliant on the ever-increasing typeface libraries of those software manufacturers, whose influence on the future of type development will be considerable as new means of electronic communication are introduced.

Without doubt the changing market will challenge those prepared to commit to a career in type design. By far the most lucrative avenues open to type designers today are those offered by businesses seeking exclusivity of branding through custom typeface production. These are the opportunities that will fund and support both pioneering and emerging independent digital typefoundries in their efforts to survive the technologically unpredictable future.

Unlike earlier times, when their predecessors had some control over end use, the real fruition of type designers' ingenuity is now largely dependent on the ability and sensitivity of others. Thus, as increasingly sophisticated software applications encourage exciting, stimulating and innovative typography at best, and anarchic abuse of base values at worst, the role of the educator in typographic communication becomes more significant. It is positive, then, to note that many of the type designers featured in this book also teach the subject.

Several of the issues confronting the type designer today are informatively addressed in the essays by successful exponents of contemporary type design that open this book. Each of the contributions reflects the passion of the author for the subject, the same passion that inspired the earliest advances in written communication. This passion for letter forms, as my foray into the lives of type designers past and present has confirmed, is the common factor that drives the majority of those featured in this book in their quest to redefine the letters of our alphabet.

Neil Macmillan

Jonathan Barnbrook
FONTS AS SELF-EXPRESSION

Like most taboos that have become openly accepted (Eric Gill and canine companions take note), typeface design used to be something that was whispered about in hushed tones rather than discussed openly. Thankfully, things have changed in the past twenty years. Once an expensive, time-consuming process only undertaken after seemingly decades of pious study and self-flagellation, it has now become something which is available to all. Hey, today many people not in the design world now even know what a typeface IS. In doing so, typeface design has become open to all kinds of influences and now has a role to play as a valuable signifier of the current ideologies and fashions in design generally – typefaces can now last a moment or a century, be authoritarian or subversive, playful or serious.

As with many other areas of design, this change was because of the introduction of the Apple Macintosh. It did what technology should do – make something 'new' possible, and make a difficult, expensive process easy. Suddenly everybody could be a type designer ... 'OH NO', bellowed many established type designers in

exasperation, believing the world would collapse under a weight of illegibility, and society would no longer function. Nobody would be able to read a sign to get out of a building if it were on fire; all books would be useless. They were wrong: there has always been bad typography and good typography, it was just that there was going to be a lot more of it around us and it should be open for everybody to try. Instead, typeface design exploded into a massive creative force that became the lifeblood of contemporary graphic design for over a decade.

It was very exciting and one of those moments when, although we were not so conscious of it at the time, something new was happening and it had nothing to do with creativity as a commodity. Rather like the 1970s punk ethic of 'record a song and release a single', the late 1980s and early 1990s became a time when anybody could start a foundry and release their fonts. Yes, there was some terrible stuff, badly drawn modular fonts, 'new' fonts that were just Photoshop-filtered rip-offs, but in all that confusion there was some really good stuff too. Suddenly, boring, dusty old font design was

False Idol

FALSE IDOL

Expletive Script

EXPLETIVE SCRIPT

Melancholia

MELANCHOLIA

MORON

MORON

being directly influenced by contemporary philosophy. Postmodernism and deconstruction were being talked about, not just the Trajan Column or Hermann Zapf. People wanted to subvert type history, to include their own immediate environment in their work; the vernacular became an important influence, as was simple, schoolboy humour.

So that was then and this is now. The digital font industry has matured, and while everybody is still welcome to have a go, many have realized that there is little financial return for the effort, and actually, if you want to do the job properly, it still takes a good deal of time and knowledge to construct a font well. Instead of the punk ethic we have a lively, divergent scene where the newcomer and the experienced professional can release their own stuff for distribution. Even the old-timers who complained have realized that, like the CD revolution in music, it has enabled them to obtain the obscure and different. Cuts of typefaces or specific letter forms that were previously unavailable can now be used. They can even release their own work, directly controlling the craft and quality and terms on which it is presented to

people. What could be a more perfect scene for a means of self-expression?

Other unexpected things happened. Suddenly the name of the typeface also became incredibly important as a means of self-expression. In the past it seemed that typefaces were either named after a place, the designer, a hero, or were a kind of 'funny one-liner' that crassly explained the concept behind a font. Now they showed the 'attitude' of the designer – a place to intellectualize or preach to a very specific audience of other designers. Some people pushed it to the limit: my own naming of a font 'Manson' after Charles Manson, the serial killer, proved too much for some and it was subsequently changed to 'Mason' (highlighting very clearly the issue of the font name in relation to its usage). The name became somewhere to link poetry, concepts and contradictions of language with the concepts of abstract visual forms. Today there are so many fonts that the naming process has become more and more difficult, a similar dilemma to Internet domain naming. Will there be a point at which all of the single words in the dictionary have been used up for naming fonts?

Erik van Blokland
LETTERROR, OR THE GHOST IN THE MACHINE

So, being part of the generation that experienced this transition and made use of it to experiment with typeface design, the question I am most often asked today is: 'Why do you continue to design fonts? Surely there are enough already?' To these people I say it is exactly because type design is such a valid means of self-expression that I/we continue to do so. Somehow in those 26 funny shapes you can express the spirit of the age, the ever-changing state of language, subvert the whole of the design industry, turn a thousand years of history on its head or make a political statement. Most importantly, drawing and releasing a typeface means you have shaped a new voice that is uniquely yours with which to speak to the world on your own terms.

LettError started more or less in 1989 when I began working together with Just van Rossum. Gerrit Noordzij introduced us, pointing out that we were both interested in using computers in design. Later on we were both employed by Erik Spiekermann, who kept us locked in a room with computers and printers. At that time the big typefoundries were digitizing their libraries to PostScript, and economics determined that they took their main, important designs first.

Just and I had studied type design at the Royal Academy in The Hague and we shared an interest in computing and writing code. It followed naturally that we applied ourselves to programming some fonts and using the new tools to build new fonts. Experiments in combining code and font technology resulted in Beowolf (EvB & JvR) and BeoSans (JvR). A modified PostScript font program caused the letter forms in the font to change once they got to a printer. To us, these fonts proved that digital type was something completely different from any type technology invented before. Fonts were data, code, open to change, dynamic characteristics and new kinds of design. Later on, because of operating system versions,

Showing of the LettError BitPull fonts. Complex but entertaining, they are not so much fonts as building blocks for bitmaps. They come with a small program, BitPuller, which helps make them less complex.

Showing of the LettError RobotFonts. These are based on a bitmap font, Python Sans, which, through programmed filters, reinterprets bitmap shapes to create interesting, and possibly unexpected, results. 'It's design by remote control,' say the designers.

12

printer drivers, font formats and changing applications for type, the real random versions of Beowolf and BeoSans stopped working. But they had shown us a direction in combining type design, typography and engineering that we are still following. In type, technology and aesthetics become the same thing. Being able to work in both areas means that problems in one might find an answer in the other.

Goofing around with early versions of Photoshop, Illustrator, Streamline and Fontographer showed a 'path' from real-world examples of type to a PostScript font. We made a list of ideas which could benefit from this sampling: handwriting, rubber stamps, typewriters, stencil lettering – shapes familiar to everyone, but until then never produced as typefaces because of high production costs. We discovered that this had changed drastically and that these fonts were relatively easy to produce. Published by FontShop, FF Trixie, Hands, Instant Types and others became unexpectedly popular.

In the early 1990s, talking about the combination of code and aesthetics, of programming and type, was not easy. For many designers, working with a computer at all

was an expression of ultimate geekery, let alone trying to program it or alter the way it worked. But that has changed – virtually all designers (of all disciplines) work with computers. Mainstream applications have scripting layers and allow extensive automation and modification of the processes. Not that designers would think of themselves as programmers.

The LettError co-operation has always focused on leveraging some discovery, a new application, format, tool, a bit of code or any kind of idea into a new project. LettError projects always seem to define themselves and do not really like to be placed directly in the context of a client project. So Just and I decided pretty early on to avoid having a real company – which would force the co-operation into a situation where it presumably would not work. From a traditional design company's point of view that does not make much commercial sense, but LettError projects and ideas reliably find their way to some sort of commercial application anyway. LettError is the research. Work is a reason to use some of it.

Our emphasis on tool development through the years has led us to a more abstract involvement in type design.

Clive Bruton
EDUCATION: THE ANSWER TO FONT THEFT?

Just develops the FontTools Python toolkit, a library of code that allows access to OpenType and TrueType fonts. Together with Tal Leming we develop Robofab, another Python library for fonts and glyphs. Both projects are open source and are used widely in the type technology industry. All development and research in the end supports new design and ideas. And that's what keeps life interesting.

Some time ago I attended a design event in London that was showcasing the work of a prominent design group. I have to say, without a shadow of doubt, this was great design, and some of it was truly ground-breaking. One of the principals of this group talked us through the show and told us of the trials and tribulations involved.

While reviewing the work I noticed a typeface designed by someone of my acquaintance. I knew he would be pleased to learn how his work was being used by others, so, at the end of the session, I approached the design group principal and remarked that I would tell my friend, the type designer, how his face was used in their design. 'Oh, don't do that,' he said, 'I never know whether we've paid for our fonts or not.' A little taken aback by this admission, I asked what he meant. It was simple, he explained, they didn't really have strict controls on who could place fonts on their server and didn't have an IT department to double-check these things, so faces turned up that they hadn't bought licences for – whether that was through people sending them files to work on, or interns bringing files in with them. Though he wanted his company to have appropriate licensing, it wasn't always easy to keep track of such issues. Thus whatever appeared on the company's servers was considered 'usable' by the design team.

A few months ago I was visiting a postgraduate course, where a well-known type designer was showing his work to the students. A portion of this touched on the piracy endemic within the type business, in terms of the copying of designs by other companies, and the widespread disregard for the efforts of type designers in the design businesses that many of these students were, or would shortly be, working for. This was a good pitch, I thought: the students were postgraduate, so most had spent at least some time working in the industry, and they were on a course that centred around typography. They could go away and think about the issues raised, and perhaps think more carefully about the way they worked in the future.

As the session finished, one of the students came over and started chatting. I had expected a few questions would arise, but the one he asked threw me a little: 'When do you need to buy a licence for a font?' Not quite sure what he meant, I asked him for clarification. He explained that he was working on a freelance job, and asked if he needed to buy a licence for the typefaces he was using for that job. At this point I decided not to get into 'How did you come to have the face on your computer anyway?', simply saying that if he hadn't paid for the face, or it wasn't bundled with software or the operating system, then he should buy a licence. It was a case of professional ethics I told him, and he agreed.

When I later related both of these stories to a couple of my colleagues they were both somewhat shocked. One was a seasoned type designer, the other a fairly recent postgraduate student who was now working. The more senior said, 'It's just a matter of education, we need to reach out to these people,' and the other agreed. 'But,' I protested, 'the graphic designer has as much experience as you or I do, he knows it's wrong, and said as much. The student may be forgiven, but he's on a specialist typography course – surely someone tells them about such things at college?' In the end we agreed, no matter how much we went out into the world and evangelized, the vast majority of type users would slip through our fingers – even in the professional realm, which would be our main target. They would never understand their obligations to license fonts, they would never grasp the damage done by those cloning other people's designs, and their companies would probably never put in place systems to ensure that unlicensed fonts did not appear on their servers.

Perhaps it is the case that the foundries of the world are their own worst enemies. Close to twenty years after the introduction of digital type on the desktop we have no sophisticated encryption schemes, no copy protection and few organized efforts to tackle piracy. The changes in the business over a similar period have not helped either. Once the business of producing type for print was an industry of large companies, often with thousands of employees. Today the typical foundry is likely to be a single designer, producing his or her own faces for retail sale and custom work for corporate and design clients. A team of five or six would be considered a large enterprise. So, here we are, at the mercy of 'professional ethics', and everyone serving in the cyclical business of design knows it's feast or famine – at once

lavish print production and trying to save small sums by avoiding one's obligations for licensing. Perhaps all we can hope for is to capture a few with 'education'.

An A–Z of type designers should introduce you to the other side of type design, assign 'faces to faces', as it were, and humanize the designers. Here you'll find people who have contributed through the centuries to the literacy of the world. Some will have designed hundreds of typefaces, others just a few – faces you may never have seen, or ones that annoy you every time you see an advertising campaign. Perhaps, through their collective work, they can convince you of the value of type design, the cause of education will be furthered, and next time you use a font you'll check that you have paid for the licence.

John Downer
TYPEFACE REVIVALS

The art of reviving a typeface can be considered a form of portraiture. It is an attempt to depict a look and a feel, in order to convey a mood. It is, moreover, an effort to capture what is ultimately an indescribable essence, a certain character within, a spirit. A good typeface revival is ordinarily an exercise in honouring the past and paying homage to a typeface that once served a particular purpose. In various ways, of course, the act of replicating or reinterpreting an existing typeface likewise differs widely from painting a portrait of a person. Portraiture is primarily concerned with the objective of creating the likeness of a human being, not re-creating the likeness of a man-made form. However, similar kinds of interpretive skills are obviously needed by both a portrait artist and a typeface revivalist. Each must try to get 'in tune' with his or her subject and strive to understand the subject in a personal and sympathetic manner.

Naturally, an appreciation of the model is essential: to see the model as an organism – or to begin to think of it as one. A printing type is, curiously, somewhat like a biological system. It fosters movement on the page; it has rhythm and cadence; it breathes in a distinct space; it has a life of its own which is meant not to interfere with the message of the text. In a sense, a workable text typeface is closely akin to a living being. It doesn't just sit. It has an effect on the viewer and on the reader. It interacts. And it behaves in a way that its form can often betray. Doing a typeface revival is an effective way of coming to grips with the rationale, and the imagination, of the person who created the original. It is a way for a contemporary type designer to look back through the eyes of a predecessor – much as a contemporary portrait artist can look back to a moment in painting through the eyes of a portrait painter who lived and painted a long time ago. There is, remarkably, an affinity among artists, artisans and various practitioners of craft that often connects the present to the past.

Inevitably, historical types are reminiscent of golden eras in printing. From the late fifteenth century up to the late nineteenth century, the evolution of printing types had been generally progressive. Each new style had been based either on the styles which had immediately preceded it or on fresh concepts. Seldom did typefounders look back very far in history for their models.

Palatino by Hermann Zapf
A highly personal calligraphic
roman typeface; a rendition
nevertheless reminiscent of
a genre of historical printing
types that was briefly
favoured in northern Italy
in the late 1400s.

Iowan Old Style
by John Downer
Typographic influences
combine with vestiges of
American sign painting in this
contemporary homage to early
Venetian punch-cutting. The
face is not strictly Venetian
in character.

Vendetta by John Downer
A revival of the general
Venetian Old Style class
of types. Tribute is not paid
to one individual punch-cutter
or to a single printing type,
but rather to a definitive
historical structure.

MiniText by John Downer
An experimental humanist
type, digitally optimized for
6 point print on rough paper
stock. The axis of the letters
and the way they stand on the
baseline identify their historical
parentage.

Humanist

Humanist

Humanist

Humanist

Abrupt changes in style were rarely influenced by achievements of the distant past. The appetite for commercial revivals of early types came from a combination of factors: the technical means afforded by photography and the advances in type manufacturing that were brought about by pantographic punch-cutting and matrix engraving equipment; the rise of the professional typographic designer or layout artist who drew (as differentiated from an artistic compositor/printer who worked at the press); and a kind of popular antiquarian book connoisseurship, which caught on in America and Europe during the second part of the nineteenth century and the first part of the twentieth century. At the time, discerning typographers were keen to re-create the appearance of pages originally set in extinct historical types, and to do so, facsimile types were needed. One of the first notable instances of a typeface revival came as early as the 1860s, with the adaptation of the Fell types, which were originally cut by Dirk and Bartholomeus Voskens in Holland, and were purchased by Bishop John Fell for Oxford University Press in the 1670s. Three decades later, William Morris based his Golden Type on a much earlier historical font, Nicolas Jenson's seminal roman type of 1470.

Ever since, type revivals have remained viable. In today's world of digital typography, the recent past is being combed for models just as extensively as the ancient past was being combed for models a hundred years ago. No longer does a market for books that are designed intentionally to 'look old' drive the economy of type revivals. Times have changed. Portraits need no longer look like portraits, only like pictures. In general, type revivals are undertaken now not because typographers wish to create modern portraits of antiquarian books, but instead because users of type have no need to know the context of type revivals. For the majority of users, the exact historical context has become irrelevant. Old types can be reinterpreted and used for new projects, without regard for the design of the pages from which the model letter forms were derived. This disregard for provenance and specific usage is pervasive. A typeface revival today is unlike a typeface revival of a century ago; it can be offered to clients who are not necessarily concerned about using a re-creation exclusively

John Hudson
GLOBAL TEXT AND TYPE: A CONSIDERED SNAPSHOT

in a manner that resembles the original page design. It is simply more fashionable today to be anachronistic. It's accepted.

The twentieth-century writer Gertrude Stein posed numerous times to have her portrait painted by Pablo Picasso. According to legend, Picasso was never satisfied with his efforts and was never able to finish a single portrait in Stein's presence. Eventually, however, Picasso did manage to paint a portrait of Stein from memory. When Stein saw the painting, she protested, noting that she didn't look like the woman in the picture. Picasso is said to have replied, 'No, but you will.'

There are between four thousand and six thousand languages spoken in the world today, depending on how one defines the difference between a language and a dialect. As many as 90 per cent of these languages face possible or certain extinction in the next hundred years, a reduction in global cultural diversity of unprecedented scale, for language is the primary carrier of culture. In the words of the philosopher Rush Rhees, language is a record of ways of living that have meant something.

At the same time as so many languages are in decline, the very forces that drive them to extinction are consolidating the importance of several hundred dominant national, regional and trade languages. It is an irony that, as so many languages are dying, the development of new typeface designs for non-Latin writing systems represents the most significant growth area in the digital font business.

Type design has always had an international flavour. Expertise in design has necessarily been linked to technical and manufacturing knowledge, and in the past it has gravitated to traditional centres of the trade.

Throughout most of the history of type, the majority of fonts for non-Latin writing systems were designed and manufactured in Europe. Today, the designing and making of type is a distributed, global business, with international communications technology providing the means for co-operation between designers and technicians in different countries, and also generating new markets for their products.

The demand of people around the world to be able to read e-mail and web pages in their own scripts and languages has required major changes in text processing and font software. The principal tools of the Western 'desktop publishing revolution' of the 1980s – single-byte character sets and Type 1 PostScript fonts – are now seen clearly as a temporary measure, hopelessly insufficient to handle most of the world's writing systems. We are now in the middle of another larger but quieter revolution of internationalization, multi-byte text encoding and smart font formats.

The groundwork for this revolution began in the mid-1980s, as the desktop revolution went into full swing. The initial aim of what was to become the Unicode Standard was to standardize encoding of East Asian character sets in an efficient way by unifying the shared characters of Chinese, Japanese and Korean writing systems. It quickly became apparent that the principles employed could be applied to other writing systems, and that the single-byte (i.e. 8-bit) character sets and fonts limited to 256 characters were as inappropriate for even the Latin script, seen in its international entirety, as they obviously were for East Asian text. So Unicode was developed as a global text-encoding standard, assigning a unique identifier, or 'codepoint', to every character needed to encode text in all the world's scripts and languages.

Obviously, this is a massive task, and two decades after work on Unicode began there remains much to be done, especially in the encoding of historical scripts. Today, however, almost all of the world's current writing systems are now encoded in Unicode, including more than 80,000 East Asian characters, plus specialist characters for science, mathematics and linguistics.

At the core of Unicode is the distinction between characters and glyphs. The latter is a new term for many in the type business, since we have largely inherited a

4 characters	1 glyph	2 glyphs	3 glyphs	4 glyphs
offi	*offi*	*offi*	*offi*	*offi*
		offi	*offi*	
		offi	*offi*	

terminology from manual and mechanical typesetting systems in which a character was understood as synonymous with a 'sort', i.e. a piece of metal or other delivery medium for a particular typeform, regardless of whether that meant an individual letter or, for example, a ligature. In today's digital typography the relationship of the character to the typeform that appears on screen or in print is complex, and requires a distinction to be made between the encoded entity (the character) stored in the memory of the computer, and how that entity is displayed (the glyph or glyphs). Text, in the dim mind of the computer, is a string of characters, of numeric codes that represent abstract semantic entities and properties such as directionality, case-mapping, etc. This text may be displayed in a variety of ways, across various media, using diverse arrangements of glyphs.

A good example of the distinction between a character and a glyph can be found in the case of ligatures. In the Caflisch Script Pro typeface by Robert Slimbach, the sequence of letters 'o f f i' is encoded as three distinct characters, but it may be displayed using one, two, three or four glyphs (see above).

The relationship of the 'plain text' encoding of Unicode characters and their display as 'rich', i.e. formatted, text is the domain of text layout engines and fonts. Text layout engines are character-handling and display software, which may be resident at the operating system level or in individual applications. Examples of these include Apple's ATSUI (Apple Text Services for Unicode Imaging) and Microsoft's Uniscribe (Unicode Text Processor) at the system level, and the Adobe core text service, which is resident in recent versions of Adobe applications. These text engines interact in various ways with fonts. The assignment of responsibilities to text engines and to fonts depends on the writing system used as well as the philosophy of the particular text-display architecture.

There are three font formats of note in terms of Unicode text and multilingual typography: OpenType, AAT and Graphite. Of these, OpenType is by far the most widely supported and important, but it is useful to consider the others in so far as they illustrate different philosophies, and because they may be useful in particular circumstances. All three of these formats exploit the extensibility of the TrueType sfnt font structure: a series of indexed tables, for which new tables can be defined with minimal impact on existing data. All three are classified as 'smart font' formats; that is, they can contain glyph-processing intelligence to affect ligature and other substitutions and/or dynamic glyph positioning. As extensions of the TrueType format, they do not suffer from the inadequate 256-character limitation of 8-bit formats such as Adobe's Type 1 format; each font can contain up to 65,536 glyphs, mapped to an appropriate number of Unicode characters.

The AAT (Apple Advanced Typography) font format is an extension of Apple's original TrueType format. AAT began life in Apple's short-lived Quickdraw GX graphics system of the mid-1990s and has survived to become a likely permanent feature of the Mac OS, even though relatively few applications or fonts take advantage of it. Central to the AAT format philosophy is the idea that the font contains virtually all the shaping intelligence necessary to a writing system. This makes the format powerful and flexible, since it requires no script- or language-specific knowledge from the generic text layout engine, but it has the considerable overhead of requiring font developers to handle not only typographic niceties but also basic script processing. This, combined with lack of support in graphical font development tools and Apple's overall small global market share (AAT glyph processing only works on Mac OS, and only in applications that make use of the core text engine – it is not, for instance, accessible in Mac versions of Adobe applications), has resulted in little interest from the type industry.

OpenType began life as TrueType Open, a Microsoft initiative providing support for complex scripts such as Arabic. In the late 1990s it was co-developed by Microsoft and Adobe to incorporate a wider range of typographic and language-shaping features (OpenType Layout), and to offer font developers a choice of whether or not to use TrueType or PostScript (CFF) outlines and hints (low-resolution rendering assistance), all within a common sfnt table structure. Unlike AAT, the text-processing philosophy of OpenType more equitably shares responsibility between the font and the text engine, with the latter performing most of the generic language shaping such as the character reordering for

بعض → ب ع ض	initial, medial and terminal forms
هبلا → هبلا	required ligatures
والامار سخ → والامار سخ	optional ligatures
تنتبتنتبتنتب → تنتبتنتبتنتب	contextual alternates assisting letter differentiation
١٤٢٥ ١٤٧ → ١٤٧ ١٤٢٥	contextual alternates positioned within enclosing signs
عبد بعض → عَبْدُ بَعْضٍ	mark-to-letter dynamic positioning
إِلَى كُتَّابِهِ → إِلَى كُتَّابِهِ	mark-to-mark dynamic positioning

22 Indic scripts and contextual analysis for Arabic. This approach has made OpenType much more attractive to font developers, as has Microsoft and Adobe's commitment to tool support and the incorporation of OpenType Layout support in popular font production programs such as FontLab and DTL FontMaster. The implementation of OpenType Layout in Microsoft's Office suite on Windows, the largest install base for multilingual text processing, and in Adobe's professional graphics applications on both Windows and Mac, has secured OpenType's position as the leading smart font format. The downside of the OpenType philosophy is that it is less flexible than AAT, since support for specific scripts, languages and typographic features is dependent on both font and text engine; font developers and users must wait on the arrival of operating system or application support, which is governed by the global strategic interest of large software companies.

Although it is not as widely supported as OpenType, the open-source Graphite format is worthy of mention. This format was developed by SIL International, a non-profit institute supporting a global force of field linguists and translators, many of them working with minority and endangered languages. Because many of these languages are written in scripts that are not within the immediate strategic sights of software companies like Microsoft and Adobe, SIL needed a more flexible solution than OpenType, following the AAT philosophy but available on Windows and Unix-based operating systems as well as the Mac. In 1999 SIL began to 'roll their own', developing Graphite fonts and also a word-processing application to support the format. Graphite, like AAT, puts the burden of script and language support on the font developer, but this is precisely its raison d'être: to be able to provide language support without waiting for text engine updates. Graphite remains largely a specialist tool, and even SIL favours OpenType support for those scripts and languages adequately supported by the major software developers. Since 2002, Graphite has been open-source software.

The specific layout capacities of the three formats also vary, and whilst it is largely possible to produce the same visual results from all three formats, the methods used may vary. The illustration above demonstrates many

Jean François Porchez
NATIONALITY AND TYPE DESIGN

of the layout possibilities in OpenType, as implemented in Arabic Typesetting, a font I co-developed with Mamoun Sakkal and Paul Nelson.

The creative potential of OpenType Layout for Latin-script typography is now being actively exploited by type companies large and small, most notably in dynamic display faces such as Linotype's Zapfino Pro, Adobe's Bickham Script Pro, Jeremy Tankard's Aspect and House Industries' Ed Interlock. Users of these fonts, who might not ever work with non-Latin scripts, might pause to consider that the new functionality they enjoy is built on a foundation of Arabic, Devanagari, Thai and other complex script text processing; whether they realize it or not, they are plugged into a truly global typography.

Nationality does not apply easily to type and culture, as Yvonne Schwemer Scheddin has said: 'The concept of "nation" is political, whereas script is connected directly to language and its geographic linguistic areas.'[1]

A couple of centuries ago, languages, scripts and the typefaces which represented them were intrinsically related to each other. Roman capitals had, during the Roman empire, become the typographic system dedicated to monumental inscriptions, whilst the Carolingian minuscule was being adopted as the official script for all of Charlemagne's empire by the early ninth century. In Ireland, the semi-uncial, as seen in the Book of Kells, was already in use. In contrast to our globalized era, during the early days of civilization there were no easy means of communication between the various parts of the world. Communication happened largely through trade and war. Later, during the Renaissance and in the early days of printing, when the main language of culture in Europe was Latin, books were set with local typefaces and exported. The mixing of type cultures probably started in Venice during the sixteenth century. In 1499, Aldus

Blado italic
Italy c.1500

Baskerville
England 1757

Bodoni
Italy c.1800

Manutius registered his narrow and economical italic typeface design for small books at a time when his competitors were using less economical roman typefaces. Two years later, in Lyon, the first copies of his edition of Virgil, including a recut of his registered italic, came out. Two decades after that, de Tournes, Estienne and others combined this italic with their roman to create an even more complete type family.

The period in the history of Western typography that followed can be understood as one of an exchange of influences between masters from different countries. Two examples are the Englishman Baskerville's influence on the Italian Bodoni, and that of the Frenchman Didot on the Englishman Bulmer. This game of influence became standardized around the seventeenth century, when all of the arts were analysed and published in large 'Encyclopedias'. Type design was included, and projects appeared that were directly connected to the intellectual needs of the period, such as the 'romain du roi' project conducted for Louis XIV by the 'commission Bignon' (1693–1718), which resulted in an official typeface being cut for the Imprimerie Royale in France.

During the early years of industrialization, typefaces used in large sizes became a tool to market new products. Thus they became more than just a tool to print ideas and thinking – their design and style began to be dictated by function, as for instance with the egyptian typefaces. This term was used to describe heavy titling faces, generally with large serifs or simply without any, not because fat faces came from Egypt, but simply because of a fascination with antiquity in all things related to the arts and architecture. A little later, in France, Louis Perrin finally decided to cut a set of 'Caractères Augustaux' (1846) for the composition of a book on the subject of Roman inscriptions in Lyon, because he disliked the association of Didot types with the subject. Reverting to the roots helped to define the recent ideas on type culture and type connotation. What is interesting about these ideas is that they became more clearly defined when humans had succeeded in building the tools of their destruction through the globalization of cultural exchange.

During the twentieth century, the emergent universalism became a clearer concept. It is still largely used

Univers
Switzerland 1957

today in the teaching of graphic design and typography, in contrast to expressionism which, from Art Nouveau to the vernacular styles of the Western world, cannot be ruled by any definition. The avant-garde and Swiss typographic waves of rationalism, taking their roots from the seventeenth-century 'romain du roi', are Utopian, desiring neutral, constructed and grid-based typefaces to combine with an ideal universal machine that can cross cultural borders. At the same time the business world, in a similar manner, seeks unique branding solutions for products it wants to sell across these borders.

Over the second half of the twentieth century, many exponents of the international style shared the belief that only a few typefaces met their requirements. Univers, designed in 1957 by Adrian Frutiger, appeared in answer to the request for large families. Ladislas Mandel, who was at the head of the Frutiger studio at Deberny & Peignot, wrote later: '[typographers] confused modular architecture with type design, and they removed all handwriting references which reflect cultural roots ... they switched to the nudity of the sans serifs without savour ... and made up to 20 alternatives

and more from a unique basic form, as a pretence at answering all the needs of typography.'[2]

While Univers can be put in the basket of rationalized typefaces, Adrian Frutiger showed us that, with all the typefaces that he designed after Univers sharing a similar style, they have become a sort of brand. What Sebastian Carter wrote – 'We should welcome typographic variety as the natural consequence of human creativity' – can be applied to Univers.[3] If we try to go further on the subjective analysis of the Frutiger style we can perhaps say that his style came from his background in Switzerland, where, at a minimum, three languages need to be taken into account when you design typefaces. Thus it sounds natural, because of his cultural background, that he should have designed quite universal typefaces (in the 1950s sense). So, what was adopted by the international style movement as the ideal and universal typeface is, in fact, just the style of its designer, which varied with all the beautiful typefaces he has designed during a long and rich career. Frutiger himself countered what was considered universal with his design of New Devanagari (in around 1970). This new

Helvetica
Switzerland 1957

Meta
Germany 1991–2003

Gill Sans
England 1927–30

typeface was in fact the traditional Devanagari writing system, based on the broad-edge pen, adapted to the Univers modular typeface system. The result, as beautiful and clear an expression of modernity as Univers was for our Western eyes (in the 1950s), never achieved popularity in India, probably because it was seen as a foreign, Western representation of local Indian culture and not as the universal design we see from our perspective.

Nothing can be considered universal, especially not typefaces. But the global influence on the Western world is such that probably any typeface designed for Latin script is now considered universal by Western people. In today's world, what is considered culturally referenced is more likely to be the effect of branding than of real cultural roots. Just take a comment by Erik Spiekermann: 'Writing this, as I do in my native Federal Republic of Germany, I often wonder why Helvetica hasn't long since been renamed Teutonica. Every decent law-abiding German company and institution specifies this, the Federal Face, for its corporate image.'[4] This was written a couple of years before he designed and published his FF Meta (1991), which has become today's 'Federal' face

of Germany. He refers mainly not to the cultural heritage of Germany, but simply to corporate identity. Still, Helvetica could be seen as Swiss, and by extension German, by foreigners during the 1970s and 1980s, just as Gill Sans is obviously seen as English. Spiekermann, during his important lectures around the world – in which he likes to make analogies and jokes to help explain what defines good typography – always refers to 'olives' when discussing French type, quoting Roger Excoffon's work as the perfect example of olive design with his Antique Olive. Whilst we understand his analogy, the Olive name doesn't come from the olives of Provence but from the name of the typefoundry in Marseilles which published Excoffon's typefaces, Fonderie Olive. He also wrote: 'what looks totally unacceptable to a North American reader will please the French reader at breakfast, while an Italian might find a German daily paper too monotonous. Of course, it's not only type or layout that distinguishes newspapers, it is also the combination of words.'[5]

Nowadays, type designers do use local cultural roots to build new typefaces but, at the same time, they are

Antique Olive
France 1962–6

Bliss
England 1996

Anisette
France 1995

also much influenced by each other via their immediate exchange of ideas through the global network. This can be understood to be achieving more of an individual *manière d'être* than a representation of a collective way of life based on local cultural habits. To take some recent examples: House Industries (USA) have long used typographic archetypes as fuel for their new designs, from their earlier Tiki Type, which used the 1960s graphic-design style from the Pacific Islands, to their invention in 2000 of the character of René Albert Chalet, a fictional Swiss fashion designer living in France and designing 'Chalet', a 'universal' sans serif that can, in fact, clearly be seen as a 1960s/1970s style of type. In addition we can read, within a typeface specimen from Jeremy Tankard, that his Bliss (1996) is a 'modern-day English typeface' and 'stylistically it was intended to create the first commercial typeface with an English feel since Gill Sans.' Myself, with my Art Deco typeface Anisette, I simply used the name of this typical French drink with the intention of giving a French appeal to the American market for the launch of the typeface by Font Bureau (USA) in 1996.

The lesson of this is that today's typeface designers, understanding that the world is now global, naturally try through their own ideas to be different from one other. They also know that, despite all of their dreams, a perfect universal typeface which suits all situations and cultures does not exist, and that, hopefully, each graphic design job needs a particular typeface that suits the local culture, the client's wishes or 'branding' considerations. Type designers like to build stories around the typefaces they design because it helps them to create a world which reflects their own dreams.

1 Yvonne Schwemer Scheddin, 'Broken Images: Blackletter between Faith and Mysticism', in *Blackletter: Type and National Identity*, The Herb Lubalin Study Center of Design & Typography 1998.
2 Ladislas Mandel, *Écriture, Miroir des hommes et des sociétés*, Atelier Perrousseaux Éditeur 1998.
3 Sebastian Carter, *Twentieth Century Type Designers*, Lund Humphries 1995.
4 Erik Spiekermann, *Rhyme & Reason: A Typographical Novel*, H Berthold AG 1987.
5 Erik Spiekermann and E M Ginger, *Stop Stealing Sheep & Find Out How Type Works*, Adobe Press 1993.

27

Erik Spiekermann
CORPORATE TYPOGRAPHY

Type is visible language; it is the way a corporation is seen to be speaking. Corporate design should be a system of integrated visual elements that can each express the voice of the corporation (or call it brand, company, institution) if seen on its own. Cover up the logo, leave out the images, print in black and white and all you have left is a typeface and a layout style, the arrangement of the page. That tectonic arrangement is like the façade of a building. It should be unique, although there are only so many ways to put doors and windows into a house without making it uninhabitable. The building bricks – to extend that metaphor even further (and for the last time) – are the typefaces. They don't look much from a distance, but close up one recognizes structure, subtle shades of colour: the character. Neglecting to choose a proper, suitable and possibly unique family of typefaces results in the corporate building (there goes the metaphor again!) looking like all the others: prefab, boring, forgettable.

Corporate typography deals with four issues: identity; design and production; distribution; and licensing.

Identity
You can design a typeface from scratch, occupy and dominate an existing one, or adapt and own an existing one. Designing from scratch is not half as expensive as most design managers think. The amount of money it takes to buy a licence for the worldwide use of a family of fonts from one of the digital typefoundries buys you one all of your own. The scarcest resource, as always, is talent. The dilemma in designing yet another typeface suitable for both text and display, to be read across diverse cultures (and we're only talking about the Roman alphabet just now), is that it has to look 95 per cent like all the other faces out there, lest it be seen to be silly, contrived and fashionable. But that is a dilemma all serious type designers face. Vanity is not a good adviser here, but neither is timid adaptation of so-called standards. Who – besides Deutsche Telekom, BMW and others – needs yet another Helvetica clone, altered enough to avoid paying a licence for the real thing but not enough

Below Corporate ASE.
Designed by Kurt Weidemann
for Daimler-Benz AG by 1990.

Right Sans and serif types
designed exclusively for Nokia.

Daimler Chrysler Corporate A · **S** · **E**

AaBbCcDdEeFfGgHhIiJjKkLlMmNnOo
PpRrSsTtUuVvWwXxYyZz1234567890

AaBbCcDdEeFfGgHhIiJjKkLlMmNnOo
PpRrSsTtUuVvWwXxYyZz1234567890

AaBbCcDdEeFfGgHhIiJjKkLlMmNnOo
PpRrSsTtUuVvWwXxYyZz1234567890

NokiaSuomi
NokiaBritain
NokiaDeutschland
NokiaItalia

NokiaFrance
NokiaArgentina
NokiaSverige

NokiaNorge
NokiaDanmark
NokiaEspaña

NokiaNederland
NokiaÖsterreich

to give it character? I am not talking about typefaces for a campaign or another limited application, but full corporate typefaces that have to last at least ten years, or until the next merger or management change.

Kurt Weidemann designed Corporate ASE (as in Antiqua, Sans Serif, Egyptian) for Daimler-Benz AG back in 1990, and it is hard to imagine that brand's communication without these typefaces. Weidemann knew that you need more than just a sans to express properly everything a company needs to say. More and more companies understand that type has not only to fit the brand, but also the content. That is why we added Utopia to Futura when we redesigned Volkswagen's identity back in 1995, and that is why even a company like Nokia had an exclusive sans and serif family designed. If you want to communicate with type across all media and audiences rather than just making your advertising look unique, you need to consider a system of co-ordinated typefaces, be they exclusively designed or simply chosen from a catalogue.

If the communication needs are simpler than those for a global brand selling a variety of goods and services,

it may be enough to take a face that is appropriate, fairly distinguishable without being silly, and legible enough for headlines and short text. Who can name the typeface used for all Marlboro ads? Neo Contact has only one weight and couldn't be used for more than a few words at a time, but it is recognized by everybody. Marlboro dominate it so much that you would think it was their exclusive, even though anybody else could choose to employ that typeface.

If designing from scratch seems too risky or too much trouble, you can always take, say, your average Univers and Times New Roman and make them your own. That is what Audi did when they repositioned themselves as a premium brand in 1994. The decision to use these two faces had been made when we came to the project, so we took the faces and tuned them to Audi's purposes. With a licence from the original foundry, you can do that with any typeface, as long as you don't resell it. One of the advantages is that you can rename the fonts so that everybody knows they are using the right typeface. Audi Sans is different from Univers, but most users wouldn't know that if it weren't for the name.

aáàäãâåæbcçdeéèêëfghiíìîïjklmnñ
oóòôöõøœpqrstuúùûüvwxyÿzß&&
AÁÀÂÄÃÅÆBCÇDEÉÈÊËFGHIÍÌÎÏJKL
MNÑOÓÒÔÖÕØPQRSTUÚÙÛÜVWXYŸZ
1234567890 $£¥€ >%‰ºª¼½¾¹²³<
(_-–—.,:;¡) {±+÷~×= ¬} «fifl„"..."ƒ»
[¶§#°*/†‡\µ #¿?¡!@©®™¯˘ˆ˙˜˝¸˛ˇ] ▶

Audi Sans Roman

áāąàäãâååăæbcçčćdđd'eęēĕěéèêëfgğǧh
iíìîïįijklłļľl'mnñņńňoōŏóòôöõøœpqrřŗŕsš
śştţuúùûüŭyůűvwxyÿýzżžźß
AĀĂÁÀÂÄÃÅÅÆBCČĆÇDĐĎE̦ĘĚĒĔĘĘÉÈ Ê
FGĞHIÍÌÎÏJĻÍIJKKĻLĽĽ'ĹMNÑŅŃŇOŐŎÓÒÔÖÕ
ØQRŘŔŖ́SŠŚŞTŤŢUÚÙÛÜŲŮŰVWXYÿÝZŻŽ

Audi Sans Roman CE
Central European

Below Neo Contact. Used effectively in Marlboro branding for over 20 years.

Right Univers retuned under licence to become Audi Sans for the company's branding requirements.

You know this brand.

Design and production

Very simply put, a corporate typeface has to be good-looking, well-built and useful.

Good-looking is difficult to define, but in the context of a corporate design programme it means that the typeface has to be in line with the brand values. It is no good taking a cuddly, cute face to a hi-tech company, or a cool, fashionable, geometric one to a manufacturer of health foods. That goes for all the other elements of the design system, but type designers seem either to be afraid of taking risks altogether and so keep constantly tweaking the same well-known outlines, or to fall victim to the latest trend. It is easy to score with clients either way, but in the long run neither serves the brand. Modesty can be a virtue when it comes to designing type, as long as it doesn't equate with boredom.

A well-built typeface has all the characters for the languages required; only English needs no accents. It has to have enough weights to make it useful in different applications. To look good on paper as well as on screen, it needs to be digitized with attention to detail, well-hinted and carefully tested across all platforms. Theoretically,

OpenType is the new font format which works on both Mac and PC. Practically, however, we still have to supply TrueType and PostScript Type 1 fonts, if only for all those users who have not upgraded to the latest Windows or Mac OS. The character set could include logos as well as special sorts like arrows for signage. Anything that could be accessed via a keyboard should be included in the corporate typeface. It needs to be easy to install, to use concise menu names and style links, and also to have sufficient, but no redundant, hierarchies.

It is usually best to identify user groups and make separate packages available for design, documentation and office communication. Not everybody needs all the weights, nor all the formats.

Distribution

It is best to appoint an agent to handle worldwide distribution, with order forms available online and different payment methods for departments, suppliers and agencies. And why not make suppliers pay for the corporate fonts? Not only will a cut of the proceeds pay towards the design and production (and often actually way more than that), but it will also make people appreciate the fact that these fonts are only to be used for that one client and according to their guidelines.

Licensing

Legally, fonts are treated as software. You do not buy a font, but acquire a licence to use it. A multi-user licence is needed for a font used on more than five CPUs or more than one output device. As those licences tend to cost quite a bit, whether you're buying them for a few or ten thousand users, it makes a lot of sense to invest that same sum in designing your own typeface. You then hold it exclusively and can either sell to your suppliers or even to the open market. That is what Daimler-Benz did with their Corporate ASE. This was against the advice of their marketing and design experts, of course, but how do you explain the value of a unique brand to a controller? Now every bucket shop in the world can have the Daimler typeface on its sign.

Type design and the production of fonts have become easy, technically. A new typeface can now be designed and produced within months rather than years. Getting the right balance between 'corporate' and unique still depends on the talent and knowledge of the designer. Whilst there are more type designers than ever, working to a brief within the constraints of a corporate system isn't everybody's scene. When it comes down to it, there are still only a handful of people who successfully straddle the disciplines of corporate design and type design.

Jeremy Tankard
DRAWING LETTERS AND TYPE: INITIAL STEPS IN DESIGNING TYPE

Opposite Drawing in a sketchbook: ideas and notes for Kingfisher.

In his book *Typologia* Frederic W Goudy wrote, 'Today the type designer who essays a new type which he hopes will be useful, novel, and beautiful sets himself no easy task.'[1] A simple and timeless observation that is still very true. In our current digital age, it can be said that the task is even harder than before. Not only is the type designer constrained to fit the outlines to the grid imposed by the computer, but also needs to be aware of various multilingual and software requirements. However, even with these additional burdens, and the benefits a computer affords, the basic roots of type design have not changed. More often than not a type aims to be legible and stylish. It needs to function well in its intended context and to offer some degree of interest to the eye. Many areas of the visual aspects of type design are subjective; others rely on the laws of optics and on traditions of perception.

One of the most difficult aspects of designing type is focusing on the idea. I keep a sketchbook for each design. In this I note my thoughts, make quick drawings, identify reference material I intend to study. In this format, removed from the constraints of the computer, all aspects of the design are given thought and review, and the design has a chance to develop freely. Generally I make notes about what I intend to achieve with the type and what use it is being designed for. As my initial ideas become more focused, questions arise: the size of the character set (will Central European languages be supported?); how many weights and widths (light to heavy, condensed to wide) the type family will have; whether the italic will be cursive or sloped; if there will be a display version. And if the font has serifs, what style could these be? At the same time I begin to sketch several key characters, taking tentative looks at character and font proportion and structure: the x-height in relation to the character width and stroke weight; the arch of the 'n' and how it joins the stem; the descender depth and ascender height to cap height and x-height.

Most of the personality of a type can be found in its lower-case, and I tend to start here, possibly with 'a, e, f, g, n'. The sketchbook is a perfect place to throw ideas down. I use a pen and treat each mark I make as a permanent visual record in the type's development. These initial notes help to focus the look and establish definite

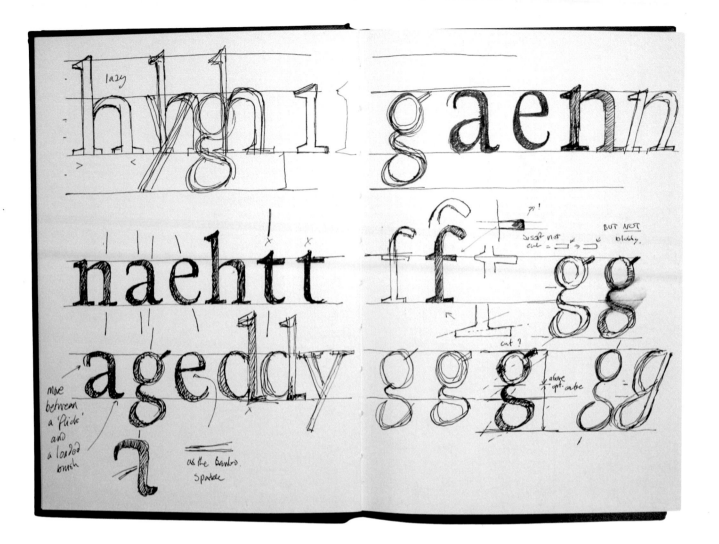

directions for the design. I move to the computer when I feel comfortable that the notes are becoming focused and the direction resolved.

I tend to approach type design as product design and the creation of letters as technical drawing. In reality one is plotting the points that describe the outline. Controlling the form on screen can be difficult. The computer should not be trusted. Always believe in your own judgement and look at the form in printouts at various sizes. It is all too easy to accept the rationalizing geometry that the computer dictates. I constantly refer back to the sketchbook and pay close attention to the notes and sketches made. Subtleties in drawing can be vital in order to remove monotony and give life to the type. A movement of one or two units to part of the outline can be perceived by the eye and can have a profound effect on the final form. This is especially true of curves. The careful placement and editing of points is vital in order to achieve a convincing natural outline. This does not mean a smooth, lifeless curve. Rather it means looking beyond the visual form and into its structure, and creating a tension between the inside and the outside lines.

It is worth remembering that the negative spaces are as important as the perceived positive form, and sometimes more so. Many problems in a form can be the result of poor counters. It is also worth mentioning that some type designs will benefit from using no straight lines. Depending on the design, it may be better not to employ straight lines, as these can often impart a rigidity that may not help the type. Other types may rely on them though.

Letters are designed individually, one at a time on the computer. However, it must always be remembered that letters are rarely treated as individual elements. A single letter that works well may not result in a successful typeface. Letters en masse behave differently from when they are seen in isolation. It is important constantly to review the letters in the context of other letters. Then decisions can be made more easily about their proportions and how the type as a whole is taking shape. The size at which the type is seen will affect its design, so review the design at various sizes. Text types seen at large sizes appear chunky; conversely, types with fine stems or serifs will appear too thin when seen small.

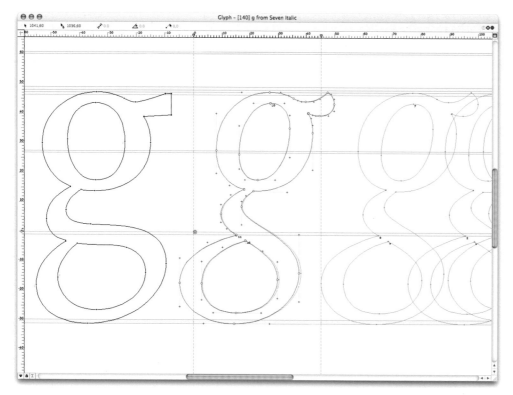

Drawing on screen with FontLab: the developing Kingfisher italic 'g'.

The various concepts of rhythm, form, balance and proportion help to inform your opinion and achieve a successful result. This takes time – time to develop a good sense of opinion and time to allow the forms to progress. Rushing doesn't help. This does not mean that designing type is an overly slow process, but a type does take time to make. Where one process is now quicker, the time saved is used elsewhere in other processes. For instance, metal-type manufacture did not need to concern itself with its on-screen appearance. I find that I work in bursts of concentration (with slow periods between) during which I test the forms together and scrutinize them intensely. It is as much relaxing as it is infuriating to study developing letter forms: tracing the edges, following the structures, finding the tension in each form and understanding the space it occupies.

1   Frederic W Goudy, *Typologia*, University of California Press 1940, p.73.

A

nanbncndnenf

nanbncndnenf

nanbncndnenf

nanbncndnenfngnhn

nanbncndnenfngnhn

nanbncndnenfngnhn

nanbncndnenfngnhninjnknlmnon

nanbncndnenfngnhninjnknlmnon

nanbncndnenfngnhninjnknlmnon

nanbncndnenfngnhninjnknlmnonpnqnrnsntnunvn
nanbncndnenfngnhninjnknlmnonpnqnrnsntnunvn
nanbncndnenfngnhninjnknlmnonpnqnrnsntnunvn

abcdefghijklmnopqrstuvwxyz
1234567890

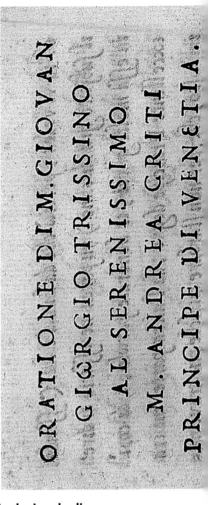

Otl **AICHER**
1922–91 D

Types
Traffic 1972
Rotis 1988
Writing
Typographie, Ernst & Sohn 1988
Further reading
Ian McLaren, 'Otl Aicher – a practical utopian', *Baseline*, no.26, 1998

A designer with a worldwide reputation in the field of corporate identity, Otl Aicher has also made a major contribution to type design and typography, not least through his writing.

He was born at Ulm in Germany and, after World War 2, studied sculpture at the Akademie der Bildenden Künste in Munich. At the Hochschule für Gestaltung in Ulm, of which he was a founder, he headed the development group, lectured on visual communications, and was for a time its principal.

He designed the typeface Traffic for use in the public transport systems in Munich and at Munich Airport, but his best-known design is the typeface family Rotis, in which he tried to combine elements of both serif and sans serif in his search for ultimate legibility.

Above: comparison of Rotis Sans, Semi-Serif and Serif from *Typographie*, 1988. (SBPL)

Jean Antoine **ALLESSANDRINI**
b.1942 F

Types
Trombinoscope 1964
Hypnos 1969
Mirago 1970–1
Alessandrini 7 1972
Graphic Man 1973
Astronef 1976
Mikado 1977
Éclipso 1982
Anarchiste 1984
Writing
Typomanie, la Noria 1977

French graphic designer, illustrator and type designer Jean Allessandrini was born in Marseilles. Studies at the Collège Technique des Arts Graphiques in Paris led to work in advertising and magazine publishing. His types, influenced by 1970s culture, were mostly decorative and ornamental. He produced types for Hollenstein Phototypo, Transfert Mécanorma and Typo Gabor.

Above: showing of Hypnos, 1969. (NM)

Ludovico degli **ARRIGHI** da Vicenza
d.1527 I

Types
Blado (revived 1923)
Arrighi/Centaur Italic (revived 1925)
Further reading
A F Johnson and S Morison, 'The Chancery Types of Italy and France', *The Fleuron*, no.3, 1923
James Wardrop, 'Arrighi Revived', *Signature*, no.12, 1929

Ludovico degli Arrighi was a writing master who later became a printer of fine editions using his own italic types.

Arrighi was the first writing master to print specimens of his scripts, which he did in *La Operina* (1522) and *Il modo de temperare le penne* (1523). *La Operina* was printed from wood blocks but the later book uses his first italic type, the earliest formal chancery italic. In 1524 he started a small press with

Charles Robert **ASHBEE**
1863–1942 GB

Lautitius Perugino, probably the cutter of Arrighi's types. They printed fine editions of short contemporary works, using type based on Arrighi's formal cursive script. Arrighi used another version of this type for books published in 1526 and 1527 after Lautitius had left the company, and it was a font of this later type that the printer Antonio Blado acquired and used for many publications.

Stanley Morison supervised an adaptation of the type as it appeared in Blado's *Nuova Poesia Toscana* of 1539. Named Blado, it accompanies Poliphilus, the 1923 facsimile of the 1499 roman of Aldus Manutius. The other type based on the Arrighi italic and named Arrighi, was designed by Frederic Warde for Monotype in 1925. Cut by Charles Plumet, it accompanies Bruce Rogers's Centaur.

Nothing is known of Arrighi after 1527 and it has been suggested that he died in the sack of Rome during that year by the Imperial armies under the Constable of Bourbon. His types, however, and his own spacious and elegant style of book design influenced many of his contemporaries.

Above: detail (actual size) from G G Trissino, *Oratione del Trissino al Serenissimo Principe di Venetia*, 1524, set in Arrighi's first italic. (ECC)

Types
Endeavour 1901
Prayer Book 1903
Writing
An Endeavour Towards the Teaching of John Ruskin and William Morris, Essex House Press 1901

Born in Isleworth on the outskirts of western London, architect, designer and social reformer Charles Robert Ashbee was a major force behind the Arts and Crafts Movement, which glorified the ideals of medieval craftsmanship.

In 1888, after Cambridge and two years in an architect's office, Ashbee founded the Guild of Handicrafts, and its attendant school. After the death of William Morris in 1896, he took over the plant and equipment of the Kelmscott Press to found the Essex House Press. Book production became the most important activity at Essex House and it was not long before Ashbee began designing type. His first effort was a set of decorated initials produced in 1899. This was followed by Endeavour, a type very much on the lines of Morris's Golden Type, and later by Prayer Book, a type specially created for the printing by Essex House of a luxurious prayer book to commemorate the accession in 1901 of Edward VII.

Above: frontispiece from *An Endeavour Towards the Teaching of John Ruskin and William Morris*, 1901, set in Endeavour. (SBPL)

37

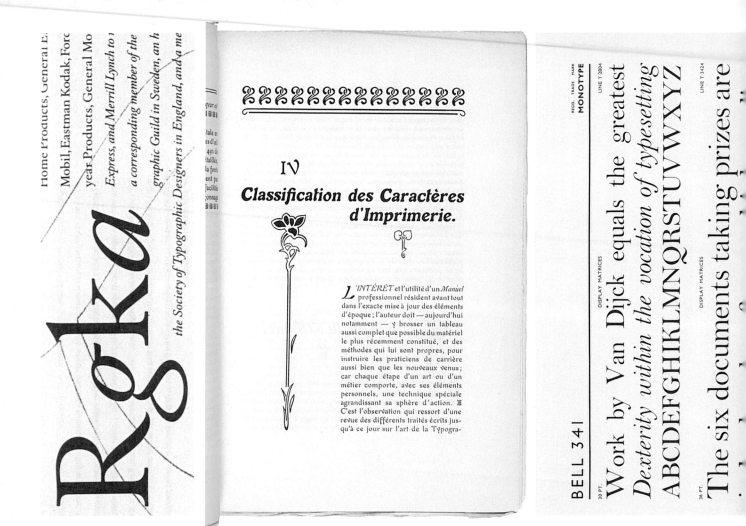

Antoine AUGEREAU
c.1485–1534 F

Antoine Augereau was a contemporary of Geoffroy Tory, the royal printer and binder to François I of France, and he was the first Frenchman to cut and print roman types in the style of Aldus Manutius. It may be the result of the brilliance of contemporaries such as Tory that Augereau has hardly featured in typographic literature. He was, however, the tutor of Claude Garamond. An active supporter of the Reformation, he was executed for heresy in 1534.

Above: detail from announcement in *U&lc* of George Abrams's Augereau revival, 1996. (NM)

Georges AURIOL
1863–1938 F

Types
Auriol 1901–4
La Français 1902
L'Auriol 1903
Auriol Champlevé 1904
Le Clair de Lune 1904–11
Le Robur 1904–11

Georges Auriol (born Jean Georges Huyot) was a French graphic artist whose work exemplifies the Art Nouveau style that was practised in Paris in the late 19th and early 20th centuries.

Auriol knew many of the artists of the period, including Van Gogh, Toulouse-Lautrec and Eugène Grasset, who designed the typeface Grasset for the typefoundry Peignot Et Sons. In 1900 Georges Peignot asked Auriol to do the same. The result was the typeface Auriol. With its distinctive 'M', Auriol was the basis for the lettering used by Hector Guimard for the entrance signs to the Paris Metro.

Other typefaces followed quickly, as did a series of typographic ornaments, but the time that Auriol spent as a type designer was short, less than three years. When Peignot Et Sons became Deberny Et Peignot and moved into new premises, Auriol designed the decorations for the front of their new factory. The typeface Auriol was re-released by Deberny Et Peignot in 1979 with a new bold.

Above: page taken from F Thibaudeau, *Manuel Français de Typographie Moderne*, 1924, set in Auriol. (SBPL)

Richard AUSTIN
c.1768–1830 GB

Types
Fry's Ornamented 1796 (revived 1949)
Scotch Roman/Scotch No.2 (revived 1907/20)
Monotype Bell (revived 1931)
Further reading
Stanley Morison, *Richard Austin, Engraver to the Printing Trade Between the Years 1788 and 1830*, Cambridge University Press 1937

Richard Austin, born in London, trained as a woodengraver with Thomas Bewick. In 1788 he joined the British Letter Foundry of publisher John Bell as a punch-cutter. Influenced by Bell's enthusiasm for contemporary French types, Austin, a skilful cutter, produced a very sharply serifed letter which Stanley Morison was to call the first English modern face. The type retains some old-style

B

characteristics and should more properly be called a late transitional. Austin went on to cut true moderns and later, in 1819, after starting a foundry of his own, he outlined the dangers of such designs being taken to extremes.

The British Letter Foundry closed in 1798 and between this date and his setting up of the Imperial Letter Foundry in Worship Street, London, Austin cut types for the Wilson foundry in Glasgow and for William Miller in Edinburgh. Austin also cut at least one decorated face: Fry's Ornamented.

The types Richard Austin cut for Bell fell out of favour in Britain, though a small amount of Bell type remained at Cambridge and, its origins forgotten, it acquired the name Georgian. In 1867 type

cast from the original matrices was taken to the USA, where it was known as Brimmer. Later D B Updike, who admired Brimmer, had Mountjoye cast in the same way. It was after learning of the origins of these types that Stanley Morison began his study of Bell, which was published by Cambridge University Press in 1930. He then supervised the cutting of the facsimile Monotype Bell, prepared in collaboration with Stephenson Blake, which was issued in 1931, the centenary of John Bell's death.

Previous page: section of page from *Specimen Book of 'Monotype' Printing Types*, n.d.; Above: Fry's Ornamented, Stephenson Blake, n.d. (both CLR)

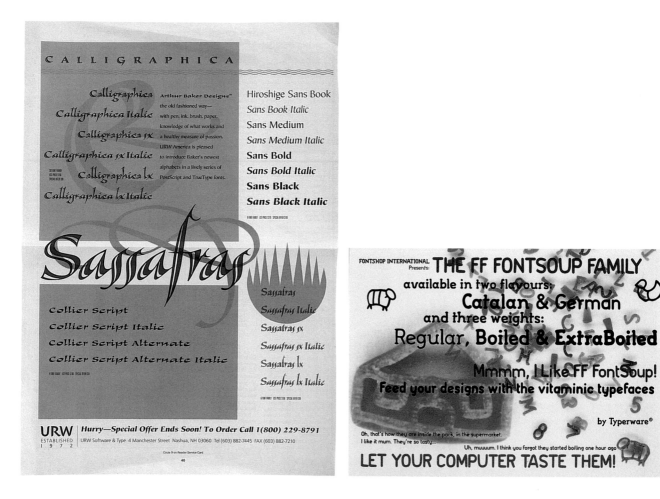

Arthur **BAKER**
USA

Types
Baker Signet 1965
ITC Tiepolo 1987 (with Cynthia
   Hollandsworth Batty)
Visigoth 1988
Amigo 1989
Marigold 1989
Oxford 1989
Pelican 1989
Kigali 1994
Cold Mountain 1995
Oakgraphic 1995
Sassafras 1995
Baker2000 Sans 2000
Calligraphica 2001
Mercator 2001
Collier Script
Daybreak
Duckweed (and Sans)
Hiroshige Sans

Arthur Baker, who currently
lives in Andover, Massachusetts, is a renowned calligrapher with over 20 books on
the subject to his credit,
including *Calligraphic
Alphabets*, a compilation of
140 alphabets. Baker's fonts
are carried by numerous
foundries and brand many
successful international
identities. The word 'Coke' in
Coca-Cola product branding
uses Baker Signet Bold.
Designed in 1965, the Baker
Signet family, with an endur-
ing quality, is still popular
today, over 40 years later.

Above: an advertisement in
U&lc for Baker's types, 1994.
(NM)

Andreu **BALIUS**
b.1962 E

Types
ITC Belter 1996
ITC Temble 1996
FF FontSoup 1997
   (with Joan Carles P Casasín)
Pradell 2001
Trochut 2003
Writing
*Type at Work: The Use of Type
   in Editorial Design*, Gingko
   Press 2003
Web
andreubalius.com

Barcelona-born graphic
designer and typographer
Andreu Balius studied Sociol-
ogy at Barcelona University,
before graduating in graphic
design at the IDEP school in
1989. He established Garcia
Fonts & Co., an experimental
type project, and co-founded
the Typerware studio in
Barcelona with Joan Carles
P Casasín in 1993. Balius, who
also teaches in Barcelona, has
contributed to the ITC and FSI
FontFont libraries. His interest
in 18th-century Spanish
typography led to Pradell,
his typeface homage to the
Catalan punch-cutter Eudald
Pradell. Pradell received
awards from Bukva:Raz! 2001
and the 2002 Type Directors
Club type-design competition.

Above: FF FontSoup
promotional postcard,
n.d. (CLR)

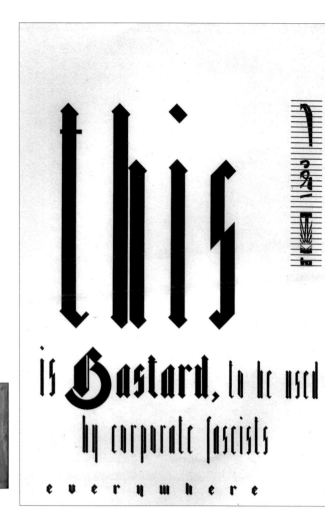

Jonathan **BARNBROOK**
b.1966 GB

Types
Bastard 1990
Exocet 1990
Prototype 1990
Mason (Manson) 1991–4
Patriot 1994
Delux 1995
Nixon Script 1995
Nylon 1996
Apocalypso 1997
Draylon 1997
Drone 1997
False Idol 1997
Prozac 1997
Newspeak 1998
Echelon 2000
Expletive Script 2000
Moron 2000
Melancholia 2001
Coma 2002
Infidel 2003
Priori Sans 2004
Priori Serif 2004
Tomahawk (Shock & Awe) 2004
Enola Gay (Shock & Awe) 2004
State Machine 2004
Further reading
Interview, *Eye*, no.15, 1994
Web
virusfonts.com

Born in Luton, England, Jonathan Barnbrook graduated from Central Saint Martins College of Art and Design in 1987 and from the Royal College of Art in 1990.

Barnbrook has since worked as a freelance designer creating high-profile designs with unconventional and groundbreaking typography for leading UK advertising agencies and design companies. His work on typographic sequences for commercials director Tony Kaye was outstanding, as were projects for both artist Damien Hirst and musician David Bowie.

Characteristics of Barnbrook's design work are the use of his own typefaces, a strong sense of decoration and the recurring use of the cross motif. Some of these feature in Barnbrook's

inscribed slab, with letters machine-cut into the stone, which is displayed in the Victoria & Albert Museum in London. Barnbrook releases his own typefaces through his digital typefoundry Virus, which he launched in 1997. As is obvious from their names, many of these comment on contemporary politics.

Above: machine-generated stone-carving, 1990; page from *Virus Late-20th Century Font Catalogue*, n.d. (NM)

John **BASKERVILLE**
1706–75 GB

Further reading
F E Pardoe, *John Baskerville of Birmingham, Letter Founder and Printer*, Muller 1976

John Baskerville was one of the first printers to use type which moved away from the old face patterns of the preceding two centuries. Although his work was frequently derided in his native England it influenced continental printers like Didot and Bodoni.

Born in Wolverley, Worcestershire, he moved to Birmingham in 1725, where he worked as a writing master and engraver for ten years before setting up in business making japanware. Following the financial success of that venture he set up a typefoundry and printing press in 1750. After a considerable period of experimentation in production processes, his

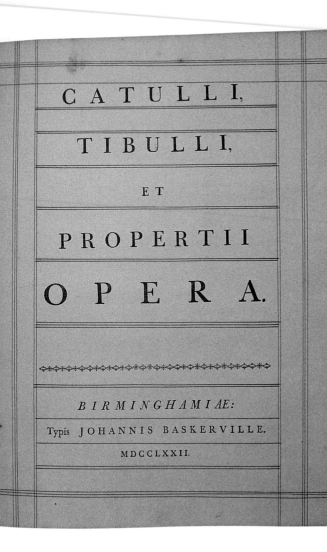

Johann Christian **BAUER**
1802–67 D

first book, Virgil's *Bucolica, Georgica et Æneis*, appeared in 1757. Baskerville became printer to Cambridge University Press in 1758, printing a grand folio Bible in 1763, which brought much acclaim on the Continent, along with a Greek New Testament for Oxford University Press in the same year. His type was cut by John Handy (d.1792), and its restraint was mirrored by Baskerville's typography, which (apart from his Bible titlepage) is notable for its lack of ornament and its sensitive use of space.

The punches for his types were sold by his widow Sarah (née Eaves) after his death in 1775 and they eventually came into the possession of the Deberny & Peignot typefoundry, which presented them to Cambridge University Press in 1953.

Successful contemporary interpretations of Baskerville's type include ITC New Baskerville by Matthew Carter and John Quaranda, Berthold Baskerville Book by Günter Gerhard Lange and, most recently, Mrs Eaves, by Zuzana Licko of Emigre.

Previous page: detail from Baskerville's Virgil, photographed for the CLR. (CLR); Above: titlepage printed by Baskerville, 1772. (CSM)

Types
Fette Fraktur 1850
Roman Extra Bold 1850
Verdi 1851 (revived 1957)

When Johann Christian Bauer, born in Hanau, Germany, started the Bauer foundry at Frankfurt am Main in 1837 it was to Great Britain, renowned as the centre of punch-cutting and typefounding expertise, that he came to learn and perfect his skills. He arrived in Edinburgh in 1839, where he worked for the firm of P A Wilson. There he applied himself to learning the art of punch-cutting and eventually he formed his own concern under the name of Bauer, Furgusson & Huie.

Returning to Germany in 1847, he renamed his company Englische Schriftschneiderei und Gravieranstalt (English

Typecutting and Engraving Works). Although by nature a craftsman rather than an industrialist (it is said that in his lifetime he cut more than 10,000 punches with his own hands), he turned his business into a worldwide concern in the 20 years before his death in 1867.

Above: detail of page from *Des Buch Druckers*, Schatz-Kästlein 1928. (SBPL)

42

60° Die Schrift wird in der Höhenfräsmaschine jetzt auf die gewünschte Höhe gebracht, während nun in der gleichen Zeit

IMPRESSUM VOLTA

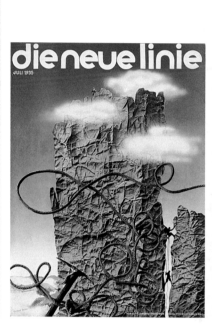

die neue linie
JULI 1935

Konrad F BAUER
1903–70 D

Types
Horizon/Imprimatur 1952–5
Alpha and Beta 1954
Fortune/Volta 1955–6
Folio/Caravelle 1956–63
Verdi 1957
Impressum 1963
Writing
Aventur und Kunst,
Bauersche Giesserei 1940

Although no relation to Johann Christian Bauer, Dr Konrad F Bauer was head of the art department at the Bauer foundry in Frankfurt from 1928 until his retirement in 1968. He designed a number of typefaces, all with Walter Baum. These include Folio, a sans-serif family based on 19th-century German models, and Fortune, the first clarendon to have a companion italic.

Konrad Bauer came from a printing family: his father had worked in two type-foundries in Altona. He studied the history of art, specializing in the history of lettering, and also learnt calligraphy, before serving a printer's apprenticeship. Bauer was interested in the history of printing and wrote several books, pamphlets and articles. He taught book design and printing at the University of Mainz and in 1962 he instigated the revival of a competition for the most beautiful German book, heading the judging panel for 13 years. He continued to work for the Bauer foundry after his retirement.

Above: Bauer Foundry type specimen, n.d. (CLR)

Walter BAUM
1921–67 D

Types
Volta 1956
Folio/Caravelle 1956–63
Verdi 1957
Impressum 1963

Born in Gummersbach, Germany, Walter Baum trained as a typesetter before studying the graphic arts at the Meisterschule für das gestaltende Handwerk in Offenbach. In 1949 Baum joined Bauersche Giesserei in Frankfurt am Main, where he became director of the graphics studio and collaborated with Konrad F Bauer on many type projects. From 1972 to 1986 he was director of the Kunstschule Westend in Frankfurt am Main.

Above: detail from Bauer Foundry type specimen, n.d. (CLR)

Herbert BAYER
1900–85 A

Types
Proposal for a Universal type 1925
Bayer Type 1933
Further reading
Alexander Dorner, *The Work of Herbert Bayer*, Wittenborn, Schultz, Inc. 1949
Arthur A Cohen, *Herbert Bayer. The Complete Work*, MIT Press 1984

Through his work at the Dessau Bauhaus as head of the workshop of graphic design and printing from 1925 to 1928 and his later, more illustrative work in the USA, Herbert Bayer was one of the most influential figures in 20th-century graphic design.

He arrived at the Weimar Bauhaus in 1921 as a student, having worked in an architect's office for two years. As a student his work was heavily influenced by Moholy Nagy and De Stijl. As a teacher he transformed

HLLIA est omnis diuisa in partes tres, quarum unam incolunt Belgae, aliam Aquitani, tertiam, qui ipsorum lingua Celtae, nostra Galli appellantur. Hi omnes lingua, institutis, legibus inter se differunt. Gallos ab Aquitanis Garumna flumen, a Belgis Matrona et Sequana diuidit. Horum omnium fortissimi sunt Belgae, propterea quod a cultu atque humanitate prouinciae longissime absunt, minimeque ad eos mercatores saepe commeant atque ea, quae ad effeminandos animos pertinent, important, proximique sunt Germanis, qui trans Rhenum incolunt, quibuscum continenter bellum gerunt. Qua de causa Heluetii quoque reliquos Gallos uirtute praecedunt, quod fere cotidianis proeliis cum Germanis contendunt, cum aut suis, finibus eos prohibent aut ipsi in eorum finibus bellum gerunt. Eorum una pars, quam Gallos obtinere dictum

est, in contin finibus quanis git ad s Galliae inferio tant in Aquita renaec quae e tat into A pur et la et T cupidi bilitati finibus rent: bus pr potiri. undiqu una ex atque

Den enso Bestans

△ 25.31 mm/72 pt¹ (27.00 mm⁰ᵐ) △ −1 H 17.28 mm

Peter **BEHRENS**
1868–1940 D

Types
Behrens-Schrift 1901–7
Behrens-Antiqua 1907–9
Behrens Medieval 1914
Further reading
H Lanzke, *Peter Behrens. 50 Jahre Gestaltung in der Industrie,* Berlin 1958
'A-Z of typographers', *Baseline,* no.38, 2001

Like Otto Eckmann, Peter Behrens was influenced by the ideals of the Arts and Crafts Movement, but purged of its medievalism. He and Eckmann were proponents of Jugendstil, their response to Art Nouveau and a style which played a pivotal role in the transition from 19th-century decorative art to the simple, functional and geometric forms of the first half of the 20th century.

A native of Hamburg, Behrens studied painting at the academies in Karlsruhe, Düsseldorf and Munich. In 1903, after a period with the Künstlercolonie in Darmstadt, he became director of the Kunstgewerbeschule in Düsseldorf.

The turning point in his career came in 1907 when Emil Rathenau, the general director of AEG, asked him to take charge of all areas of the company's visual identity, including architecture, industrial design and graphic design. His work for AEG was the first example of a co-ordinated corporate identity. For a period Walter Gropius was his assistant, and it is likely that through him Behrens had an influence on the Bauhaus movement.

Above: page from Rudhardsche Gießerei specimen book, n.d. (SBPL)

Georg **BELWE**
1878–1954 D

Types
Belwe Roman 1907 (revived by Alan Meeks in 1976)
Fleischmann 1927
Shakespeare Medieval 1927–9

Georg Belwe, who co-founded the Steglitzer Werkstadt with F H Ehmcke and F W Kleukens in 1900, was an influential teacher, typographer and type designer. He studied at the Königliches Kunstgewerbemuseum in Berlin, where he was born, and later became a teacher there. In 1906 he became head of typography at the Leipzig Akademie für Graphische Künste und Buchgewerbe.

Above: Linotype specimen of Belwe Roman, 1990. (NM)

44

the Bauhaus: out went lithographs and woodcuts, in came movable type and mechanical presses; out went serifs, black-letter and capital letters, in came sans-serif lower-case: asymmetric, simple and direct. What is thought of as 'Bauhaus typography' comes from these years. Both his typeface designs reflect these beliefs and a strict adherence to geometric principles; they are rigorous in application and stark in appearance.

Bayer left the Bauhaus in 1928 and moved to Berlin. In 1938 he fled from the Nazis to the USA, becoming an inspiration for post-war American designers.

Previous page: magazine cover designed by Bayer, 1935. (CLR); Above: revival of Bayer Type by The Foundry, 1993.

ITC BENGUIAT (BEN-GAT)

Edward **BENGUIAT**
b.1927 USA

Types
ITC Souvenir 1970
ITC Korinna 1974
   (with Victor Caruso)
ITC Tiffany 1974
ITC Bauhaus 1975
   (with Victor Caruso)
ITC Bookman 1975
ITC Benguiat 1978
ITC Benguiat Gothic 1979
ITC Barcelona 1981
ITC Modern 216 1982
ITC Caslon 224 1983
ITC Panache 1988
ITC Century Handtooled 1993
ITC Cheltenham Handtooled
   1993
ITC Garamond Handtooled
   1993
ITC Edwardian Script 1994

An American type designer
with over 500 typefaces to
his credit, Ed Benguiat was
vice-president of International Typeface Corporation,
where he worked with Herb
Lubalin on the influential
U&lc magazine, doing much
to develop its style.

Son of a display director
at Bloomingdale's, he trained
at the Workshop School of
Advertising Art and studied
calligraphy under Arnold
Bank and Paul Standard.
After becoming associate
director of *Esquire* magazine
in 1953 he opened his own
design studio. In 1962 he
joined Photo-Lettering Inc.,
where he was typographic
design director and editor of
its promotional publication
Plinc. He has taught in New
York at the School of Visual
Arts and Columbia University
for over 30 years.

Above: ITC specimen book
cover, c.1978. (CLR)

Linn Boyd **BENTON**
1844–1932 USA

Types
Century 1894
   (with Theodore L De Vinne)

In their different ways, both
Linn Boyd Benton and his son
Morris Fuller Benton made
enormous contributions to
the development of type
design. Born in Little Fall,
New York, Linn Boyd Benton,
from a young age, developed
a fascination for machinery.

His career started as a
'printer's devil', rolling the
forms in the style of the day,
and in this humble capacity
he soon put his mechanical
inventiveness to work by
developing a method of
handling the sheets which
shortened the time at press.
His next job was in a paper
store and typefoundry, where
he eventually became the
senior partner in the firm
which became known as
Benton Waldo & Co.

Throughout his time
with the company (it was
eventually absorbed into
ATF) his mechanical flair
and inventiveness ran
parallel with his design and
punch-cutting skills. His
masterpiece was undoubtedly
the Benton automatic punch-
cutter. This invention came
in the nick of time for
Mergenthaler Linotype,
which at that particular
moment in its history faced
failure unless it could find
an adequate method of providing matrices for its new
typesetting machine. Indeed,
it is said that without
Benton's punch-cutter,
Linotype setting would not
have been possible.

Although as a type
designer he is undoubtedly
overshadowed by his son,
Linn Boyd was famed as a
punch-cutter and among his

45

Benton

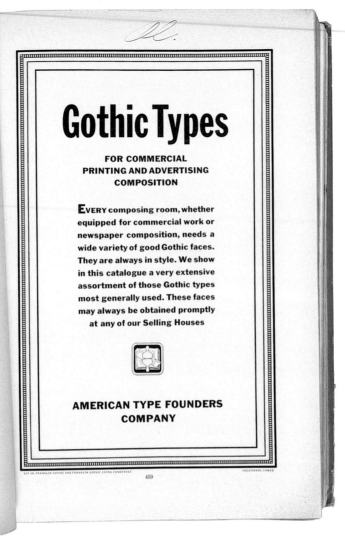

Morris Fuller BENTON
1872–1948 USA

many achievements was the cutting of Century for Theodore L De Vinne's *Century* magazine.

When Benton Waldo et Co. was absorbed into ATF, Robert Nelson, ATF's director, asked Benton to set up a type-design department, the first in a foundry, and it was here that Morris Fuller Benton joined his father as his assistant.

Previous page: showing of Century Expanded derived from Benton's Century in ATF specimen book, 1923. (NM); Above: Benton Modern by The Font Bureau based on Century Expanded, 1997. (CLR)

Types
Cloister Old Style c.1897
Alternate Gothic 1903
Franklin Gothic 1903
Bold Antique/Whitin Black 1904
ATF Bodoni 1907
Clearface 1907
News Gothic 1908
Hobo 1910
Garamond 1917
  (with T M Cleland)
Century Schoolbook 1924
Bulmer 1928
Chic 1928
Modernique 1928
Novel Gothic 1928
Parisian 1928
Broadway 1929
Louvaine 1929
Bank Gothic 1930–3
Agency Gothic 1933
Benton/Whitehall 1934
Tower 1934
Phenix 1935
Empire 1937

Morris Fuller Benton is accredited with being the most prolific type designer in American history, with an output twice as great as that of Frederic Goudy (although in fairness Goudy did not start his career until a later age). The fact that Benton's father worked at the foundry until an advanced age did in all probability place an added strain on the younger man, but seems not to have diminished his remarkable output. A factor in his relative anonymity was his position as an in-house designer, but it was a position that suited his retiring character: when pressed he would put his successes down to 'Lady Luck'.

Benton has been credited with inventing the concept of the type family and although this is not the case he did do his best work expanding faces into families and adapting existing type styles for ATF. Between 1900 and 1928 he designed 18 variations on Century, including the popular Century Schoolbook. Morris Benton also worked closely with his contemporary at ATF, Henry Lewis Bullen, collector of the company's famous library and mentor of type publicist and scholar Beatrice Warde.

Above: Franklin Gothic types from ATF specimen book, 1923. (NM)

David Berlow & Roger Black

and all the **Font Bureau** designers cordially invite you to a cocktail reception **to celebrate ATypI '95** 8:30 pm Saturday, 23 September 1995 Museu Frederic Marés, Placa de Sant Lu No.56 Barcelona

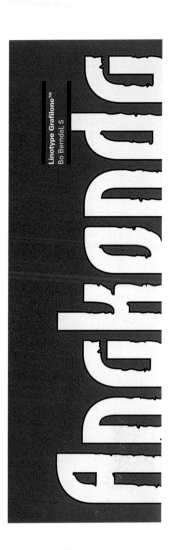

David BERLOW
b.1955 USA

Types
New Caledonia 1979
New Century Schoolbook 1980
Belizio 1987–98
Bureau Grotesque 1989–93
Eagle 1989–94
Empire 1989–94
Millennium 1989–96
Agency 1990–5
Numskill 1990
Romeo 1990–1
Belucian 1990–4
FB Phaistos 1991
   (with Just van Rossum)
Yernacular 1992
Giza 1994
Meyer 1994
Village 1994
Californian 1994–9
Esperanto 1995
Hitech 1995
Nature 1995
Online Gothic 1995
Throhand 1995
Truth 1995
Zenobia 1995
Techno 1995–7
Gadget 1995–8
Rhode 1997

Further reading
Font Bureau Type Specimens,
   3rd edition, Font Bureau
   2001
Web
fontbureau.com

David Berlow was born in Boston, Massachusetts. He obtained a bachelor of science in art at the University of Wisconsin, Madison. His career as a type designer began in 1978 at Mergenthaler, Linotype, Stempel Æt Haas, where he was involved in a number of major projects, including revisions of Dwiggins's Caledonia and many of the ITC faces released by Mergenthaler.

After leaving Linotype in 1982 he joined Bitstream Inc., the independent digital typefoundry newly formed by Matthew Carter and Mike Parker, where he worked in the type design, technical and marketing departments as a senior designer and director. After leaving Bitstream in 1989, he co-founded Font Bureau with Roger Black, a digital typefoundry offering custom typographic solutions to the new generation of Macintosh-using designers. As this market expanded to include newspapers, the demand for Font Bureau's expertise increased and the company used the skills of highly trained in-house and independent type designers to create an ever-expanding retail library that now influences every area of typographic design.

Above: invitation using Giza type, 1995. (NM)

Bo BERNDAL
b.1924 S

47

Types
Åhlens 1959
Nouveaulic 1964
Boscribe 1989
Bosis 1991
Art Gallery 1992
Carl Beck 1992
Läckö 1993
Boberia 1994
Grafilone 1994
Sabellicus 1998
Berndal 2003
Siseriff 2004
Writing
Typiskt typografiskt,
   Fisher & Co. 1990

Bo Berndal, born in Stockholm, started his career during World War 2 in the composing room as a Linotype operator. A prolific and award-winning calligrapher, his fascination with letter forms has also resulted in the design of an abundance of typefaces, a selection of which is listed above. Success as a graphic designer enabled

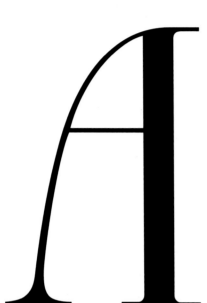

BERNHARD MODERN
roman & *italic*

AMERICAN TYPE FOUNDERS

Lucian **BERNHARD**
1883–1972 D

him to establish the Swedish advertising agency, BIGG, in the 1980s. Berndal also co-owned Hålet, a gallery dedicated to the typographic arts, and, although retired, he continues to design typefaces in a wide range of styles.

Previous page: from Linotype Library TakeType 2·1 promotion for Grafilone, 1998.; Above: Boberia from Linotype Library TakeType catalogue, 1998. (both NM)

Types
Bernhard Antiqua 1912
Bernhard Fraktur 1912–22
Bernhard Privat 1919
Bernhard Cursive/Madonna 1925
Lucian 1925
Bernhard Hand Brush Script 1928
Bernhard Fashion 1929
Bernhard Gothic 1929–30
Lilith 1930
Negro 1930
Bernhard Tango 1934
Bernhard Modern 1937
Bernhard Roman 1937
Aigrette 1939

Further reading
Steven Heller, 'The master who couldn't draw straight', *Print Magazine*, March/April 1993

A graphic artist with an international reputation for innovative posters, Lucian Bernhard achieved his effect by using few words – frequently only one – and simple images. In his minimal designs he tried to achieve a distillation of the message to its simplest elements. Self-taught, he became a major force in poster design, a medium which had much greater significance in the first half of the 20th century than it does today.

Born in Stuttgart, and educated in Zürich, he became professor of fine arts at the Akademie der Künste in Berlin before adopting America as his home. In 1929 he started designing typefaces for American Typefounders. True to the design principles demonstrated in his poster work, his typefaces are often economical and rational.

Above: Cover of ATF specimen, n.d. (CLR)

Raffaello **BERTIERI**
1875–1941 I

Types
Inkunabula 1911
Sinibaldi 1926
Paganini 1928
   (with Alessandro Butti)
Iliade 1930
Ruano 1933

Raffaello Bertieri, who was primarily a printer and publisher, played a leading role in the development of higher standards of print in Italy at the start of the last century. Born in Florence, he left school to become apprenticed to a small local printing office. At the age of 27 he became a technical editor at a printing and publishing house in Milan. It was here that he began to develop his ideas in publishing. His first title was the journal *Il Risorgimento Grafico* (*Renaissance of the Graphic Arts*), which rapidly became Italy's most influential publication in this field.

Geneva Chicago Lucida

a g n

Charles BIGELOW
b.1945 USA

His company, Bertieri & Vansetti, published the works of Gabriele D'Annunzio and *L'arte di G B Bodoni* and many art books for leading French and German publishers. His typeface Inkunabula, released by Nebiolo, is a roman based on the work of the German printer Erhard Ratdolt, who worked in Venice in the late 15th century.

Above: page from O Simon and J Rodenberg, *Printing of Today*, Peter Davies 1928, set in Inkunabula. (NM)

Types
Leviathan 1979
(with Kris Holmes)
Syntax Phonetic 1980
(with Hans Eduard Meier)
Lucida 1984–95
(with Kris Holmes)
Apple Chicago 1991
Apple Geneva 1991
Writing
(Editor), *Fine Print on Type*,
Lund Humphries 1989

Charles Bigelow is a partner in the design studio of Bigelow & Holmes and a professor of digital typography at Stanford University.

A native of Michigan, he developed an early interest in typography as a result of his experience as a writer and editor at Cranbrook Academy, Michigan. At Reed College in Oregon, where he graduated, he studied typography with Lloyd Reynolds and later with Jack Stauffacher in San Francisco.

With Kris Holmes, his partner, he has designed a number of typefaces including Lucida, an extended family of serif, sans-serif, script, black-letter, greek, scientific and linguistic alphabets designed for laser printing. In collaboration with Hans Eduard Meier he produced Syntax Phonetic, a phonetic typeface design for Native American languages. Bigelow is also a writer and a poet.

Above: Macintosh versions of three types worked on by Charles Bigelow.

Peter BILAK
b.1973 CS

49

Types
FF Craft 1994
Champollion 1995
FF Atlanta 1995
FF Masterpiece 1996
FF Orbital 1997
FF Eureka 1998
FF Eureka Sans 2000
FF Eureka Mono 2001
Fedra Sans 2001
Fedra Mono 2002
Fedra Serif 2003
Writing
Illegibility 1995
Transparency 1997
Web
peterb.sk

Peter Bilak, born in the former Czechoslovakia, runs his own graphic design studio in The Hague, Netherlands. He co-founded *Dot-dot-dot* magazine and his work has featured in others such as *ID*, *Items*, *UE&lc*, *HOW* and *Graphics International*.

Above: detail from Typotheque specimen booklet, 2003. (CD)

Nederland heeft in de ontwikkeling van drukletters altijd een grote rol gespeeld. Het zetten en drukken met losse loden letters was een Nederlandse uitvinding. Misschien dat Laurens Janszoon Coster (1405–1468) de uitvinder was ofwel een andere, onbekend gebleven, drukker. In de zeventiende eeuw was Nederland het typografisch centrum van de wereld. De bekendste Nederlandse stempelsnijder uit de gouden eeuw is Christoffel van Dijck,

Nederland heeft in de ontwikkeling van drukletters altijd een grote rol gespeeld. Het zetten en drukken met losse loden letters was een Nederlandse uitvinding. Misschien dat Laurens Janszoon Coster (1405–1468) de uitvinder was ofwel een andere, onbekend gebleven, drukker. In de zeventiende eeuw was Nederland het typografisch centrum

8/10   9/12

Evert **BLOEMSMA**
1958–2005 NL

50

Types
FF Balance 1993
FF Cocon 1998–2001
FF Avance 2000
FF Legato 2004

A graduate of the Kunst Acadamie in Arnhem, Evert Bloemsma has created four type families that have contributed considerably to the success of FSI's FontFont library. His first, FF Balance, which he developed whilst working on digital font production at URW in Hamburg, is a sans serif that explores the feasibility of top-heavy letter forms initiated by Roger Excoffon with his Antique Olive types of the early 1960s. Bloemsma's type production over the next ten years continued to reflect this studious approach to type design.

Bloemsma worked as a printer and graphic designer in his native Netherlands before joining URW, the inventors of Ikarus software. He gained further experience of specialized font production as a typographer with the Dutch company Océ, before establishing himself as a freelance graphic designer, typographer and photographer in 1991. He advised FontShop and Monotype on technical issues, taught type design in Breda and Arnhem, and contributed many articles on his interests to magazines and journals.

Much to the dismay of the type industry, Evert Bloemsma died suddenly in April 2005 at the age of 41.

Above: Cover of FF Balance specimen designed by Bloemsma, 1993. (NM)

Frank E **BLOKLAND**
b.1959 NL

Types
Bernadette
DTL Documenta 1986
DTL Haarlemmer 2002
Writing
Kalligraferen, de kunst van het schoonschrijven, Stichting Teleac 1990
Web
dutchtypelibrary.nl

Frank Blokland, born in Leiden, studied graphic and typographic design at the Koninklijke Academie van Beeldende Kunsten in The Hague. Whilst a student in 1980 he co-founded the influential working group Letters, which was to produce many of today's successful Dutch type designers.

After graduating Blokland worked on many lettering assignments and in 1985 his typeface Bernadette won Chartpak's type-design contest. In 1987 he succeeded Gerrit Noordzij on his

retirement from the Koninklijke Academie. He continues to teach lettering and type design there.

In 1990 Blokland's book, *Kalligraferen, de kunst van het schoonschrijven*, sold 16,000 copies. In that same year he founded the Dutch Type Library, Holland's first digital typeface publishing company.

Above: detail from Dutch Type Library Documenta specimen (actual size). (DTL)

PROFORMA

NEW EXHIBITION OPENS TUESDAY

MEDIUM
Contemporary Photographs from Southeastern Europe, Turkey & Russia

LIGHT ITALIC
Modern Cantilever Structures

ULTRA LIGHT
INTERSECTION OF 36TH STREET AND BROADWAY

SEMIBOLD ITALIC SMALL CAPS
NEW BRIDGE WILL CONNECT FINANCIAL DISTRICT DIRECTLY TO NINTH CIRCLE OF HELL

BOOK ITALIC SMALL CAPS
Tolls on the new bridge are expected to be heavy, but only for round trips

MEDIUM ITALIC
ORPHEUS AND EURYDICE TOUR LINES

BOLD
STAY FOR ONE, TWO, OR THREE NIGHTS, OR FOR ALL ETERNITY WITH OUR PACKAGE TOURS

Erik van BLOKLAND
b.1967 NL

Types
FF Beowolf 1990
 (with Just van Rossum)
FF EricRightHand 1991
FF Trixie 1991
F Niwida 1992
FF Kosmik 1993
F WhatYouSee 1994
 (with Just van Rossum)
FF Zapata 1997
LTR Critter 1997
LTR Federal 2000
LTR Bodoni Bleifrei 2001
 (with Just van Rossum)
LTR Salmiak 2001
Writing
LettError, Rosbeek 2000
Further reading
David Earls, 'Erik van Blokland',
Designing Typefaces,
RotoVision SA 2002
Web
letterror.com

Born in Gouda, Holland, Erik van Blokland studied at the Koninklijke Academie van Beeldende Kunsten in The Hague, graduating in graphic and typographic design in 1989. Whilst there he was introduced to fellow student Just van Rossum by type-design tutor Gerrit Noordzij, who knew they shared an enthusiasm for computers and programming. Together they formed *LettError*, initially a college magazine, but soon an outlet for their innovative exploitation of digital type technology.

Van Blokland and van Rossum worked with Erik Spiekermann at MetaDesign in Berlin from 1989 to 1990. That connection led to the release of a series of their informal fonts, now described as 'modern classics', in the early 1990s through FontShop's FontFont label. Since then, combining their understanding of computer codes and scripts with typographic invention has enabled the LettError partnership to produce unique and exciting typefaces.

Believing that designers should be their own programmers, van Blokland, who is based in The Hague, and van Rossum, who works from Haarlem, continue to practise what they preach, applying their many talents to the goal of self-programmed graphic expression. In the year 2000, as LettError, they were recipients of the Charles Nypels Award.

Above: LTR Federal promotion, 2000.; FF Kosmik specimen for FSI, 1994. (both NM)

Petr van BLOKLAND
b.1956 NL

51

Types
Proforma 1984
Productus 1992
Deforma 1999

The elder brother of Erik, Petr van Blokland also studied at the graphic and typographic design department of the Koninklijke Academie van Beeldende Kunsten in The Hague, graduating *cum laude* in 1979. Work experience with Total Design and Studio Dumbar followed before he set up as an independent designer in 1980. He taught at the Academie voor Beeldende Kunsten in Arnhem from 1984 until 1989 and currently teaches at his alma mater in The Hague.

His first typeface, Proforma, a contemporary interpretation of old style commissioned by the Danish company Purup, was issued for general use by Font

Here is an important new book and periodical face, 'Monotype' EMERSON roman *and italic,* in 24 pt.: abcdefghijklmnopqrstuvwxyz1235567890£ *abcdefghijklmnopqrstuvwxyz 1234567890 .,:;-!?''*

18 point Emerson compared with 18 point Caslon 128 and Bodoni 135

A quick brown fox jumps over the lazy dog *after*

A quick brown fox jumps over the lazy dog *after*

A quick brown fox jumps over the lazy dog *after*

'Monotype' Emerson, shown here in 14 pt., is a versatile face, strong enough for coated paper and admirably adapted to offset or photogravure reproduction.

LA GERUSALEMME LIBERATA CANTO VIGESIMO.

52

Bureau in 1994. A companion sans, Productus, was issued by the same foundry in 2001. Van Blokland was awarded ATypI's coveted Prix Charles Peignot in 1988 for his work on Proforma. He and his wife, Claudia Mens, work from their studio in Delft, where they specialize in information design and corporate identity projects.

Previous page and above:
Font Bureau specimen page,
1994. (NM)

Joseph BLUMENTHAL
1897–1990 USA

Types
Spiral/Emerson 1930–6
Writing
The Art of the Printed Book,
Pierpont Morgan Library
1973
*Typographic Years, a Printer's
Journey through Half a
Century 1925–75,*
Sandstone Press 1982

Joseph Blumenthal was a printer, historian and author, as well as the designer of the typeface Spiral/Emerson.

Blumenthal took a great interest in the work of the private presses, particularly that of Meynell's Nonesuch Press, and admired the work of Bruce Rogers and D B Updike. He worked for publishers B W Huebsch Inc. (as a sales representative), William E Rudge (as a compositor) and then briefly for A G Hoffman at the Marchbank Press. Together, Hoffman and Blumenthal set

up a press called Spiral. When the Depression forced a temporary shut-down of Spiral he sold up and left his native America for Europe. It was during this period that he designed the typeface Spiral. This face was cut for him by Louis Hoell of the Bauer foundry in 1930 and later cut for Monotype with the addition of an italic in 1936 when the name was changed to Emerson.

On his return from Europe the Spiral Press reopened, using the new typeface, and continued printing until 1971. From then until his death in 1990 Blumenthal wrote on type and organized exhibitions.

Above: detail from a Monotype Emerson advertisement, *Alphabet & Image*, no.6, 1948. (NM)

Giovanni Battista
BODONI
1740–1813 I

Types
Bodoni c.1790
Writing
Manuale Tipografico, Parma
1818

Bodoni was one of the first to cut a modern face, that is, a typeface which has hairline serifs at right angles to the uprights, vertical stress and abrupt contrast between thick and thin strokes. He took French types, such as those of Fournier and the Didots, as his model. Bodoni was, in his day, the best-known printer in Europe.

Bodoni was born in Turin in 1740, the son of a printer. At 18 he became a compositor at the press of the Vatican's Propaganda Fide in Rome, and at 28 was made director of the press of the Duke of Parma. His early types are based on those of Pierre Simon Fournier, whose

L'Egizio assal; ma nell assalto ei porta,
Portando vita altrui, morte a sè stesso.
Premuto è chi premea; ma Dio comporta
Che col Soldan giaccia Aladino oppresso;
Ch' agli empj il cielo ed ai fedeli apporta
D'ardir van, d' ardor vero il fin promesso:
Onde già scioglie il voto il popol misto,
Che'l gran sepolcro liberò di Cristo.

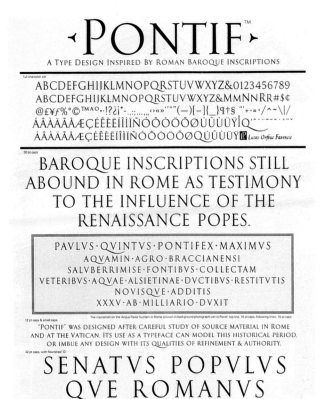

Garrett **BOGE**
b.1951 USA

Types
Spring 1988
Florens 1989
Spumoni 1990
Tomboy 1990
Wendy 1990
Visage 1993
Bermuda 1995 (with Paul Shaw)
Didot LP 1995
Cresci 1996 (with Paul Shaw)
Pietra 1996 (with Paul Shaw)
Pontif 1996 (with Paul Shaw)
Web
letterspace.com

Garret Boge's digital typefoundry, LetterPerfect, one of the earliest to be established, was founded in 1986. Born in Spokane, Washington, Boge worked early on as a lettering artist and type designer at Hallmark Cards in Kansas City. This created the impetus for a career during which, with the assistance of his partner and fellow lettering artist Paul Shaw, he has released over one hundred typefaces in a variety of styles through LetterPerfect, now based in Seattle. He has also contributed fonts to Agfa Monotype, Viacom, Microsoft and Apple Computer. His most successful designs to date are mainly his scripts, which reflect his early experience of lettering for greetings cards. However, his contemporary serif family Visage has proved popular for magazine text, and the exuberant and playful Spumoni equally so with the advertising fraternity.

Above: LetterPerfect Pontif specimen, 1996. (CLR)

Jelle **BOSMA**
b.1959 NL

Types
WTC Cursivium 1986
Forlane 1991
Cambria 2004

A native of Rijswijk, Jelle Bosma studied graphic and typographic design at the Koninklijke Academie van Beeldende Kunsten in The Hague. After graduating, Bosma, working independently as a type designer, contributed WTC Cursivium, an egyptian cursive, to the New York-based World Typeface Center. He worked for a spell in Hamburg with typesetting systems manufacturer Scangraphic, who issued his serif family Forlane. He joined Monotype Typography in 1992.

Bosma works for Monotype Imaging from his home in The Hague, where he uses his design and programming skills on a variety of type

53

work he admired, but he experimented with these letter forms to create his own. The roman letter he cut in 1798 is what we generally mean by a Bodoni. The contrast of light and shade in his types can produce a sparkling effect on the page. The books he printed reveal a taste for large sizes of type, generous use of white space and few ornaments. In addition to his romans, he also produced a great many script types.

Bodoni set out his principles of typography (although stated in vague terms) in his *Manuale Tipografico*. This book was completed by his wife, who published it in 1818, five years after his death. In 1963 the Bodoni Museum opened in Parma.

Above: detail from a four-page printed extract of a book printed by Bodoni. (CLR)

vuum™

Ein effektiver grafischer Entwurf kan
n eine vielflächige Gemme sein. Ge
nau wie bei einem Diamanten, hän
EIN EFFEKTIVER GRAFISCHER E

The successful graphic design can
be a multifaceted gem. Like a dia
mond, its beauty and value de
pend on the number of facet

e ITC
eras

Albert **BOTON**
b.1932 F

projects. These include OpenType fonts for complex scripts, mobile phone bitmap fonts and, not least, font hinting, of which he is one of the foremost exponents. He has developed his own software program, FontDame, for TrueType font editing.

Collaborating with Microsoft in 2004, Bosma created the OpenType family Cambria for the company's ClearType project.

Previous page and above: WTC Cursivium showing from *Ligature* magazine, vol.4, no.1, June 1986. (NM)

Types
Chadking 1958
Roc 1959
Brasilia 1960
Eras 1961
     (with Albert Hollenstein)
Primavera 1962
Rialto 1964
Black Boton 1970
Zan 1970
Pharaon 1971
Hillman 1972
Chinon 1973
Hudson 1973
Pampam 1974
Elan 1985
Boton 1986
Navy Cut 1986
Agora (Memo) 1990
Carré Noir 1990–5
Scherzo 1990–5
Linex Sweet 1996
Pompei 1996
Kit 1999
FF Bastille Display 2002
FF Page Sans 2003
FF Page Serif 2003
FF Tibere 2003

In his early twenties Albert Boton's study of graphic design and calligraphy under Adrian Frutiger resulted in his becoming an apprentice type designer with the Deberny ε Peignot foundry in Paris. There he worked and studied with both Frutiger and Ladislas Mandel, contributing eventually to the design of Univers in 1957.

Boton left Deberny ε Peignot in 1957 to work in various advertising agencies and design companies, including Hollenstein and Delpire, during which time he designed hundreds of typefaces and logos. From 1981 until retirement in 1997, Boton was art director responsible for brand image at the Carré Noir design company. He also taught at École Nationale Supérieure des Arts et Design and the Imprimerie Nationale in Paris, passing on to fortunate students his knowledge and skills in design, lettering and calligraphy. Boton continues to design typefaces and in recent years has made an eclectic contribution to the FontFont library.

Above: Agora specimen, Berthold Types 189, n.d. (NM); cover of ITC Eras specimen, 1976. (CLR)

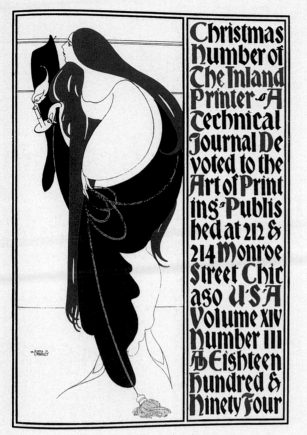

35 Cover design December 1894

Nederland heeft in de ontwikkeling van drukletters altijd een grote rol gespeeld. Het zetten en drukken met losse loden letters was een Nederlandse uitvinding. Misschien dat Laurens Janszoon Coster (1405–1468) de uitvinder was ofwel een andere, onbekend gebleven, drukker. In de zeventiende eeuw was Nederland het typografisch centrum van de wereld. De bekendste

9/12

Will **BRADLEY**
1868–1962 USA

Types
Bradley 1895
  (by Herman Ihlenburg
  after Bradley's lettering)
Wayside 1900
Bewick Roman 1904
Missal Initials 1904
Further reading
Paul A Bennet, *Will Bradley.*
  His Chap Book, The
  Typophiles 1955
Clarence P Hornung and
  Roberta W Wong, *Will*
  Bradley. His Graphic Art,
  Dover 1974

Will Bradley, born in Boston the son of a newspaper cartoonist, is recognized as the dean of American designers and art editors. He started his career as a printer's devil at the age of 12. Six years later he became an apprentice in the art department of Rand McNally.

His illustrious career as a designer kicked off when he went freelance in 1889. He quickly achieved recognition for his cover designs, drawings and posters for popular publications. Inspired by Morris's Kelmscott Press he set up the Wayside Press in 1895, taking every opportunity there to indulge his love of Caslon's types. It was in 1900, after giving up printing and publishing, that he created his typeface Wayside (named this by ATF), based on Scotch Roman, for use in the *Ladies' Home Journal*. Bradley worked for ATF in the early 1900s creating type publicity, and writing and designing their style-setting Chap Books.

Bradley was acknowledged as an inspiration by many legendary American typographers, including Frederic Goudy, to whom he sold his early printing equipment, W A Dwiggins, Oswald Cooper and T M Cleland.

Although magazine art direction dominated his career, Bradley applied his skills to many areas, including writing and directing movies. Although he finally retired in 1930 he remained active in many areas, designing type ornaments for ATF in 1953 at the age of 85.

Above: *Inland Printer* cover from 1894 designed by Bradley including lettering on which the Bradley type was based, from *Will Bradley*, Dover 1974. (NM)

Chris **BRAND**
b.1921 B

Types
Albertina 1965–98

Chris Brand was born in Utrecht, Belgium, and after studying calligraphy worked in Brussels from 1948 to 1953. He has taught design and typography in various academies and designed several typefaces, of which the best known is Albertina. This was first used for a catalogue of the work of Stanley Morison, which was exhibited at the Albertina Library in Brussels in 1966. Brand has also designed a Hebrew font, many book covers and a masthead for a national newspaper.

Above: detail (actual size) from Dutch Type Library Albertina specimen. (DTL)

55

Colin **BRIGNALL**
b.1942 GB

Types
Aachen 1969
Lightline 1969
Premier Lightline 1969
Revue 1969
Octopuss 1970
Premier Shaded 1970
Harlow 1977
Italia 1977
Superstar 1977
Romic 1979
Corinthian 1981
Edwardian 1983
Epokha 1992
Figural 1992 (with Michael Gills)
Retro Bold 1992

Born in Warwickshire, Colin Brignall began his career in press photography in London's Fleet Street. In 1963 this led him to join Letraset's type design studio as a photographic technician. It was there that he began to take an interest in letter forms and where he also began to experiment with his own ideas in type design.

Among his early works for the Letraset dry transfer range are display styles such as Aachen, Harlow, Premier Shaded and Superstar. In addition he designed typefaces suitable for both text and display, including Italia and Romic. In 1980 he became Letraset's type director.

Esselte Letraset acquired the International Typeface Corporation (ITC) in 1986, and as their type scout Brignall's ability to source marketable types and to encourage and direct their designers came to the fore. It was this talent as well as his own design skills that led to the Type Directors Club of New York awarding him their coveted Gold Medal in 2000.

Above: cover of *Baseline*, no.1, 1979. (NM)

Neville **BRODY**
b.1957 GB

Types
Arena/Stadia 1989
Avanti/Campanile 1989
Industria 1989
F State 1991
FF Typeface 4 1991
FF Typeface 6 & 7 1991
FF Blur 1992
FF Gothic 1992
FF Pop 1992
FF Dome 1993
FF Harlem 1993
FF Tokyo 1993
FF World 1993
FF Autotrace 1994
FF Dirty 1994

Further reading
Jon Wozencroft, *The Graphic Language of Neville Brody*, Thames & Hudson 1988
—, *The Graphic Language of Neville Brody No.2*, Thames & Hudson 1994

Web
researchstudios.com

Neville Brody's work for *The Face* magazine between 1980 and 1986 revolutionized magazine design. He grew up in North London, studying at the London College of Printing, and began his career working on record-sleeve designs. He was eventually appointed art director of Fetish Records.

Shortly after *The Face* was launched he became art director and rapidly turned his attention from image creation to experimentation with type. His work was characterized by bold typography with logos and display type both featuring hand-drawn letters. In 1987, whilst art director of *Arena*, he started to work with the Macintosh and his synergy with this medium shaped his graphic future. In 1988, the Victoria & Albert Museum hosted a show of his work which travelled internationally. The accompanying *The Graphic Language of Neville Brody* was one of the best-selling art books of the year.

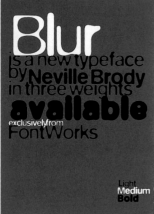

verdigris (ver-dig-rees) *n* a green or bluish coating which forms on copper, brass, or bronze that has been exposed to damp. [Old French *vert de Grice* green of Greece]

Above: page from *Bruce's Abridged Specimen Book*, 1869. (SBPL)

Mark van
BRONKHORST
b.1965 USA

Types
MVB Brünnhilde 1992
MVB Magnesium 1992, 2003
MVB Bovine 1993
MVB Magnolia 1993, 1998
MVB Celestia Antiqua 1993–6
ITC Conduit 1997, 2002
MVB Verdigris 2003
Web
mvbfonts.com
typobrand.com

The eclectic types of Californian Mark van Bronkhorst reflect a relaxed West Coast lifestyle. His editorial design work, which has graced *U&lc* and FSI's *font*, reveals a real affinity with type and typography. MVB fonts, based in Albany, California, has produced successful custom font solutions for many major US companies. His company, Typobrand, is dedicated to providing custom type services.

Above: showing of text family MVB Verdigris. (NM)

David BRUCE Jr
1802–92 USA

Types
Hancock Script
Ionic
Madisonian
Rimmed Shade
Writing
History of Typefounding in the United States, The Typophiles 1981

David Bruce Jr, born in New York, was the son of Scottish immigrant David Bruce who, with his brother George, founded the New York Type Foundry in 1813. It was there as a young man that he learnt the art of typefounding. David Bruce Jr, who by his early twenties had progressed to cutting typefaces, designed and cut display, text and titling typefaces for the family's firm. He also invented an automatic type-casting machine – the Pivotal Typecaster – which, after modification, was taken on

Four of the typestyles Brody created for *The Face* were developed and released by Linotype. In 1990, with Erik Spiekermann, he was instrumental in the establishment of digital font distributor FontShop International. He contributed to, and directed with Spiekermann and others, the creation of the FSI FontFont type library. In 1991, with Jon Wozencroft, Brody launched *Fuse*, 'an interactive magazine which explores new ideas about typographic and visual language in the digital realm'. Although his focus is now on electronic communication, Brody continues to experiment with digital typefaces.

Above: poster for a Toronto event showing Brody types, 1993. (NM); Fontworks promotions, early 1990s. (CLR)

by the Boston Type and Stereotype Foundry, and was soon licensed around the world. In 1846, using eight of these machines, he established his own foundry. Madisonian was revived and extended by Thierry Puyfoulhoux in 1999.

ABCDEFGHIJKLMNOPQRSTUVWXYZ
abcdefghijklmnopqrstuvwxyz
1234567890
ABCDEFGHIJKLMNOPQRSTUVWXYZ
abcdefghijklmnopqrstuvwxyz

aße Hüls
EÑOR ÉPI
avità, aff
VÄLGÅNC
onâtren
& ¡Libros
KE HØJSk

För alla nya sti
In elk letterc
Em todo o
In ciascu
En cac
Den e

Walter **BRUDI**
1907–87 D

Types
Orbis 1953
Brudi Medieval 1953–4
Pan 1954

Brudi, who was born in
Stuttgart, studied at the
Akademie der Bildenden
Künste in his home town
for four years from 1925.
A talented book designer,
calligrapher, illustrator and
typographer, he taught at
several schools in Germany,
finally becoming head of
typography and book design
at the Stuttgarter Akademie
where he served from 1949
until 1970. His work has
been exhibited in Europe
and the USA.

Above: Brudi Medieval from
Jaspert, Berry and Johnson,
An Encyclopedia of Typefaces,
1970. (PB)

Chris **BURKE**
b.1967 GB

Types
Pragma ND 1992–5
FF Celeste 1994–7
FF Parable 2002
FF Celeste Sans 2004
Writing
*Paul Renner: The Art of
    Typography*, Hyphen Press
    1998
Web
hiberniatype.com

Chris Burke, typographer,
type designer and type
historian, worked with
Monotype Typography before
studying for a PhD in the
Department of Typography
and Graphic Communication
at the University of Reading
in England. After gaining his
doctorate in 1995, he taught
at the university, as well as
planning and directing its
MA course in type design,
until 2001. Burke's Pragma,
designed whilst studying
at Reading, is a sans-serif
family of neo-humanist
proportions with calligraphic
influences featuring a true
italic. His contemporary serif
family, Celeste, also available
for Central European and
Greek typesetting, offers the
advantage of additional fonts
for small text use. A companion sans serif has recently
been released. His types are
issued by Neufville Digital
and FSI FontFont. Burke now
lives in Barcelona, where he
runs Hibernia Type.

Above: from Pragma specimen,
1995. (NM)

Jackson **BURKE**
1908–75 USA

Types
Trade Gothic 1948–60
Majestic 1953–6
Aurora 1960

As director of typographic
development at Mergenthaler
Linotype from 1949 to 1963,
Jackson Burke oversaw the
production of the typefaces
in which the vast majority of
American newspapers were
set for nearly half a century.
Born in San Francisco, he
was educated in Oregon and
at the University of California
in Berkeley. After serving in
World War 2, Burke spent a
short period as a private
printer. He then joined
Mergenthaler Linotype as
successor to C H Griffith,
who had been there since
1906. During his time with
the company Jackson Burke
designed or commissioned
a number of new types,
including Trade Gothic and

bestäms alfar

werp wordt

senho del

na seriw

a tipor

nsas

Alessandro **BUTTI**
1893–1959 I

the newsprint faces Majestic and Aurora.

When photocomposition was developed in the 1950s Burke insisted on editing or redesigning all the company's newsprint typefaces rather than allow them to be committed to photocomposition without appropriate modification. Another of his achievements was the extensive development of typefaces for Indian scripts, including various forms of Devanagari, Gujarati and Sinhalese.

One of his last responsibilities with the company was the cutting of the Helvetica series. He was succeeded at Mergenthaler by Mike Parker.

Above: Linotype Trade Gothic specimen, 1990. (NM)

Types

Paganini 1928
   (with Raffaello Bertieri)
Quirinus 1939
Landi Echo 1939–43
Athenaeum 1945
   (with Aldo Novarese)
Normandia 1946–9
   (with Aldo Novarese)
Rondine 1948
Cicogna 1950
Augustea 1951
   (with Aldo Novarese)
Fluidum 1951
Microgramma 1952
   (with Aldo Novarese)

A native of Turin, Alessandro Butti was art director of the Turin-based Nebiolo typefoundry. He designed a diverse range of typefaces, many of which have enjoyed wide popular appeal, such as Microgramma and Augustea, both of which were designed with Aldo Novarese.

Butti also taught at the Scuola Tipografica Giuseppe

Vigliandi Paravia in Turin. He was succeeded as art director of Nebiolo by Novarese in 1952.

Above: packaging for *Omaggio ad Alessandro Butti, Creatore di Tipi*, Alberto Tallone Editore 2002, published for the 2002 ATypI Conference in Rome. (CD)

C

ABCDEFGH
IJKLMMNN
OPQRRSTU
VWXYZ&Ç
ÀÖÜ.!?¡¿—†‡°
1234567890

Max CAFLISCH
b.1916 CH

Types
Columna 1955

Writing
William Morris, der Erneuerer der Buchkunst, Bern 1959
Fakten zur Schriftgeschichte, Zürich 1973
Schrift und Papier, Grellingen 1973
Typographie braucht Schrift, Kiel 1978

Further reading
A Berlincourt *et al.*, *Max Caflisch. Typographia practica*, Hamburg 1988

Max Caflisch was born in Winterthur, Switzerland. From 1932 to 1936 he trained as a compositor in the printing works of Studer-Schläpfer in Horgen, near Zürich. During this period he attended classes at the Kunstgewerbeschule in Zürich, where he was noted as an outstanding pupil.

In 1938 Caflisch moved to Basel to work as a senior compositor at Benno Schwabe and later Birkhäuser, where Jan Tschichold and Imre Reiner were also employed, and remained there until 1941. His work in the field of education began during World War 2 with the Allgemeine Gewerbeschule in Basel from 1941 to 1942. He was art director at Benteli AG in Bern with overall responsibility for production from 1943 until 1962, when he became head of the graphics department at the Kunstgewerbeschule in Zürich. He continued to teach there, and at the neighbouring Technikerschule der graphischen Industrie, until 1981.

In 1955 he created the typeface Columna for the Bauer foundry and later, because of his outstanding knowledge of typography, he was appointed to advise IBM and the Bauer foundry in Frankfurt on type's relationship with computer technology.

Max Caflisch was one of the first to appreciate the need for original alphabets for use with digital typesetting technology. From 1972 to 1989 he directed the type-design programme at Rudolf Hell in Kiel. Since 1990 he has been a member of the type advisory board of Adobe Systems Inc.

Above: Bauer Columna specimen, n.d. (CLR)

ah

WTC Carnase Text Light

WTC Carnase Text Regular

WTC Carnase Text Medium

WTC Carnase Text Bold

WTC Carnase Text Extra Bold

WTC Carnase Text Light Italic

WTC Carnase Text Regular Italic

WTC Carnase Text Medium Italic

WTC Carnase Text Bold Italic

WTC Carnase Text Extra Bold Italic

c

Margaret **CALVERT**
b.1936 ZA

Types
Transport 1958–63
   (with Jock Kinneir)
Calvert 1980
F A26 1994
Bic Medium 2003

Margaret Calvert came to England from South Africa in 1950. She studied illustration at Chelsea School of Art before being invited by Jock Kinneir, her former tutor, to join him in work on signing for Gatwick Airport.

After the success of the Gatwick Airport project, Kinneir and Calvert worked on lettering and signage systems for the UK's motorways and roads, railways, airports, hospitals and armed services. The company was renamed Kinneir Calvert Et Associates in 1966 when she became a partner. Their last project, in 1977, was for the Tyne Et Wear Metro. Calvert was awarded a DEtAD Silver Award for book typography in 1978. After the retirement of Kinneir in 1979 she started her own practice.

The typeface Calvert was adapted from the Tyne Et Wear Metro signing alphabet and released by Monotype in 1980. In 1994 she designed A26 for Neville Brody's *Fuse* project. Bic Medium was designed for the Pentagram Ballpoint exhibition in 2003.

Margaret Calvert taught at the Royal College of Art and was head of their Department of Graphic Arts and Design from 1987 until 1991, becoming a Senior Fellow in 2001. She was awarded an honorary fellowship by University of Arts London in 2004.

Above: differences between the Tyne & Wear Metro alphabet (in green) and Calvert, *Monotype Recorder*, no.2, 1980. (PB)

Tom **CARNASE**
b.1939 USA

Types
ITC Avant Garde Gothic 1970
   (with Herb Lubalin)
ITC Gorilla 1970
ITC Grouch 1970
ITC Honda 1970
ITC Machine 1970
ITC/LSC Manhattan 1970
ITC Milano Roman 1970
   (with Ronne Bonder)
ITC Tom's Roman 1970
   (with Ronne Bonder)
ITC Pioneer 1970
   (with Ronne Bonder)
WTC Carnase Text 1982
WTC Goudy 1982
WTC 145 1983
WTC Favrile 1984
WTC Our Bodoni
   (with Massimo Vignelli)
LSC Caslon No.223
LSC Book
WTC Our Futura

Tom Carnase was born in New York City in 1939. Before going freelance with Ronne Bonder in 1964 at Bonder Et Carnase Inc., he spent five years in the design division of Sudler Et Hennessey Inc., where he met Herb Lubalin. In 1969 he joined Lubalin and Ernie Smith at Lubalin, Smith, Carnase Inc. Ten years later he left to become an independent type consultant.

A brilliant lettering artist and type designer, Carnase founded World Typeface Center Inc. in 1980 to design, produce and market new typefaces for computerized typesetting systems. To promote WTC types Carnase published *Ligature* magazine, an equally dynamic alternative to International Typeface Corporation's *UEtlc*. He has also contributed logotypes and other graphic solutions to the identities of many large American corporates, including Coca-Cola.

Above: WTC Carnase specimen from *Ligature* magazine, vol.2, no.2, September 1983. (NM)

SEVENTY-2 PT.
SIXTY 60 POINT
FIFTY-FOUR PT 54
FORTY-EIGHT PT
FORTY-Two POINT
THIRTY-SIX POINT
THIRTY (30) POINT
TWENTY-4 POINT
TWENTY POINT
EIGHTEEN PT
FOURTEEN PT
TWELVE PT
STOP!

80-FOUR PT
9TY·SIX PT
108 PT
120 PT
144

Ron CARPENTER
b.1950 GB

Types
Cantoria 1986
Calisto 1987
Amasis 1990

Ron Carpenter, who was born near Dorking, Surrey, joined Monotype in 1968 and trained there as a typeface draughtsman. In 1975 he became responsible for quality control as a technical checker. His first experience of typeface design came when he assisted Robin Nicholas with the italic for his Nimrod. He became a senior designer in 1984 and was responsible for, amongst other typefaces, Cantoria, Calisto and new weights of Times New Roman. In 1996 Carpenter joined Bruno Maag at Dalton Maag, where he continues to be involved in type projects.

Above: from *Monotype Recorder*, no.7, 1988. (CLR)

Matthew CARTER
b.1937 GB

Types
Snell Roundhand 1965
Cascade Script 1966
Auriga 1970
Gando Ronde 1970
   (with Hans Jorg Hunziker)
Olympian 1970
Shelley Scripts 1972
CRT Gothic 1974
Helvetica Compressed 1974
   (with Hans Jorg Hunziker)
Video 1977
Bell Centennial 1978
Galliard 1978
Bitstream Charter 1987
Elephant (Big Figgins) 1992
Mantinia 1993
Sophia 1993
Skia 1993–9
Big Caslon 1994
Alisal 1995
Georgia 1996
Verdana 1996
Miller 1997–2000
Nina 1999
Further reading
Charles Bigelow, 'Galliard',
Fine Print on Type,
   Lund Humphries 1989

Sebastian Carter, *Twentieth Century Type Designers*, Lund Humphries 1995

The career of Matthew Carter, the son of printing historian Harry Carter, has been closely allied to the changes in typesetting and design technology that have taken place over the past 30 years.

At 19, Carter spent a year in Holland being taught by Jan van Krimpen's assistant, the punch-cutter P H Rädisch. In 1961 he used the skills he had acquired to cut a semi-bold for Dante under the direction of John Dreyfus of Monotype and Dante's designer Giovanni Mardersteig.

Returning to London, Carter freelanced for a while before becoming a typographical adviser to Crosfield Electronics. In 1965 he left Crosfield for Mergenthaler Linotype in New York to work

with Mike Parker. Carter stayed with Linotype for six years and after returning again to London he maintained his connection with the company, designing Bell Centennial for them in 1978. It was also in that year that Carter, assisted by Mike Parker, designed Galliard, which is modelled on the types of Robert Granjon.

Parker and Carter set up Bitstream in 1981 to develop and supply digital outline masters for desktop publishing and image setting. After ten years Carter left to set up Carter & Cone Inc. with Cherie Cone. Based in Cambridge, Massachusetts, they provide custom type solutions for a variety of clients, including Apple, Microsoft, newspaper and magazine publishers and cultural institutions. Carter & Cone expanded Galliard

The italic with the powerful punch

K Klang Bold

designed by

Will Carter

produced by

Stephenson Blake

Will CARTER
1912–2001 GB

Types
Klang 1955
Dartmouth 1961
Octavian 1961
 (with David Kindersley)

Will Carter devoted a lifetime to type design and its execution in a wide variety of print, from the humblest ephemera to the most prestigious commissions.

A major influence on Carter was a visit he made to the studio of Rudolf Koch. Koch had died in 1934, and the studio in those pre-World War 2 days was run by his son Paul, who had worked extensively with his father as a punch-cutter. Here Carter met many famous artists, including Hermann Zapf, whose skill he admired and who was to have a lasting influence on his own work.

By 1949 Carter was able to devote himself entirely to his own printing house, the Rampant Lion Press, now run by his son Sebastian. At about this time he designed Klang, which was first cut by Monotype in 1955 and which displays the influence of his prewar calligraphic studies and his visit to the Koch studio. Dartmouth, commissioned by the New England College, and Octavian, which he designed with David Kindersley, were produced in 1961.

Above: Klang specimen cover, n.d. (CLR)

and complemented the family with the beautiful display type Mantinia.

As well as his appointment as Royal Designer for Industry in 1981, Matthew Carter has received the Goudy Award for outstanding contribution to the printing industry, the Middleton Award from the American Center for Design and a Chrysler Award for Innovation in Design. He is currently a senior critic at Yale's graphic design faculty.

In addition to the types listed above, Matthew Carter has designed a number of non-Latin types. Carter's types successfully embrace every area of typographic communication.

Previous page: Carter & Cone specimen booklet, 1993. (NM); Above: ampersands from Bitstream Charter and Sophia.

The CASLON family
GB

63

Types
Caslon 1725
the first sans serif c.1816

William Caslon I (1692–1766) was the first British typefounder of any renown and was responsible for ending the dependence of British printers on imported Dutch types which (with some French types) had dominated the market throughout the 17th century.

Born in Worcestershire, William Caslon began his career in London engraving and chasing gun barrels (occasionally also cutting brass letters for bookbinders) until a printer called William Bowyer, after seeing some of his letters, encouraged him to try punch-cutting. Bowyer lent him £500 to start his own foundry, which he opened in London's Vine Street probably in 1722 or

Caslon old face

face

Types to

they that be of
the craft are as
things that be
alive. He is an
ill worker that
handleth them
not gently and
with reverence

72-point
Caslon Old Face

EXTRACTS FROM A CHAPTER ON ENGLISH
TYPES, 1500-1800, BY DANIEL BERKELEY UPDIKE,
THE MERRYMOUNT PRESS, BOSTON, U.S.A., IN
HIS RECENT TREATISE ON "PRINTING TYPES,
THEIR HISTORY, FORMS & USE."

"Why
are William Caslon's
types so excellent &
so famous?
"To explain this and
make it really clear

60-point
Caslon Old Face

16

17

64

1723. His first type was possibly a Hebrew, cut for Bowyer around 1722. In the same year he received a commission for a new Arabic font.

His first roman type, the Pica Roman of around 1725, was based closely on a Dutch type owned by the widow of the Amsterdam punch-cutter Dirck Voskens. It was followed two years later by Caslon's English. The foundry moved from Vine Street to Ironmongers' Row in 1727, and during the next two years three more types appeared: Small Pica No.1, Long Primer No.2 and the celebrated Great Primer Roman. An italic for the Great Primer followed in 1730.

In 1734 the foundry moved to Chiswell Street, where Caslon published his famous

specimen sheet showing almost a full range of the roman types he cut. Unlike those of the slightly later John Baskerville, Caslon's designs were not innovative (similar types were in use a hundred years earlier), but it was his skill as an engraver that distinguished him. His fonts, which mark the end of the old face classification, became the standard roman for British printers well into the 19th century. In 1776 the Oxford University Press felt the need to supplement the Fell collection of Dutch types with Caslon's roman.

His work found particular favour in America, and Caslon type was used by Mary Katherine Goddard of Baltimore for printing the Declaration of Independence.

William Caslon I was undoubtedly the most

important member of the family and made the greatest contribution to the development of type design. However, the Caslon family continued in the business of typefounding well into the 19th century until the death of the last male Caslon in 1873. The foundry continued under their name until 1937.

William Caslon II (1720–78) worked with his father at the Chiswell Street foundry, taking over the business on his father's death in 1766 and managing it until 1792. His son William Caslon III (1754–1833) sold his share in the foundry to his mother and sister-in-law in 1792 and with the proceeds purchased Joseph Jackson's foundry in Salisbury Square (Jackson died in 1792). In turn he was succeeded by his son, William IV (1780–1869), who

managed the business from 1807 until 1819, when the foundry was purchased by Blake Garnet & Co. (later to be known as Stephenson Blake & Co.).

Meanwhile the original Caslon foundry remained in business under Mrs William Caslon II and Mrs Henry Caslon (Henry Caslon had died in 1788) until Henry Caslon II took over in 1809. Under the name of Caslon Son & Livermore, and later H W Caslon & Co. Ltd, the foundry remained in existence until 1937, when the matrices and type, including the now-celebrated Caslon Old Face, were purchased by Stephenson Blake & Co., who thereafter added 'the Caslon Letter Foundry' to their name.

Previous page and above: pages from George W Jones's specimen book, 1924. (NM)

ALPHABET
DEMI-GRAS CORPS 60

A A B b C c D d E e F f G g

H H I i J j K k L l M m N n

O o P p Q q R r S s T t U u

V v W w X x Y y Z z

1 2 3 4 5 6 7 8 9 0
1 2 3 4 5 6 7 8 9 0

A M CASSANDRE
1901–68 USSR

Types
Bifur 1929
Acier 1930
Acier Noir 1936
Peignot 1937
Touraine 1947
  (with Charles Peignot)
Cassandre 1968
Further reading
R K Brown and S Reinhold,
  *The Poster Art of A. M.
  Cassandre*, E P Dutton 1979
Henri Mouron, *Cassandre*,
  Rizzoli 1985

A M Cassandre was one of the most influential poster artists of the 20th century. Combining his typographic sensitivity with a fine art background, his work is typified by simple, elegant imagery and strong sans-serif (capitals-only) lettering.

He was born Adolphe Jean-Marie Mouron in Ukraine. His family moved to Paris in 1915 and in 1918 he began to study fine art. To help pay for this he turned to poster design, changing his name to avoid any embarrassment.

Cassandre's typefaces all reflect his poster work; they were not commissions but personal statements about aspects of typography and communication. His first typeface, Bifur, dates from a period when his posters where characterized by the use of capitals-only, sans-serif typography. Peignot, named after Charles Peignot who commissioned it, is his most famous typeface, and was a reaction to what he saw as the deformation of the lower-case alphabet.

After the end of World War 2 his graphic work became more fluid, as typified by the Yves Saint Laurent logo drawn in 1963 and still used today. His last typeface design reflected this fluidity, being based on the current architectural forms of the ellipse and the trapezoid. It was proposed for the signage for Charles de Gaulle Airport in Paris but not used. Still unreleased, it was named Cassandre after he took his own life in 1968.

Above: Peignot specimen, 1937, and Bifur specimen, n.d., from Deberny & Peignot. (both CLR)

William CAXTON
1421–91 GB

William Caxton introduced the art of printing with movable type to England. Caxton was a businessman who became involved in printing when he retired from commerce and engaged himself in translating and publishing. As a businessman he had occupied the important post of governor of the House of English Merchants at Bruges, and it was during this time that he acquired a knowledge of printing. His first types were certainly imported, and the standard of his printing was not as good as that of his contemporaries on the Continent. In contrast to the lighter roman types of Sweynheym & Pannartz or Jenson in Italy, Caxton's types were based on the north European black-letter.

He first started printing in 1475 at Bruges, working

65

Above: page from Boethius, *De consolatione philosophiae*, c.1478. (SBPL)

TRAJANUS

NACH ZEICHNUNGEN VON WARREN CHAPPELL

Warren **CHAPPELL**
1904–91 USA

Types
Lydian 1938–46
Trajanus 1940
Writing
Anatomy of Lettering,
  Loring & Mussey 1935
*A Short History of the Printed
  Word,* André Deutsch 1972

in partnership with Colard Mansion, who owned a press. Although most of Colard's books were in French, two were printed for Caxton in English: *Recuyell of the Historyes of Troie* and *The Game and the Playe of the Chesse.* These are the first printed books in the English language.

A year later Caxton returned to England. He set up a press in London, in Abbey Precinct, Westminster, by the sign of the Red Pale, where in 1477 he produced *The Dictes or Sayengis of the Philosophres,* the first book to be printed in England with a date and place of printing. His early types, brought from the Continent, soon became worn, and there is evidence that by 1480 he was using fresh type which had been cut in England; this was in fact his fourth type.

Caxton also printed what is probably the first advertisement printed in England. He printed more than one hundred books before his death in 1491. His types were passed to his foreman, Wynkyn de Worde, who continued to use them until about 1493, when he developed a type of his own.

Warren Chappell was one of America's most outstanding and versatile figures in the field of type design, graphic art and book illustration, and was also a distinguished writer and editor on the subject of the printed word. He graduated from the University of Richmond, Virginia in 1926 and studied under Allen Lewis and George Bridgeman before taking a post in a New York printing office. But his most important training at this time was at Offenbach in Germany, where he studied punch-cutting under Rudolf Koch. Koch was a powerful influence on many who were to become leading figures in type design in the post-war years.

In 1938 Chappell rapidly took the centre stage in America with the design of Lydian, a sans-serif face inspired by calligraphic letter forms. Cut for ATF, it became one of the most popular typefaces of the period. His other typeface, issued by Linotype, was Trajanus, a roman letter in the Renaissance style.

Above: Stempel specimen, n.d. (CLR)

Thomas Maitland **CLELAND**
1880–1964 USA

Types
Della Robbia/Westminster Old
  Style 1902
Garamond 1917
  (with Morris Fuller Benton)
Writing
'Harsh Words', in *Books and
  Printing: A Treasury for
  Typophiles*, The World
  Publishing Company 1951
The Fine Art of Printing,
  The New York Public Library
  1960

Thomas Maitland Cleland was
a painter, scenic designer,
book designer, illustrator and
master designer of period
typography, who was
inspired by the work of
William Morris and Will
Bradley at the Wayside Press.

Born in Brooklyn, New
York, he attended the Artist
Artisan Institute in Chelsea,
New York City, before work-
ing as a designer at the
Caslon Press. He later started
his own Cornhill Press in

Boston where he met
D B Updike, for whom he
undertook design work for
the Merrymount Press.

The stone-cut letters
of the 15th-century Italian
sculptor Luca della Robbia
were the inspiration for the
typeface Della Robbia. It was
designed for the Bruce Type
Company, which in 1902
became part of American
Type Founders. Cleland
worked with Morris Fuller
Benton at ATF on their
revival of Garamond.

From 1907 to 1908 he
was art editor for *McClure's
Magazine* and in 1925 worked
on the publication *Westvaco
Inspirations*, the house journal
of the international paper
manufacturer Westvaco
Corporation, a post later
held by Bradbury Thompson.

Above: Della Robbia from 1923
ATF specimen book. (NM)

Charles Nicolas **COCHIN**
1715–90 F

Types
Cochin/Moreau-le jeune/
  Gravure (revived 1912)

During a life which spanned
both the death of Louis XIV
and the storming of the
Bastille, Charles Nicolas
Cochin was one of the
greatest influences on the
illustrative arts in France
and beyond.

He was born into a family
of artists in Paris. Both his
parents were successful
engravers, and by the age
of 22 Cochin himself was
an accomplished artist and
engraver. Cochin's talent was
soon recognized and in 1739,
at the age of 24, he was given
an important artistic position
at the court of Louis XV.

Like all engravers of his
time, Cochin took a special
interest in the letter forms
used for the text which
invariably accompanied

an engraving. To this end he
created a series of graceful
alphabets in a style which,
for sharpness and elegance,
exceeded anything which
could be attempted by typefounders of the day. Although
these alphabets were not
bookfaces in the conventional
sense they were an important
source of inspiration to
Baskerville, and later,
Didot and Bodoni. Cochin
was revived and issued by
Deberny ɛt Peignot in 1912.

Above: page from Deberny &
Peignot specimen, 1955. (SBPL)

Sovereign Roman		
	Light	*Light italic*
SOVEREIGN	Regular	*Regular italic*
is an unusual family	Medium	*Medium italic*
with SERIF CAPS and	Demi Bold	*Demi Bold italic*
semi-serif lower case which	**Bold**	***Bold italic***
work perfectly well together.	**Extra Bold**	***Extra Bold italic***
Tapered stems and	**Black**	***Black italic***
calligraphic-influenced serifs		***...and italics***

give plenty of movement and
character, and of course
it can be used for both
text and display.

THIS IS
Sovereign

JANUARY 2004

Sovereign is a "work in progress".
It is going to be an extensive family
of seven weights with italics,
headline, small caps
and condensed styles.

Nick Cooke
01943 461 808
Email:
nick@g-type.demon.co.uk

g
TYPE

Simon de COLINES
1480–1546 F

68

Simon de Colines and his contemporary, 'the great scholar printer' Robert Estienne, made considerable contributions to the development of roman type in France. Simon de Colines was assistant to Henri Estienne, head of the famous Estienne family and father of Robert Estienne. When Henri died in 1520, de Colines married his widow and carried on the business of printing and publishing. When Robert came of age, de Colines started his own press. Although it is uncertain that de Colines was himself a designer of types, he produced several roman types based loosely on the work of Aldus Manutius. His italic type, influenced by Arrighi, was considered a fine design.

Above: titlepage from Flavio Biondo, *De Roma Triumphante*, 1533. (SBPL)

Vincent CONNARE
b.1960 USA

Types
Comic Sans 1995
Trebuchet 1995
Wildstyle 1995
Magpie 2000

Vincent Connare, designer of the ubiquitous Comic Sans, was born in Boston, Massachusetts. He has worked as an in-house type designer and typographic engineer at Microsoft Corporation (for whom he designed Comic Sans and Trebuchet) in Redmond, Washington State, and at Agfa of Wilmington, Massachusetts. His typeface Magpie was designed as part of the MA degree in typeface design at the University of Reading. Connare joined custom font specialists Dalton Maag in the spring of 2001.

Above: from Magpie specimen book, 2000. (NM)

Nick COOKE
b.1961 GB

Types
FF Penguin 1995
ITC Dartangnon 1998
Geetype 1999
Gizmo 1999
Houschka 1999
Nubian 1999
Digitalis 2000
Accent Graphic 2001
Precious Sans 2001
Amulet 2002
Precious Serif 2002
Chevin 2003
Sovereign 2004

Nick Cooke, who was born in Hyde, Cheshire, studied at Accrington College of Art and at Blackpool Et Fylde College of Art Et Design.

He started work as a designer/lettering artist for David Cox Studios in London in 1982, where he learnt how to craft type by hand for book jackets, and where his interest in type developed. Cox is the great-nephew of Eric Gill.

Cooke's first type family, the Japanese-influenced Penguin, was followed by the script font ITC Dartangnon. His G-Type foundry, which was launched in October 1999, offers an eclectic collection of Cooke's sans, serif and script fonts.

Above: detail from G-Type Sovereign specimen, 2004. (NC)

been doing had a normal serif, but his super-bold had a more or less rounded serif. It was suggested that he try a rounded serif for his normal roman so as to relate it more closely to the bold. Cooper elected to do this first and make

36 Point COOPER Oldstyle
ABCDEFGHIJKLMNOPQRS TUVWXYZ&
abcdefghijklmnopqrstuvwxyz $12457890!?

PLATE I

First proof of Cooper Oldstyle, October 22, 1918. All of the caps were recut heavier — half of the caps, several of the lower case and all of the figures were redrawn by Cooper.

it the basis for the heavy faces to follow. When shown, it was called simply Cooper for the reason there was doubt about the innovation of a rounded serif, and the name Cooper Oldstyle was reserved for a possible future design. Introduced as an advertising type, it proved to be an excellent text type, and Cooper seemed content to let the design stand as his contribution to the galaxy of oldstyles. He suggested that it be renamed Cooper Oldstyle to save confusion. The letters are closely fitted, which method was revived by Goudy and proved in his Kennerley to be the ideal for oldstyle roman text type. Be-

77

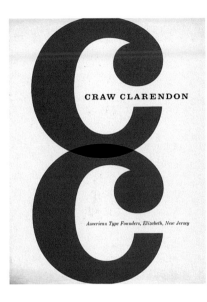

CRAW CLARENDON

American Type Founders, Elizabeth, New Jersey

Oswald Bruce COOPER
1879–1940 USA

Types
Cooper Oldstyle 1919
Cooper Black 1922
Cooper Italic 1924
Cooper Black Condensed 1925
Cooper HiLite 1925
Cooper Black Italic 1926
Pompeian Cursive 1927
Cooper Fullface (Modern) 1928
Further reading
The Book of Oz Cooper, Society of Typographic Arts 1949
'The Wizardry of Oz', *Baseline*, no.3, 1981

Oswald Bruce Cooper was a pupil of Frederic Goudy at the Frank Holme School of Illustration in Chicago. He was part of a circle of artists and designers active in Chicago in the early 1900s. Also in the circle were Will Ransom and W A Dwiggins.

In 1904 'Oz' Cooper formed Bertsch & Cooper, a partnership with Fred Bertsch. The company carried out general typography, newspaper advertisements, and book and magazine layouts, with Cooper specializing as a hand-lettering artist. In 1913 Cooper had his first notable success when he designed lettering for the Packard Motor Company. The design was considered very original and was granted a design patent and was eventually cut by ATF.

To supplement their lettering and layout services, the company added typesetting in 1914 and five years later Cooper designed Cooper Oldstyle, probably the first type with a rounded serif and the model for many heavy, round-serif types to follow. A companion italic was created in 1924.

Cooper Black ('for far-sighted printers with near-sighted customers') was designed in 1922, followed by HiLite, a variation with simulated highlights in white. The family was further extended with Cooper Black Condensed and Cooper Black Italic in 1925 and 1926.

Oz Cooper, a shy man of strong character who did not care for ceremony, died of cancer on 17 December 1940. A well-deserved appreciation in the form of *The Book of Oz Cooper* was published by Chicago's Society of Typographic Arts in 1949.

Above: first showing of Cooper Oldstyle as shown in *The Book of Oz Cooper*, Society of Typographic Arts, Chicago 1949. (NM)

Freeman CRAW
b.1917 USA

69

Types
Craw Clarendon 1955–60
Craw Modern 1958–64
Ad Lib 1961
Canterbury
Chaucery
Classic
Cursive
CBS Didot
CBS Sans

As well as being an important contributor to typeface design, Freeman Craw has also been a major figure in the creation of complete visual identity programmes for some of the world's leading companies. As vice-president and art director of Tri-Arts Press, he was responsible for the complete graphic control of some of the most impressive printed material in America.

Craw's early typefaces were created for ATF, most famously Ad Lib, designed in 1961, which drew on

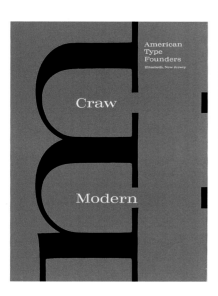

Enrico **CROUS-VIDAL**
1908–87 E

Wim **CROUWEL**
b.1928 NL

nineteenth-century wood lettering and the crude shapes of paper cut-outs, but from the 1970s his designs were primarily associated with photocomposition. He designed the proprietary CBS Didot and CBS Sans types, and in 1988 was awarded the TDC Medal for his contribution to typography.

Previous page and above: ATF specimens, early 1960s. (CLR)

Types
Catalanes 1952
Flash 1953
Paris 1953
Ilerda/Champs Elysées 1954
Île de France 1960

Enrico Crous-Vidal studied at art schools in Lérida, where he was born, and Barcelona. In 1933–4 he was the founder and art director of *Art* magazine. In 1939 he went into exile in France, working as a graphic artist. In 1959 he set up his own studio, producing several type designs for the Fonderie Typographique Française over the next ten years. At the end of the 1950s he turned to painting. Several of his typefaces have been released by Neufville Digital of Barcelona as part of their Grafia Latina collection.

Above: Fundición Tipográfica Nacional booklet showing Flash, 1955. (CLR)

Types
New Alphabet 1967
Fodor Alphabet 1969

Wim Crouwel was born in Groningen, where he studied at the Minerva Akademie and later at the Instituut voor Koonstnijverheidsonderwijs in Amsterdam. In 1952 he started his own design studio and in 1963, with Frisco Kramer, Paul Schwartz and Benno Wissing, founded Total Design – the first group of its kind in the Netherlands – a group which undertook major projects for the Amsterdam Airport Authority and the Dutch postal and telecommunications services.

An ardent supporter of lower-case typography, he proposed a single-alphabet typeface following the introduction of electronic typesetting devices. Some of the characters bore no

resemblance to existing ones and, although it was the subject of much attention, it was not taken up with any seriousness. Two years later, in 1969, he created Fodor Alphabet, a typeface designed for use in the posters and catalogues of Amsterdam's Fodor Museum.

From 1965 to 1978 he taught at Delft University and was professor there from 1972 to 1978. For a time he was design consultant to the Stedelijk Museum in Amsterdam and director of Museum Boijmans Van Beuningen in Rotterdam. Since 1993 Wim Crouwel has been working as a graphic designer in Amsterdam.

Above: showing of New Alphabet.

D

Den ensarn

△ 21.09 mm/60 pt¹ (22.50 mm^DIN) △ 0 H 13.20 mm

Bestemm

△ 25.31 mm/72 pt¹ (27.00 mm^DIN) △ −1 H 15.84 mm

42 Point   4 A 7 a

BEGIN
Restful

36 Point   4 A 7 a

MARCH
Eminent

30 Point   5 A 10 a

QUICKER
Indemnity

Carl DAIR
1912–67 CDN

Types
Cartier 1967
Writing
Design with Type, University of
Toronto Press 1967

A native of Welland, Ontario,
Carl Dair, who trained as a
compositor, was a lifelong
student of type and a gifted
and natural writer. His book,
Design with Type, first
published in 1952 but later
reissued, was chosen as one
of 50 best books of the year
by AIGA in 1967. In that
same year his only typeface,
Cartier, was also released
by Mono Lino Typesetting
for photocomposition.

Above: Linotype specimen of
Cartier, 1990. (NM)

Theodore Low
DE VINNE
1828–1914 USA

Types
Century 1894
    (with Linn Boyd Benton)
Writing
The Invention of Printing,
    New York 1878
Plain Printing Types,
    New York 1900
The Practice of Typography,
    1899–1904, New York 1902

Theodore Low De Vinne was
America's greatest scholar-
printer. Starting out as
a compositor, he rose to
the highest levels of his
profession.

   After serving his apprenticeship De Vinne worked as
a compositor with Francis
Hart & Co. and later became a
junior partner in the firm.
When the owner, Henry Hart,
died he purchased the whole
of the company and changed
the name to Theodore L De
Vinne & Co. He was responsible for the production of the
Century Magazine and also

Mail

High

ROBE

Squad

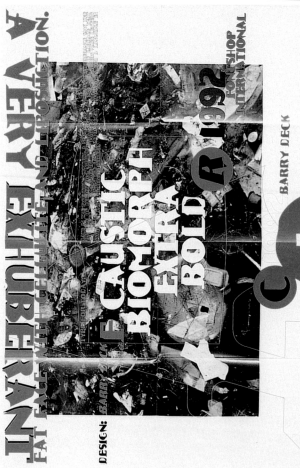

Barry DECK
b.1962 USA

Types

Barry Sans Serif 1989
Canicopulus Script 1989
Mutant Industry Roman 1989
Bombadeer 1990
Industry Sans 1990
Template Gothic 1990
Arbitrary Sans 1992
Caustic Biomorph 1992
Cyberotica 1994
Truth 1994
Traitor 1997
Eunuverse 1999
FauxCRA 2002
Moderne Sans

After graduating from Northern Illinois University, Barry Deck, who was born in Mount Pleasant, Iowa, began his career in graphic design in 1986 in Chicago. A period of freelancing for clients in Los Angeles, Chicago and New York was followed by further studies at the California Institute of the Arts. His experience there influenced his approach to type design. Reacting against perceived standards, and armed by the digital revolution, Deck produced mutilated and distorted letter forms which were embraced by the music industry and style magazines. This approach, which excited a new generation of graphic as well as type designers, was a major influence on typography in the 1990s. In 1995 Deck set up his own company, Dysmedia, in New York.

Above: poster from *Fuse*, no.4, 1991. (NM)

MORE

Quality

TYPOGE

Ernst F DETTERER
1888–1947 USA

Types

Eusebius Roman 1923 (with Robert Hunter Middleton)

Designer, teacher and calligrapher Ernst F Detterer was born in Wisconsin. After attending art colleges in Pennsylvania and studying lettering under Edward Johnson, he became associated with the revival of interest in the typefaces of the 15th-century Venetian printer Nicolas Jenson. Working for the Ludlow Typographic Company in Chicago, he designed a typeface based on these much-admired Jenson models. This typeface was created in 1923 and was called Eusebius after Eusebius Pamphili, the author of the book in which Jenson's type appeared for the first time in 1470.

While lecturing on the printing arts at the Chicago

72

collaborated in the creation of Century, the typeface which was specially cut for the magazine by Linn Boyd Benton.

As well as being a practical printer, De Vinne was also a distinguished writer about the historical and practical aspects of print. One of his most important books is *The Invention of Printing*, in which he set out to show that the invention of movable type was the work of Johann Gutenberg. Another work, *Plain Printing Types*, is the fruit of his long study of typefounders' specimen books.

Previous page and above: showing of Century Expanded (based on De Vinne's type) from 1923 ATF specimen book. (NM)

HER 5

class 5

Length of lower-case alphabet: 730 points

HIGH 7

splays 7

Length of lower-case alphabet: 606 points

PHIC 12

LE CID,

TRAGÉDIE.

ACTE PREMIER.

SCENE I.

CHIMENE, ELVIRE.

CHIMENE.

Elvire, m'as-tu fait un rapport bien sincere?
Ne déguises-tu rien de ce qu'a dit mon pere?

ELVIRE.

Tous mes sens à moi-même en sont encor charmés:
Il estime Rodrigue autant que vous l'aimez;
Et, si je ne m'abuse, à lire dans son ame,
Il vous commandera de répondre à sa flamme.

CHIMENE.

Dis-moi donc, je te prie, une seconde fois
Ce qui te fait juger qu'il approuve mon choix;
Apprends-moi de nouveau quel espoir j'en dois prendre:
Un si charmant discours ne se peut trop entendre;

LE SAINT
ÉVANGILE
DE JÉSUS CHRIST
SELON SAINT MATTHIEU.

CHAPITRE PREMIER.

Généalogie de Jésus Christ. L'ange instruit Joseph
de la conception de son épouse. Naissance de
Jésus Christ.

1. Livre de la généalogie de Jésus Christ,
fils de David fils d'Abraham.
2. Abraham engendra Isaac.
Isaac engendra Jacob.
Jacob engendra Juda et ses frères.
3. Juda engendra, de Thamar, Pharès et
Zara.
Pharès engendra Esron.
Esron engendra Aram.

a ij

François-Ambroise DIDOT
1730–1804 F

Art Institute, Detterer met Robert Hunter Middleton, who was a student in his class. Detterer and Middleton started to work together on the Eusebius typeface and subsequently Middleton was employed by Ludlow to see the typeface through its production stages. By 1929 Middleton had created matching bold, italic and open versions of Eusebius.

Above: page from Monotype specimen book, n.d. (CLR)

François-Ambroise was the son of the founder François Didot (b.1689 in Paris), who was a bookseller before he started his own printing works. François-Ambroise worked there with his brother Pierre-François until 1789, when the latter left to set up a printing office of his own, and later a paper mill. Inspired by Baskerville in England, Pierre-François was to use this mill to produce the first French wove paper.

Both men enjoyed royal patronage: François-Ambroise was printer to the comte d'Artois, later to become Charles X, whilst his brother Pierre was printer to the comte de Provence, later to become Louis XVIII. As a result of François-Ambroise Didot's reputation, Benjamin Franklin sent his grandson to him to learn punch-cutting.

François-Ambroise was also the director of the Imprimerie Nationale and in this capacity he revised Fournier's point system. His name survives in the continental Didot point.

François-Ambroise Didot initially printed with Garamond types but later began to produce his own. The exact date for this change is uncertain, but 1775 has been put forward by D B Updike, amongst others. Certainly a new Didot type, a light transitional roman, was in use in 1782 and was used the following year in three quarto editions of French classics. Firmin Didot took over the foundry when his father retired in 1789.

Above: page from *Le Cid*, printed in Maigre roman type, designed by François-Ambroise Didot 1783. (ECC)

Firmin DIDOT
1764–1836 F

Types
Didot Floriated Capitals c.1820
Didot 1784 (revived 1908)

The Didot family dominated the French book world in the late 18th and early 19th centuries. The most important family member as far as type design is concerned was Firmin Didot, the founder's grandson, who is generally agreed to have produced the first modern face in 1784. As a result, Didot roman types became standard book types in France during the 19th century and are still in use today.

In 1783 Firmin Didot, son of François-Ambroise, took over from his father's previous punch-cutter, Pierre-Louis Wafflard. In 1784 he produced the first modern face, characterized by thin serifs, a marked vertical stress and abrupt shading from thick strokes to thin.

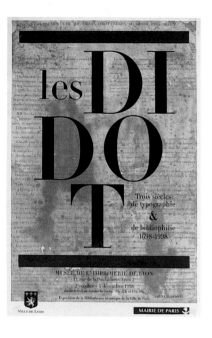

DIETHELM-ANTIQUA

93294 – 36

ABCDEFGHIJKLMNO
PQRSTUVWXYZ

VI

*Of the inhabitants of LILLIPUT; their learning, laws,
and customs, the manner of educating their children. The Author's way
of living in that country. His vindication of a great lady.*

ALTHOUGH I INTEND TO LEAVE THE DESCRIPTION OF THIS empire to a particular treatise, yet in the meantime am content to gratify the curious reader with some general ideas. As the common size of the natives is somewhat under six inches high, so there is an exact proportion in all other animals, as well as plants and trees: for instance, the tallest horses and oxen are between four and five inches in height, a sheep an inch and a half, more or less; their geese about the bigness of a sparrow, and so the several gradations downwards until you come to the smallest, which to my sight were almost invisible; but nature hath adapted the eyes of the Lilliputians to all objects proper for their view: they see with great exactness, but at no great distance. And to show the sharpness of their sight towards objects that are near, I have been much pleased with observing a cook pulling a lark, which was not so large as a common fly; and a young girl threading an invisible needle with invisible silk. Their tallest trees are about seven foot high; I mean some of those in the great royal park, the tops whereof I could but just reach with my fist clenched. The other vegetables are in the same proportion; but this I leave to the reader's imagination.

I shall say but little at present of their learning, which for many ages hath flourished in all its branches among them: but their manner of writing is very peculiar, being neither from the left to the right, like the Europeans; nor from the right to the left, like the Arabians; nor from up

18 point, 2 point leaded

Walter J DIETHELM
1913–86 CH

Types
Diethelm-Antiqua 1948–50
Sculptura 1957
Writing
Signet, Signal, Symbol, Zürich 1970
Form + Communication, Zürich 1974
Visual Transformation, Zürich 1982

Walter Diethelm was art director for the Swiss type-foundry Haas. He trained at the Kunstgewerbeschule, Zürich, at the Académie Rauson, and, with Ferdinand Léger, at the Grande Chaumière in Paris. For ten years he was art director for a major printing company in Zürich. He ran his own design studio, which he started in 1954. His book *Signet, Signal, Symbol* won wide acclaim in the advertising world.

Above: page from *Type*, SGM Books, St Gallen 1949. (CD)

Cristoffel VAN DIJCK
1601–69 NL

Types
Van Dijck (revived 1936)

One of the greatest of all Dutch punch-cutters was Cristoffel van Dijck (also van Dyck), who was intimately associated with the golden age of Dutch printing. He became the leading type-founder of Amsterdam in the 17th century and his work did a great deal to establish the reputation of Dutch types throughout Europe.

Born in Dexheim, Holland, van Dijck began working as a goldsmith in Amsterdam around 1640. A few years later he set up a typefoundry there. He was a superb craftsman, and the great Dutch publishing house of Elzevir used his types to the exclusion of all others. William Caslon is thought to have used his roman as the model for his own. Van Dijck died in the winter of 1669. In 1935 Stanley Morison commissioned Jan van Krimpen to advise on the design of a Monotype version of a van Dijck type. Monotype Van Dijk was issued in 1936.

Above: from Monotype Van Dijk specimen, n.d. (CLR)

74 By this time the Didots were using wove paper and an improved printing press, allowing the fine details of such type to be reproduced.

Firmin took over the foundry when his father retired in 1789, and continued the production of new types. He favoured neo-classical designs with increasingly fine hair serifs. In 1811 Firmin was made printer to the Institut Français and in 1814, royal printer. He retired in 1827, leaving his sons Ambroise-Firmin and Hyacinth to continue the business.

Previous page: St Matthew's Gospel in type cut by Firmin Didot 1793. (ECC); Above: poster for Museum of Printing, Lyon, 1998. (CLR)

Pierre DI SCIULLO
b.1961 F

Types
Basnoda 1993
FF Flèches 1993
FF Minimum 1993–5
F Scratched Out 1995
Gararond 1995
Quantange 1995
Sintaitik
Tifinar
Toutunepiesse
Web
quiresiste.com

Paris-born graphic designer Pierre di Sciullo has demonstrated his love of working with text and images in his own publication *Qui? Résiste*. He has designed typefaces for the FontFont library, Creative Alliance, Neville Brody's *Fuse* project and the Tuareg people in their traditional writing system. A teacher in Strasbourg, he also gives lectures at home and abroad.

Above: from a poster for F Scratched Out, *Fuse*, no.5, 1992. (NM)

Tony DISPIGNA
b.1943 I

Types
ITC Lubalin Graph 1974
    (with Herb Lubalin and
    Joe Sundwall)
ITC Serif Gothic 1974
    (with Herb Lubalin)
Fattoni
Playgirl
WNET

An emigrant to the USA from Forio d'Ischia in Italy, Tony DiSpigna studied at the New York City Community College and Pratt Institute. His first design job was with Ronne Bonder and Tom Carnase. In 1969 he joined Lubalin, Smith, Carnase Inc. and from 1973 ran his own studio in New York before becoming vice-president of Herb Lubalin Associates in 1978. In 1980 he started Tony DiSpigna Inc. Involved in almost every area of graphic communication, he has won many awards.

Above: ITC specimen cover, 1974. (CLR)

Bram de DOES
b.1934 NL

Types
Trinité 1, 2, 3 1978–81
Lexicon 1990–1
Further reading
Mathieu Lommen, *Bram de Does: Typographer & Type Designer*, De Buitenkant 2003

Bram de Does, who was born in Amsterdam, trained as a typesetter and printer. After studying at the Amsterdamse Grafische School, he followed in the footsteps of Jan van Krimpen and Sem Hartz, supervising typographic design at the Enschedé typefoundry in Haarlem. He founded Spectatorpers, his private press, in 1961. His type designs Trinité and Lexicon are particularly popular with book designers, and he has won many awards for book typography.

Above: reproduction of original analogue photographic version of Trinité as printed in *Types Asa*, no.2, June 1982. (CLR)

Dick DOOIJES
1909–98 NL

Types
Rondo 1948
    (with Stephan Schlesinger)
Mercator 1957–61
Contura 1966
Lectura 1966
Bronletter
Writing
Mijn leven met letters, Amsterdam 1991

Typographer, critic and type designer Dick Dooijes was taught type design at the Lettergieterij Amsterdam (Typefoundry Amsterdam) by S H de Roos. He was de Roos's assistant for a time and worked with him on the designs for Egmont and De Roos Roman. From 1968 to 1974 he was director of the Gerrit Rietveld Akademie Amsterdam.

Dooijes's Lectura is a loose adaptation of the 16th-century Dutch faces which William Caslon had

Roman
abcdefghijklmnopqr
stuvwxyz
ABCDEFGHIJKLM
NOPQRSTUVWX
YZ1234567890!

Italic
abcdefghijklmnopq
rstuvwxyz
ABCDEFGHIJKLM
NOPQRSTUVWX
YZ 1234567890!

Bodies
Roman (all sizes available)
8 10 12 14 18 24 30 Sm 30 Lg
Italic (available shortly)
8 10 12 14 18 24 30 Sm

INTRODUCING:
6 NEW FONTS
DESIGNED BY JOHN DOWNER
BROTHERS
REGULAR, **BOLD**, *SUPER SLANT* AND 87 WORD LOGOS
AND
COUNCIL
REGULAR AND 182 WORD LOGOS
TO ORDER CALL 1.800.944.9021 OR GO TO: EMIGRE.COM

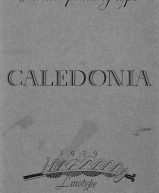

EMBLEMS AND Electra

A new printing type
CALEDONIA
1939
Linotype

used as models for his own types, whilst his Mercator is based on the 19th-century grotesks. Dooijes added to Rondo, a face principally designed by Stephan Schlesinger. His Bronletter was a private design commissioned for the printers Gooi Et Stickl.

Previous page and above: from Stephenson Blake specimen, n.d. (CLR)

John **DOWNER**
b.1951 USA

Types
Triplex Italic 1985, 1990
Roxy 1990–3
Iowan Old Style 1991, 2001
Ironmonger 1991–3
SamSans 1993–6
Sermone (Simona) 1996
  (with Jane Patterson)
Brothers 1996–9
Vendetta 1997–9
Council 1999
Paperback 2005
Writing
'Copping an Attitude: Part 2',
Emigre, no.38, 1996

John Downer, who was born in Tacoma, Washington, served an apprenticeship as a sign painter and showcard writer. Many of his type designs reflect that heritage. On becoming a journeyman, Downer studied at Washington State University, graduating with a degree in fine art before going on to the University of Iowa, where he achieved two advanced

degrees (MA and MFA) in painting. He now lives and works in Iowa City. His types are published by Emigre, Font Bureau, Bitstream, and the Italian foundry Design Lab, with whom he collaborated on the production of his Simona family. His lectures and writings show an enlightened and often humorous approach to the history of type design and typography.

Above: from Emigre specimen book, 1999. (NM)

William Addison **DWIGGINS**
1880–1956 USA

Types
Metro 1929–30
Electra 1935–49
Caledonia 1938
Eldorado 1951
Falcon 1961
Writing
Layout in Advertising, Harper and Brothers Publishers 1928
Further reading
MSS. by WAD,
  The Typophiles 1947
'Typographic Treasures: The Work of W A Dwiggins',
  Baseline, no.8, 1986

W A Dwiggins was a man of many talents. He excelled at calligraphy, type design, book design, illustration and writing. Born in Martinsville, Ohio, he studied at the Frank Holme School of Illustration in Chicago. There he met Frederic Goudy, his lettering tutor. They began a friendship which eventually led to Dwiggins following Goudy to

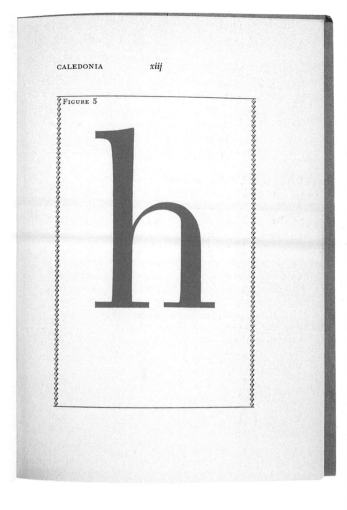

Hingham, Massachusetts, to where Goudy was to move his Village Press. Dwiggins had attempted a printing business in Ohio in 1903 but without success. Goudy moved on to New York in 1906 but Dwiggins remained in Hingham until his death. He pursued a successful career in advertising design for 20 years until, dissatisfied and looking for a new challenge, he chose to focus on book design and illustration. He began a long association with the publisher Alfred A Knopf, for whom he designed 280 books over 30 years.

In 1928 Dwiggins's *Layout in Advertising* was published and a comment therein about the need for better sans-serif types led Mergenthaler Linotype to invite him to design one. Metroblack, which he drew himself, was issued in 1929. Other weights of Metro followed, designed by Linotype under Dwiggins's supervision. Impressed with these types, Mergenthaler Linotype offered Dwiggins a contract. He worked with them for 27 years, producing 12 type designs, five of which were issued to the trade.

At home in Hingham, Dwiggins satisfied many of his skills with puppetry. He designed magnificent puppets, built a puppet theatre, wrote plays, designed tickets and posters and gave shows. It was at home, too, that he ran the Püterschein-Hingham Press, in collaboration with Dorothy Abbe, from 1947 until his death in 1956.

Previous page: cover of Linotype Electra specimen, 1935, and Linotype Caledonia specimen, 1939.; Above: from Linotype Caledonia specimen. (both NM)

Den ensartede Bestemmelsen

△ 25.31 mm/72 pt¹ (27.00 mm^DIN) ▷ −1 H 18.10 mm

Erbar Grotesk fett

8 Cicero

LUDWIG & MAYER
Schriftgiesserei und Holzgerätefabrik
Frankfurt am Main

Un certain

Comme une

Que lorsqu'

Nous devons,

Afin que d

Et qu'on

Otto **ECKMANN**
1865–1902 D

Types
Eckmann 1900

Born in Hamburg, Otto Eckmann was a painter, graphic artist and type designer. He was a contemporary of Peter Behrens and a collaborator with him in the creation of Jugendstil. This movement, a response to Art Nouveau, was named after the Munich-based journal *Jugend*, for which both did graphic work. His brush-script-based typeface, Eckmann, issued by the Klingspor foundry in two weights, combines Jugendstil with the traditional German black-letter. Eckmann died of tuberculosis in 1902 at the age of 37.

Above: from Linotype specimen, 1990. (NM)

Jakob **ERBAR**
1878–1935 D

Types
Feder Grotesk 1910
Erbar and variants: Lucina, Lumina, Lux and Phosphor 1922–30
Koloss 1923
Candida 1936

After training as a compositor in Düsseldorf and having studied type under Fritz Helmut Ehmcke and Anna Simons, Jakob Erbar spent most of his life working and teaching in Cologne, first at the Städtischen Berufschule, and then at the Kölner Werkschule.

In 1910 Erbar designed his first type, Feder Grotesk, and he went on to create a number of typefaces for the Frankfurt typefounders Ludwig & Mayer. The best known of these is the one which bears his name, Erbar. One of the first geometric

sans serifs, Erbar pre-dates both Paul Renner's Futura and Rudolf Koch's Kabel.

According to Walter Tracy in his book *Letters of Credit*, Erbar's aim was to design a printing type which would be free of all individual characteristics, possess thoroughly legible letter forms, and be a purely typographic creation. His conclusion was that this could only work if the typeface was developed from a fundamental element, the circle. There are four weights of Erbar, and the family also includes Lucina (a set of white on black capitals), Lux (a version with contrasting outlines) and Phosphor (an inline version of the bold Erbar weight).

Above: Ludwig & Mayer specimen cover, n.d. (CLR)

Roger **EXCOFFON**
1910–83 F

Types
Chambord 1945
Banco 1951
Mistral 1953
Choc 1955
Diane 1956
Calypso 1958
Antique Olive 1962–6

Roger Excoffon, like many creators of type in the 20th century, approached his subject from the standpoint of graphic design, and in doing so achieved a subtle blend of eloquence and economy which perfectly suited the mood of the period.

After university education at Aix-en-Provence, Roger Excoffon, born in Marseilles, went to Paris to study painting, but here his preference turned increasingly towards graphic art and the design of letter forms. In 1947 he formed his own advertising agency in Paris and, at about the same time,

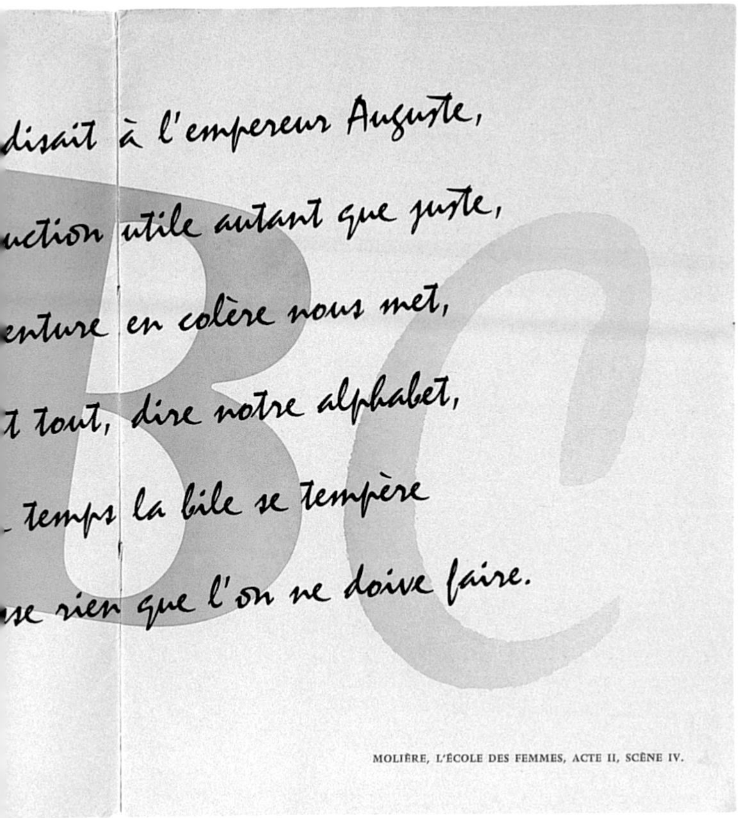

disait à l'empereur Auguste,

...uction utile autant que juste,

...enture en colère nous met,

...t tout, dire notre alphabet,

...temps la bile se tempère

...se rien que l'on ne doive faire.

F

became design director
of a small but ambitious
Marseilles typefoundry,
Fonderie Olive.

As a freelancer he had
already worked for the
Fonderie Olive and had
designed Chambord, a typeface modelled on Cassandre's
Peignot, but in his position
as design director new typefaces appeared rapidly and
to enthusiastic acclaim.
In addition, he helped in
the design of another type,
François Ganeau's Vendôme,
which was modelled on
17th-century French types.

Between 1962 and 1966 he
designed his most successful
face, Antique Olive. This was
a response to the increasing
demand for sans-serif faces
following the success of
Haas's Helvetica and Deberny
ɛt Peignot's Univers, which
were intended to give the

clean contemporary (some
would say lifeless) look of
the 1960s. These new and
exciting typefaces gave
French advertising and
graphic design much of the
vigour and exuberance for
which it was acclaimed at
the time.

Above: spread from Fonderie
Olive specimen, n.d. (CLR)

To pass the time on a rowing expedition from Folly Bridge to Godstow on July 4, 1862, Carroll began a story, plopping 'my heroine straight down a rabbit-hole, to begin with, without the least idea what was to happen afterwards.' Present on the occasion were the three daughters of Dean Liddell – Lorina ('Prima'), Alice ('Secunda'), and Edith ('Tertia') – and the Reverend Robinson Duckworth, then a fellow of Trinity. Later, 'to please a child I loved,' Carroll wrote out the story, the original version of ALICE'S ADVENTURES IN WONDERLAND, *called* ALICE'S ADVENTURES UNDER GROUND. *Though the Meteorological Office records indicate that a good deal of rain fell in the twelve hours prior to 2 a.m. on July 5, Duckworth, Dodgson, and Alice each remembered the day as sunny and warm. Their recollections are expertly supported and the confusion cleared up by H. B. Doherty in an essay in* WEATHER *(1968). We can now be assured that it indeed was warm and sunny, a 'golden afternoon.'*

Alfred FAIRBANK
1895–1982 GB

Types
Narrow Bembo Italic 1923
Writing
A Handwriting Manual,
 The Dryad Press 1932
A Book of Scripts, Penguin
 1949, Faber & Faber 1977

Undoubtedly Alfred Fairbank was the man who did more than any other to revive the use of the italic cursive hand. A brilliant calligrapher himself, he was renowned as a teacher and writer on handwriting, and his *Handwriting Manual* is considered to be the definitive work on the subject.

He was also a type designer. His Narrow Bembo Italic was commissioned by Monotype to complement their Griffo revival, Bembo. It was considered, however, that this beautiful italic worked better alone, and another, based on the letter forms of Tagliente, replaced it as the standard accompaniment to Bembo. Although he would have liked to create more usable types, it was unfortunate that he lived at a period when, in England at least, carvers rather than calligraphers were preferred as type designers.

Above: showing of notes set in Narrow Bembo Italic from *Alice's Adventures in Wonderland*, illustrated by Barry Moser, Pennyroyal Press 1982. (NM)

Dave FAREY
b.1943 GB

Types
ITC Beesknees 1991
ITC Johnson 1991–2001
ITC Oswald 1992
Torino Modern 1992
ITC Highlander 1993
Ringworld 1993
Blackfriar 1994
Subway 1994
Aries 1995
ITC Golden Cockerel 1996
Stellar 1996
Cachet 1997
La Gioconda 1999
Collins 2000
Comedy 2000
Ersatz 2001
Zemestro 2002
Azbuka 2004
Writing
'The Last of the Elite. London's
 Historic Typefoundries',
 Baseline, no.20, 1995
The Liberated Letter,
 Mark Batty 2003

Londoner Dave Farey's prolific contribution to type design – he has been involved in the creation of over two hundred typefaces – began after an early experience with sign painting. He then joined Letraset in 1961 in a junior capacity, assisting with negative retouching, film processing, stencil cleaning, and, of course, also making the tea. He progressed to stencil-cutting and, having achieved the skill level demanded by this most exacting process, his first task was to cut Aldo Novarese's Augustea Open.

Over the many years since, Farey's fascination with letter forms and his resulting knowledge has led to the introduction and revival of a huge variety of type designs.

Now based at HouseStyle Graphics in London, Farey and partner Richard Dawson are specialists in typeface design for every area of typographic communication.

FTF12

FTF MORGAN TOWER TWO 580 PT

KCB

FTF MORGAN TOWER THREE 170 PT

SQUADRON

FTF Morgan Tower; one, two three, four
Four fonts designed in 2001

3-line Pica Roman

Man that is born
of a woman is of
few days and full

Mário **FELICIANO**
b.1969 P

Types
Aurea 1997
Bronz 1997
Cepo 1997
Escrita 1997
Gazz 1997
MexSans 1997
DeBula 1998
Strumpf 1999
BsKombat 2002
BsMandrax 2002
FTF Morgan Project 2002
FTF Rongel 2002
FTF Stella 2002
FTF Merlo 2004
FTF Morgan Avec 2004
FTF Grotzec Headline 2004

Mário Feliciano was born in
Caldas da Rainha, Portugal,
in 1969. He began work as
a graphic designer for *Surf
Portugal Magazine* in 1993.
In 1994 he founded his own
design studio in Lisbon,
Secretonix. He has been
heavily involved in type
design since. A versatile
designer, he has made
typefaces that range from
contemporary display
and text fonts to classic
interpretations of early
Spanish types. Before establishing his own foundry in
2001 he designed typefaces
for Adobe, T26 and Psy/ops.
His typefaces are used
prominently in many
Portuguese and international
publications. A winner of two
Type Directors Club awards,
he is the Portuguese country
delegate for ATypI.

Above: FTF Morgan from
Feliciano Type Foundry
specimen, 2004. (NM)

John **FELL**
1625–86 GB

Types
Fell types c.1672

Dr Fell was bishop of Oxford,
dean of Christ Church and
vice-chancellor of Oxford
University. Between 1670
and 1672 he imported types,
punches and matrices, which
were bought in Holland on
his behalf by Thomas
Marshall. These included
some Granjon types and
some supplied by van Dijck.
With three others (and for an
annual payment of £200) he
took over the management
of Oxford University Press in
1672. In 1676 he set up a typefoundry attached to the press
and, after employing Dutch
type-cutter Peter Walpergen,
published a specimen sheet
in 1693.

The types cast from his
collection, known as the Fell
types, became neglected until
their revival by C H O Daniel

Clients, of which there
are many in the publishing
world, include *The Times*
newspaper for whom Farey
and Dawson designed the
display and text type, Times
Classic.

Previous page: first edition of
The Times using Times Classic.
(CLR); Above: Faces promotion,
1999. (CD)

FOUR LINES PICA IN

FURNIT

FIVE LINES PICA AN

MANK

FOUR LINES PICA (

MAIDST

TWO LINES NONPAREIL A

ABCDEFGHIJKLMNOPQRS

---

at his private press from 1877 onwards. In 1915 Francis Meynell persuaded the controller of Oxford University Press to let him have two cases of Fell type, with which Meynell and Stanley Morison printed two books.

Previous page and above: details of Fell's 3-lines Pica roman, photographed for the CLR. (CLR)

Ed FELLA
b.1938 USA

Types
OutWest (on a 15° ellipse) 1993
Further reading
Edward Fella: Letters on America, Photographs and Lettering, Princeton Architectural Press 2001

A recipient of many prestigious awards, Ed Fella is an artist, teacher and graphic designer. After 30 years as a commercial artist in Detroit, where he was born, he studied at Cranbrook Academy of Art for an MFA in design. He has taught since at the California Institute for the Arts. Fella's work is featured in the National Design Museum and Museum of Modern Art in New York. He drew his typeface OutWest by hand using a 15 degree ellipse on an architectural template, hence its full name.

Above: detail from Emigre broadsheet, 1993. (NM)

Vincent FIGGINS
1766–1844 GB

Types
Gresham 1792 (revived 1925)
Figgins Shaded c.1815 (revived 1937)
Egyptian 1817
Further reading
Berthold Wolpe, *Vincent Figgins Type Specimens*, Printing Historical Society 1967

Vincent Figgins, born in Peckham, England, was one of the influential early 19th-century typefounders working in London and was responsible for the introduction in 1817 of the first typeface in the egyptian style.

He started at the age of 16 as an apprentice in the foundry of Joseph Jackson in London. When Joseph Jackson died in 1792, Figgins was to take over the business, but lack of finance made this impossible and the entire foundry was purchased by William Caslon III. Determined to succeed on his own,

Figgins was eventually able to start his own business in Swan Yard, Holborn Bridge, London.

One of his most important commissions was the production of a facsimile type for Macklin's Bible, for which Jackson had originally cut the type in 1789. When the printer Bensley had partly completed the work he decided to renew the type and chose not to go to Caslon, who now held the Jackson matrices, but instead asked Figgins to cut a font to correspond with the original. Figgins obliged by cutting a perfect match. The reputation of Figgins was now well established and a succession of roman types followed, for both English and Scottish printers. He was also successful with newspaper types, which were undergoing

URE,
ND
INE,
WXYZ,;:.-'

V. FIGGINS.

BERLING

Johann Michael
FLEISCHMANN
1701–68 D

Karl Erik FORSBERG
1914–95 S

Types
Parad 1936
Lunda 1938
Berling 1951–8
Carolus 1954
Ericus 1964

radical changes with the introduction of the steam press; one of the first was adopted by *The Times* in 1814.

It is for his work with display types, however, that Figgins is chiefly remembered. His later specimen books show that he could compete with the new foundries such as Stephenson Blake by producing a range of powerful display types, including the very first egyptians (named after his original typeface), which matched the new mood of the Industrial Revolution. This first truly original design of advertising type was brought out in 1817; with its heavy, slab serifs and even weight it has been described as a typical expression of the machine age.

Above: detail from 1967 facsimile of Figgins's specimen book, 1815. (NM)

Johann Fleischmann was born in Wöhrd near Nürnberg, where he trained in the craft of punch-cutting. He lived for some time in Frankfurt am Main, working at the Egenolff-Luthersche typefoundry, before moving to Holland around 1728. There he was employed by several typefounders before establishing his own foundry in Amsterdam.

In 1735 Fleischmann sold out to the printer Rudolph Wetstein and eventually went into the employment of the Enschedé foundry of Harlem. During a 20-year period at Enschedé, he cut an enormous amount of types in a wide variety of styles, often difficult small types, often with accompanying titles and ornaments cut by Jacques-François Rosart. Fleischmann was honoured on his death by

the foundry's issue of a special type specimen.

Fleischmann's roman types, which were influenced by the 'romain du roi' of Philippe Grandjean, achieved a degree of innovation which later inspired the renowned French punch-cutter, Pierre Simon Fournier.

Above: page from Enschedé specimen book, 1931. (NM)

Karl Erik Forsberg, born in Munsö near Stockholm, trained in typography, calligraphy and as a compositor in Basel, a combination which, not surprisingly, led him to design types. He worked for Almquist & Wiksell, printers to the University of Uppsala, as head designer, before becoming head of another Swedish publishing company, P A Norsted & Sons, where he succeeded fellow type designer Akke Kumlien.

Berling is his best-known typeface. It was called after the foundry that produced it, Berlingska Stilgjuteriet of Lund. Forsberg's Carolus and Ericus are alphabets of

Pierre Simon **FOURNIER** (le jeune)
1712–68 F

capitals, whilst Lunda was designed for use in advertising.

An outstanding book designer and calligrapher, Karl Erik Forsberg also designed magazines and postage stamps. He taught design and calligraphy at a number of colleges of graphic arts and, in 1983, he was awarded the honorary degree of doctor of philosophy by the University of Uppsala.

Previous page and above: detail from Castcraft specimen, c.1950s. (CLR)

Types
Fournier (revived 1925)
Barbou (revived 1968)
Writing
Dissertation sur l'origine et les progrès de l'art de graver en bois, Barbou 1758
Manuel Typographique
(2 vols.), Barbou 1764–8

Pierre Simon Fournier, also known as Fournier le jeune, made several important contributions to type design. He set up his own foundry in Paris, where he cut and founded all the types himself, pioneered the concept of the type family and is said to have cut 60,000 punches for 147 alphabets of his own design. He created new print-ers' flowers and ornaments that caught the mood of the age. He broke a monopoly on music printing in France and improved existing methods of printing music. He also invented a point system for standardizing music type and published its first version when he was only 25. Not surprisingly perhaps, Fournier's death at 56 was attributed to overwork.

Pierre Simon Fournier was the youngest son of a printing family and, although he initially studied painting, became involved in type design through work he did for his eldest brother. He started off engraving wood blocks and large capitals, later moving on to fonts of type. In 1736 Fournier began his own foundry, and pub-lished the first version of his point system the following year. In 1742 he published a specimen book, printed by Jean Joseph Barbou, part of a long association between the two men.

The two main influences on Fournier's types were the celebrated 'romain du roi' cut by Grandjean for the Imprimerie Royale in 1702, and the narrow letters, particularly those by Johann Fleischmann, favoured in Holland and Germany. Fournier took a keen interest in the history and theory of printing and typography and he wrote several papers on aspects of these subjects, including his *Dissertation* advancing Schöffer over Gutenberg as the inventor of printing. His most famous work is the two-volume *Manuel Typographique* dated 1764 and 1766 (though the second volume was actually published in 1768).

Fournier is probably best remembered as the designer of one of the early transi-tional faces. His St Augustin (14pt) Ordinaire served as the model for the Monotype

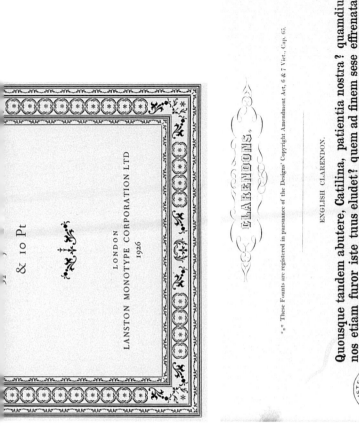

transitional face Fournier, released in 1925. Another version of this face, Barbou, was cut by Monotype at the same time, in 13d/14pt. Although used in *The Fleuron* in 1930, it was not released to the trade until 1968, the bicentenary of Fournier's death.

Previous page: titlepage from *Manuel Typographique*, 1764–8, photographed for the CLR.; Above: from *Monotype Recorder*, March/April 1926. (both CLR)

Benjamin FOX
d.1877 GB

Types
The first Clarendon c.1845

An exceptionally gifted punch-cutter, Benjamin Fox cut the original Clarendon series, which was basically an egyptian with bracketed serifs. Clarendon proved extremely popular because it met the demand for a compact dictionary type, an application for which it is still used to this day.

Fox went on to cut the Medieval series, a revival of Miller & Richard's Old Style, which was popular as an alternative to the romans of Isaac Moore and Joseph Fry.

Fox was a partner in the firm of R Besley & Co., the typefoundry of Robert Besley. Besley himself had previously been a partner in the typefoundry of William Thorowgood. Besley acquired ownership on Thorowgood's

retirement, when he changed the firm's name.

Benjamin Fox died in 1877, and the stock of the foundry was eventually purchased by Stephenson Blake in 1905.

Above: detail from 1848 specimen book. (SBPL)

Tobias FRERE-JONES
b.1970 USA

Types
Armada 1987–94
Garage Gothic 1992
Cafeteria 1993
Epitaph 1993
Nobel 1993
F Reactor 1993
Reiner Script 1993
    (after Imre Reiner)
Stereo 1993
    (after Karlgeorg Hoefer)
Interstate 1993–9
F Fibonacci 1994
Hightower 1994
Niagara 1994
Asphalt 1995
Citadel 1995
F Microphone 1995
Pilsner 1995
Mercury Text 1999
Gotham 2001
    (with Jesse Ragan)

New Yorker Tobias Frere-Jones was an artist from a young age, exhibiting paintings, sculptures and photographs in his home city from the age of 14. Son of an ad agency copywriter and a

Adrian FRUTIGER
b.1928 CH

print buyer, Frere-Jones, not surprisingly, discovered an affinity with letter forms, which led him to study at the Rhode Island School of Design. An exceptional student there, he drew the attention of Matthew Carter, who directed him, after graduation in 1992, to Font Bureau in Boston.

During seven years at Font Bureau Frere-Jones learnt his craft under the experienced eye of David Berlow and contributed considerably to their library. His sans-serif Interstate family, based on US highway signage, was one of the most successful types of the 1990s. Between 1993 and 1995 he designed three types for Neville Brody's experimental *Fuse* project.

In 1999 Frere-Jones left Font Bureau to join forces with friend Jonathan Hoefler

at the Hoefler Type Foundry which they renamed Hoefler & Frere-Jones Typography. There they satisfy the demand for custom type designs of the highest quality from major magazine, newspaper and design clients.

Previous page: Gotham, detail from *Hoefler Type Foundry Catalogue*, no.7, 2003. (NM); Above: Interstate, detail from *Font Bureau Type Specimens*, 2nd ed., 1997. (NM)

Types
Phoebus 1953
Ondine 1954
President 1954
Meridien 1955
Univers 1957
Opéra 1959–60
Egyptienne 1960
Apollo 1964
Serifa 1967
OCR-B 1968
Iridium 1975
Frutiger 1976
Glypha 1979
Breughel 1982
Icone 1982
Versailles 1982
Centennial 1986
Avenir 1988
Herculanum 1990
Linotype Didot 1991
Vectora 1991
Pompeijana 1993
Rusticana 1993
Frutiger Stones 1998
Frutiger Symbols 1998
Linotype Univers 2000
Linotype Frutiger Next 2001
Linotype Avenir Next 2004
  (with Akira Kobayashi)

Writing
Schrift, Ecriture, Lettering, Zürich 1951
Der Mensch und seine Zeichen (3 vols.), Frankfurt am Main 1978–81
Type Sign Symbol, Zürich 1980
Signs and Symbols: Their Design and Meaning, London 1989

Further reading
Charles Bigelow, 'Philosophies of Form in Seriffed Typefaces of Adrian Frutiger', *Fine Print on Type*, Lund Humphries 1989
Sebastian Carter, 'Adrian Frutiger', *Twentieth Century Type Designers*, Lund Humphries 1995

Adrian Frutiger is considered to be one of the most important type designers of the 20th century and continues to influence typographic communication in the 21st century. He is best known for his sans serifs Univers and Frutiger.

abcd(abcdef abcde(abcc

ABC(ABCDE ABCD ABC

abcdef abcdefgh abcdefgl abcde

ABCDI ABCDEF ABCDEF ABCD

abcdefg abcdefghij abcdefghi abcdef

ABCDE(ABCDEFGI ABCDEFG ABCDE

abcdefghij abcdefghijklm abcdefghijkl abcdefg

ABCDEFG ABCDEFGHIJ ABCDEFGHI ABCDEF

abcdefghijkli abcdefghijklmnop abcdefghijklmno abcdefghij

ABCDEFGHI ABCDEFGHIJKL ABCDEFGHIJKL ABCDEFGI

abcdefghijklmno abcdefghijklmnopqrst abcdefghijklmnopqrs abcdefghijklm

ABCDEFGHIJKL ABCDEFGHIJKLMNO ABCDEFGHIJKLMN ABCDEFGHIJ

abcdefghijklmnopq abcdefghijklmnopqrstuvw abcdefghijklmnopqrstuv abcdefghijklmn

ABCDEFGHIJKLMN ABCDEFGHIJKLMNOPQ ABCDEFGHIJKLMNOPQ ABCDEFGHIJKL

abcdefghijklmnopqrstu abcdefghijklmnopqrstuvwxyza abcdefghijklmnopqrstuvwxy abcdefghijklmnop

ABCDEFGHIJKLMNOF ABCDEFGHIJKLMNOPQRST ABCDEFGHIJKLMNOPQRST ABCDEFGHIJKLM

abcdefghijklmnopqrstuvw abcdefghijklmnopqrstuvwxyzabcde abcdefghijklmnopqrstuvwxyz ab abcdefghijklmnopqrs

ABCDEFGHIJKLMNOPQR ABCDEFGHIJKLMNOPQRSTUVW ABCDEFGHIJKLMNOPQRSTUVV ABCDEFGHIJKLMNO

abcdefghijklmnopqrstuvwxyz a abcdefghijklmnopqrstuvwxyzabcdefgh abcdefghijklmnopqrstuvwxyz abcdefghijklmn abcdefghijklmnopqrs
ABCDEFGHIJKLMNOPQRSTUVWXY ABCDEFGHIJKLMNOPQRSTUVWXYZ12 ABCDEFGHIJKLMNOPQRSTUVWXYZ1 ABCDEFGHIJKLMNOPQF

abcdefghijklmnopqrstuvwxyz abcdefg abcdefghijklmnopqrstuvwxyz abcdefghijklmnopqrs abcdefghijklmnopqrstuvwxyz abcdefghijklmnop abcdefghijklmnopqrstuvwxyza
ABCDEFGHIJKLMNOPQRSTUVWXY ABCDEFGHIJKLMNOPQRSTUVWXYZ123456789 ABCDEFGHIJKLMNOPQRSTUVWXYZ1234567 ABCDEFGHIJKLMNOPQRSTU

univers

LEEDS

Ten Lines Pica.

Frutiger was born in Switzerland in 1928 near Interlaken. He was apprenticed in that town to the printers Otto Schaeffli as a compositor after his father refused to allow him to train as a sculptor. Frutiger has said that his enthusiasm for sculpture has persisted and finds expression in the types he designs. Between 1948 and 1951 Frutiger studied at the Kunstgewerbeschule in Zürich, where his subjects included calligraphy.

Charles Peignot recruited Frutiger for Deberny Et Peignot after seeing a brochure he had produced, *History of Letters*, which used his wood-engraving skills. The typefounders Deberny Et Peignot were connected with the Lumitype/Photon photosetting machine, which needed typefaces adapted to suit. Charles Peignot wanted Frutiger to adapt Futura and this provided the impetus for Univers. Frutiger found Futura too geometric for his taste. He also wanted to create a large, matched family of faces of different weights. The 21 members of the Univers family were all designed before the first matrix was struck. Many founders followed Deberny Et Peignot in producing large sans-serif type families of their own; Haas, for instance, developed Helvetica.

Although Frutiger has said that all his types have Univers as their skeleton, he felt, when he came to design a face for the Charles de Gaulle Airport, that Univers seemed dated, with a 1960s feel. His airport face, originally known as Roissy but renamed Frutiger for its issue to the trade by Mergenthaler Linotype in 1976, is a humanistic sans serif that has been compared to Gill and Johnston types. In 1986 Frutiger received the Gutenberg Prize for technical and aesthetic achievement in type.

Since the late 1990s Frutiger has supervised the digital recutting of his sans serifs Univers, Frutiger and Avenir, using the latest technology. The completely recut Linotype Univers now has 63 weights. Frutiger Next offers additional weights and true italics. Working with Linotype Library type director Akira Kobayashi, Frutiger reworked the weights of Avenir, also adding condensed versions to create Avenir Next.

Above: from Deberny & Peignot Univers specimen, n.d. (CLR)

Joseph **FRY**
1728–87 GB

Types
Fry's Baskerville 1768
Old Face Open 1788
(revived 1928)

Joseph Fry established the Fry foundry, later taken over by his two sons. Type Street (now Moore Street, London) was so called because it became home to this foundry.

Joseph Fry was inspired to take up typefounding by the example of Baskerville, and there are some similarities between the two men. Fry, like Baskerville, was a Birmingham man by birth who came to typefounding relatively late in his career, after having been successful in other fields. Amongst his numerous ventures he started Fry's Chocolates.

In 1764, whilst living in Bristol, Fry went into partnership with a local printer. He set up a foundry attached to the works. Isaac Moore was taken on to cut types, later becoming a partner. Moore cut his types after Baskerville's and the foundry's early types are all of this kind. In 1766 they published their first specimen sheet and two years later moved to London as Isaac Moore ɛt Co., one of many renamings.

Fry's two sons Edmund and Henry joined the firm in 1782. In 1787, when Fry retired, Dr Edmund Fry, the eldest son, ran the foundry, renaming it Edmund Fry ɛt Co. The company was again renamed in 1788, becoming the Type Street Foundry. In 1828 Edmund retired and sold his stock to William Thorowgood of Fann Street.

Previous page and above: details of Fry's 10-lines Pica type from 1785 specimen, photographed for the CLR. (CLR)

François GANEAU
1912–80 F

Types
Vendôme 1951–4

François Ganeau was born in Paris and was principally a sculptor and theatre decorator with numerous public commissions to his credit. He was a friend of Maurice Olive, the proprietor of the Fonderie Olive in Marseilles, where Roger Excoffon was the chief designer. François Ganeau's typeface Vendôme was cut at the Fonderie Olive in 1951–4. It is believed that Roger Excoffon assisted in the design of this face.

Above: detail of Fonderie Olive Vendôme specimen cover, n.d. (CLR)

ABCDEFGHIKL
MNOPQ RSTV
XYZ abcdefghil
mnopqrsſtuvxyz

laricationes noſtras
warum ⲧῶϡακαλων αυ
cis noſtræ ſuper eum
os ſicut' oues erraui-
auit,& Garamond on
im. O der eſſus fuit',
Sicut' D.Stempel AG
m tondente ſe obm.

Claude **GARAMOND**
c.1500–61 F

Types
Garamond
(revived from 1924)
Grecs du Roi c.1549
Further reading
Paul Beaujon, 'The "Garamond"
Types', *The Fleuron*, no.5,
1926
Stanley Morison, 'Garamond
roman', *A Tally of Types*,
Cambridge University Press
1973

Claude Garamond's roman letters, designed at his Paris foundry, took the roman of Aldus Manutius as their model and were much copied. By the end of the 16th century they had become the standard European type and they were still in use in the 18th century.

Little is known of Garamond's early life, but he may have worked with several punch-cutters before embarking on a career of his own. In the late 1520s he was approached by the scholar and printer Robert Estienne to cut types, and Garamond's first roman appears in the 1530 edition of *Paraphrasis in Elegantiarum Libros Laurentii Vallae* by Erasmus.

The model Garamond used for this type was the 1455 *De Aetna* roman of Aldus Manutius, but Garamond refined the type to suit his own tastes. Following the success of the roman, King François I commissioned a greek for his exclusive use from Garamond, which is now known as the 'grecs du roi'.

In 1545 Garamond began publishing on his own account, using types of his own design that included a new italic cut in two sizes. His first book was the *Pia et Religiosa Meditatio* of David Chambellan.

After Garamond's death in 1561 his punches and matrices were sold off. A principal buyer was Christopher Plantin of Antwerp, but type also found its way to Frankfurt, where it appeared in a 1592 specimen of the Egenolff-Berner foundry.

Garamond's types were much revived in the past century and several versions exist under his name; most, however, are based on the Caractères de l'Université in the Imprimerie Royale in Paris, which Beatrice Warde (under her pseudonym Paul Beaujon) proved in 1925 to be the work of the later Jean Jannon. These revivals include the ATF Garamond of 1918 by Morris Benton; Goudy's Garamont for Lanston issued in 1921; Monotype Garamond of 1922; and the Italian foundry Simoncini's Garamond issued in 1958.

Accurate revivals of Garamond-style type include Stempel's Garamond of 1924, based on the Egenolff-Berner sheet; G W Jones's Granjon of 1928–31, so named to avoid confusion with all the other Garamonds; and the Adobe Garamond of Robert Slimbach issued in 1989.

Above: Garamond Canon from Plantin-Moretus Museum, Belgium, photographed for the CLR.; Stempel specimen, n.d. (both CLR)

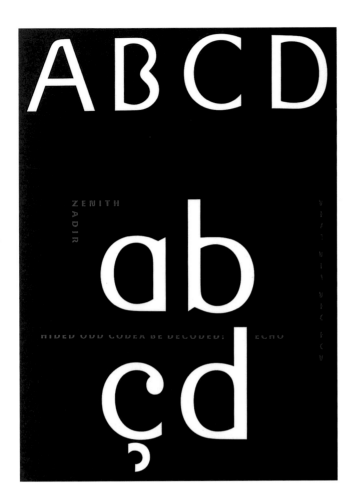

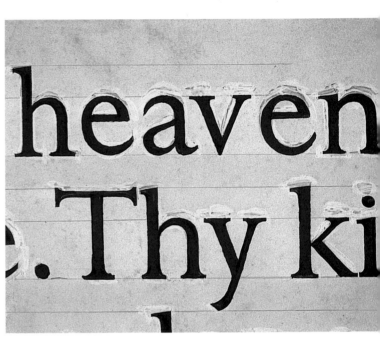

Karl GERSTNER
b.1930 CH

Types
Gerstner Programm 1967
Gerstner Original 1987
Writing
Kalte Kunste?, Teufen 1957
Die Neue Graphik, Teufen 1959
  (with Markus Kutter)
Programme Entwerfen,
  Teufen 1964
Kompendium für Alphabeten,
  Teufen 1972
Typographisches Memorandum,
  St Gallen 1972
The Designer as Programmer,
  Hatje Cantz 2002

Graphic designer, typographer, painter and writer Karl Gerstner, who was born in Basel, studied at that city's Allgemeine Gewerbeschule under Armin Hoffman and Emil Ruder. It was there, too, that he trained in graphic design with Fritz Bühler's studio. He opened his own studio in 1953 following a period of freelancing. Gerstner was a contributor to the influential 'Swiss typography' of the 1950s. He was a co-founder of the successful GGK advertising agency in 1962, which numbered Swissair, Volkswagen and IBM amongst its many international corporate clients.

Gerstner assisted Berthold in the standardization of the classic sans serif Akzidenz-Grotesk, and it was their Bodoni that he chose for the outstanding corporate identity he created for IBM. His Gerstner Original family, a sans serif featuring many experimental letter forms, was released by Berthold in 1987. Now in retirement, Karl Gerstner continues to pursue visual art through his love of painting.

Above: Berthold Exklusiv Gerstner Original specimen, n.d. (NM)

Eric GILL
1882–1940 GB

Types
Gill Sans 1927–30
Golden Cockerel Press Type
  1929
Solus 1929
Perpetua 1929–30
Joanna 1930–1
Aries 1932
Floriated Capitals 1932
Cunard/Jubilee 1933–4
Bunyan/Pilgrim 1934
Writing
An Essay on Typography (1931),
  5th ed., Lund Humphries
  1988
Art, Devin-Adair 1934
Reading
R Brewer, *Eric Gill, the Man who
  Loved Letters*, Frederick
  Muller 1973
Robert Harling, *The Letterforms
  and Type Designs of Eric Gill*,
  Eva Svensson 1976
Fiona MacCarthy, *Eric Gill*,
  Faber & Faber 1988

Arthur Eric Rowton Gill, letter-cutter, sculptor, wood-engraver and type designer, was one of the most prominent and controversial figures of his day.

Born in Brighton, Gill studied at Chichester School of Art before being apprenticed to an ecclesiastical architect in London. Whilst there he attended the classes of the calligrapher Edward Johnston at the Central School of Arts and Crafts. Thus he became involved in the small world of scribes and illuminators and the Arts and Crafts Movement, embarking on a career as a stone-cutter and letterer.

In 1905 Gill moved to Hammersmith, home to William Morris, and a haven of the private press movement. Gill's work at this time was varied: inscriptions, tombstones, head-pieces and initial letters for private presses, including Emery Walker's Doves Press and

The Versatile Gill Family of Type Faces

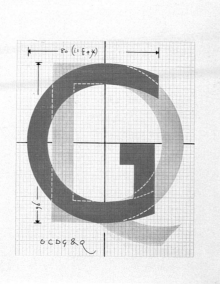

Gill Sans (262)
Gill Sans Bold (275)
Gill Sans Light (362)
Gill Sans Extra Bold (321)
Gill Sans Ultra Bold (442)
Gill Sans Condensed (485)
Gill Sans Bold Condensed (343)
Gill Sans Bold Extra Condensed (468)
Gill Sans Titling (231)
Gill Sans Bold Titling (317)
Gill Sans Extra Bold Titling (526)
Gill Sans Bold Condensed Titling No. 1 (373)
Gill Saps Bold Condensed Titling No. 2 (525)
Gill Sans Shadow Titling (304)
Gill Sans Shadow No. 1 (406)
Gill Sans Shadow No. 2 (408)
Gill Sans Shadow No. 3 (338)
Gill Sans Shadow Line (290)
Gill Sans Poster (353)
Gill Sans Cameo (233)
Gill Sans Cameo Ruled (299)
Gill Sans No. 2 (349)
Gill Sans Bold No. 2 (350)
Gill Sans Light No. 2 (662)

The Monotype Corporation Limited

Avalanche
Charlotte
Charlotte Sans
Gilgamesh
Spiderman

Michael GILLS
b.1962 GB

Harry Kessler's Cranach Press in Weimar.

The Gills left Hammersmith in 1907 and set up the first of their three craft-based, self-sufficient religious communities, at Ditchling in Sussex. (The others were at Capel-y-ffin in Wales, 1924–8, and Pigotts in Buckinghamshire, 1928–40.)

Gill designed his first typeface at the invitation of Stanley Morison of the Monotype Corporation. The drawings for the type, Perpetua, were begun in 1925. Charles Malin cut the type before the work was passed to Monotype for production.

Gill Sans, designed during the same period, was based on the same sources as the Johnston sans serif. Gill had painted san-serif lettering on Douglas Cleverdon's Bristol Bookshop in 1927 and it was

this that suggested the idea of a Gill sans serif to Morison. Joanna was cut by the Caslon foundry; one of its first uses in 1931 was for Gill's own *Essay on Typography*. These three typefaces are from his most creative period; he was also working for Robert Gibbings's Golden Cockerel Press, where he designed the typeface of that name.

In 1935 Gill was made an associate of the Institute of British Architects. Two years later he was made an associate of the Royal Academy and in 1936, with J H Mason, was amongst the first to be given the title Royal Designer for Industry. He died at home in 1940 after a lung operation.

Previous page: detail of Perpetua design, photographed for the CLR.; Above: Monotype Gill specimen from the mid-1950s. (both CLR)

Types

Avalanche Script
Iris 1990
Isis 1990
Prague 1991
Charlotte 1992
Charlotte Sans 1992
Elysium 1992
Figural 1992
Hand Drawn 1993
Gilgamesh 1994
Katfish 1994
Fling 1995
Frances Uncial 1995
ITC Forkbeard 1998
Spidercave 2000

Web
gillsey.clara.net

After an apprenticeship in engineering, Michael Gills's interest in letter forms led to studies in design at Suffolk College. He joined Letraset as a type designer in 1988 where, during seven years, he made a considerable and varied contribution to their library. His most successful types are the sans serif

Charlotte and its companion serif, which he created directly on the screen. Influenced and inspired by earlier German and Czech type designers and calligraphers, he has revived several of their types, particularly those of Oldrich Menhart. Although now more involved in graphic design, Gills retains his enthusiasm for letter forms.

Above: a selection of types by Michael Gills. (MG)

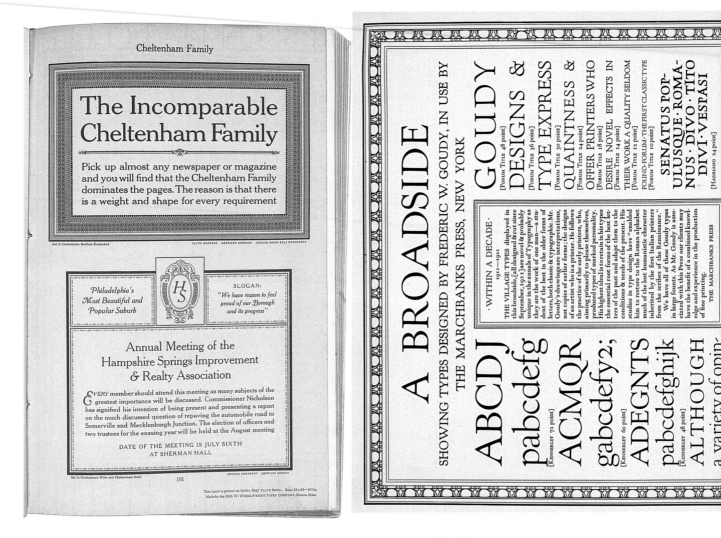

Above: from 1923 ATF specimen book. (NM)

Bertram Grosvenor **GOODHUE**
1869–1924 USA

Types
Merrymount 1894
Cheltenham 1896

A distinguished American architect, Bertram Grosvenor Goodhue was the designer of Cheltenham, one of the most successful American typefaces. Produced in 1896 for Ingalls Kimball of the Cheltenham Press in New York, 'Chelt' was probably the first typeface to be designed with the sole objective of achieving maximum legibility by the application of logical design principles: leading is an aid to legibility; ascenders are more important than descenders.

Cheltenham was also one of the first designs to be produced by pantographic punch-cutting, and was an immediate success. It was acquired by American Type Founders in 1902, having been further refined by Morris Fuller Benton, and has remained consistently popular ever since.

Goodhue also designed Merrymount for the Merrymount Press, the private press run by D B Updike.

Frederic W **GOUDY**
1865–1947 USA

Types
Copperplate Gothic 1901
Pabst 1902
Powell 1903
The first Village Type 1903
Kennerley Old Style 1911
Forum Capitals 1912
Goudy Antique/Lanston 1912
Goudy Old Style 1915
GoudyType 1916
Goudy Modern 1918
Goudy Open 1918
Hadriano 1918
Goudy Antique 1919
Garamont 1921
Goudy Newstyle 1921
Frenchwood Ronde/Italian Old
    Style 1924
Goudy Extra Bold 1926
Cushing Antique 1927
Goudy Text and Lombardic
    Capitals 1928
Deepdene 1929–34
Kaatskill 1929
Mediæval 1930
Goudy Sans Serif 1930–1
Goudy Village 1936
Californian 1938
Goudy Thirty 1946

Writing
The Trajan Capitals,
    Oxford University Press 1936
*The Alphabet and Elements of
    Lettering*, University of
    California Press 1952
Typologia, University of
    California Press 1940
*A Half-Century of Type Design
    & Typography 1895–1945*,
    Typophile Chapbooks XIII
    and XIV, 1946

Further reading
Melbert B Cary Jr,
    *A Bibliography of The Village
    Press 1903–1938* (1939),
    new ed., Oak Knoll Press 1981
D J R Bruckner, *Frederic Goudy*,
    Abrams 1990

Frederic Goudy, one of the best-known and most prolific of type designers, designed, by his own reckoning, 123 faces. Born in Bloomington, Illinois, he worked in various cities before founding the Booklet Press in Chicago in 1895 with equipment bought from Will Bradley. Renaming

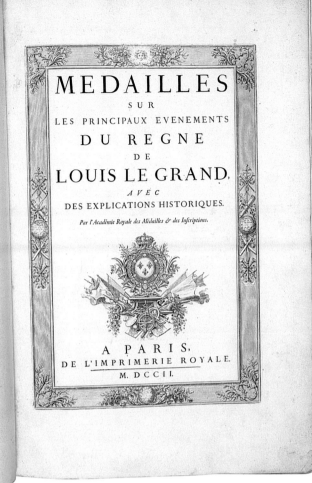

Philippe **GRANDJEAN**
1666–1714 F

Types
Romain du Roi 1702

The Romain du Roi was a significant development in the history of typography because it was the first real departure from the old-style faces in use in Europe at the time, and as such can be considered the first transitional typeface.

Philippe Grandjean de Fouchy was born into an old Mâcon family in 1666. A visit to a printing office in Paris led the young Grandjean to design a set of capitals. A Monsieur de Ponchartin, who was shown his early attempts, recommended him to Louis XIV, and Grandjean was summoned to start working for the Imprimerie Royale under its director Jean Anisson. Later Grandjean was to run the foundry and change its location as he moved house so it was always close to his home.

In 1692 Louis XIV appointed a committee from the Académie des Sciences to draw up plans for a new typeface which would be the exclusive property of the Imprimerie Royale. The committee, headed by Nicolas Jaugeon, studied types then in use, historical manuscripts and principles of geometry. The letter designs it then drew up were based on divisions of the circle. The type was to be called the Romain du Roi, the King's Roman.

Grandjean was assigned to cut the new type and, whilst guided by the drawings, he did not follow them slavishly. The type established his reputation. He worked on it from 1694 to 1702, and it appeared in its first size in 1702 in *Medailles sur les principaux*

---

it Camelot Press, he printed the journal *American Chap-Book* before selling his interest a year later. The sale of a set of capitals of his own design to the Bruce Type Foundry, Boston, encouraged him to become a freelance lettering artist. He taught at the Frank Holme School of Illustration, developing an interest in the English private presses. The Village Press was started with Will Ransom in 1903. It moved to Hingham, Massachusetts, before going to New York in 1906. When the workshops were destroyed by fire in 1908 Goudy returned to his work as a lettering artist and designer.

His breakthrough with type design came in 1911. He designed Kennerley Old Style for the publishers Mitchell Kennerley on the understanding that he could sell it to the trade. He set up the Village Letter Foundry to cast and sell Kennerley and a titling font, Forum. These established his reputation, and American Type Founders commissioned Goudy Old Style, regarded as one of his finest designs. In 1920, with 40 types to his name, Goudy was appointed by Lanston Monotype as art adviser, working on the Garamond revival Garamont.

The Village Press and Letter Foundry moved to New York State in 1923. Four years later, Robert Wiebking, who had cut the matrices for most of Goudy's types, died. Goudy learnt about typefounding and in the 12 years until his second workshop fire in 1939 he produced 60 typefaces. He died at his home, a watermill on the Hudson River, in 1947.

Above: Marchbanks Press broadside, 1921. (NM)

Previous page and above: pages from *Medailles sur les principaux événements du règne de Louis le Grand*, 1702. (SBPL)

Robert **GRANJON**
active 1545–88 F

Types
Civilité 1557

événements du règne de Louis le Grand. It was finally completed, in 21 sizes of roman and italic, in 1745. Jean Alexandre, Grandjean's assistant, took over the task of cutting it, and was succeeded in turn by Louis Luce, who also designed types in his own right.

As an attempt to protect the Romain du Roi from copying, one letter was given a distinctive mark. It was reputedly Louis XIV who decided that this letter should be his initial: 'l'. In the lowercase, the l has a little projection on the left-hand side (a feature taken from a calligraphic 'l'). In practice the Romain du Roi was copied anyway, sometimes with this special l, sometimes with the projection removed.

The design of the Romain du Roi is a step towards the modern face because it has shading which is closer to the vertical than that of an old-face type and also has intensified contrast between the thick and the thin strokes. Its serifs are flat and unbracketed but not hairline (though it is unlikely that printing technology could have reproduced a hairline serif anyway at this time). Grandjean's italic also differs from the italic of the old-face types. He regularized the slope and modified some of the letters. The Romain du Roi continued to be used throughout the 18th century and, despite being protected by law, it was much copied (notably by Fournier and Didot).

Robert Granjon began his career as a printer in Paris in 1549, as a partner to Michel Fezendat, and began supplying types around the same time. He moved to Lyon in 1557, later to Antwerp, and finally to Rome, where his clients included the New Vatican Press. Nothing is known of him after 1588.

Granjon designed and cut a great many types, but he is best known for his italics and for the script type which he called the 'lettres Françaises', but which acquired the name Civilité through its use in books of manners. Henri II granted a ten-year monopoly on the type to Granjon, but on the expiry of the monopoly the type was not taken up by others in the way its creator had hoped. Granjon had designed Civilité as a rival to italic, a truly French one since it was based on current French handwriting, but italic was too well established for Civilité to be a threat. The type did prove popular in Holland, and a Dutch version was created. In France it continued to be used occasionally until the mid-18th century.

Granjon's types were adopted enthusiastically by other European printers of the day, most notably by Plantin, and in the 20th century provided the basis for Plantin, Times New Roman and Galliard. Granjon, the face that was named after him in G W Jones's 1924 Linotype revival, was subsequently found to have been based on a Garamond type.

Above: from H G Carter and H D L Vervliet, *Civilité Types*, Oxford University Press 1966. (SBPL)

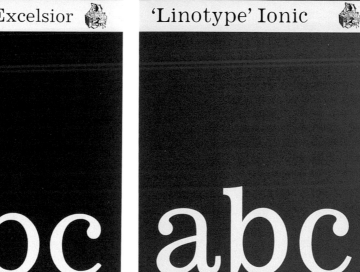

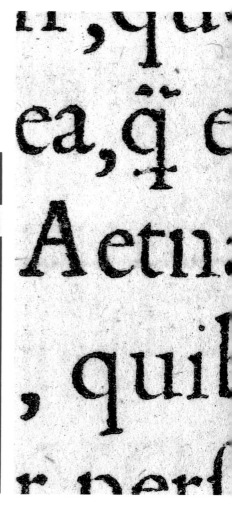

Chauncey H GRIFFITH
1879–1956 USA

Types
Ionic 1922–5
Poster Bodoni 1929
Excelsior 1931
Paragon 1935
Opticon 1935–6
Janson 1937
Bell Gothic 1938
Corona 1941
Monticello 1946

In his position as vice-president of typographic development for the Mergenthaler Linotype Company of New York, Chauncey H Griffith was responsible for instigating many new designs, of which the best known is the Legibility Group: Ionic, Excelsior, Paragon, Opticon and Corona, all designed for the rigours of newspaper printing.

Griffith started his career as a journeyman compositor and pressman. When he joined Mergenthaler Linotype in 1906 it was as part of their sales force. He was made sales manager and assistant to the president before taking charge of the company's typographical development programme. Two designers who worked for him were W A Dwiggins and Rudolph Ruzicka. During his period at the company he issued revivals of Granjon, Baskerville and Janson, plus a large number of oriental scripts, and designed Bell Gothic for the Bell Telephone Company. The Legibility Group was begun in 1922 with Ionic, which was first used by the *Newark Evening News* in 1926. Excelsior, the second in the series, has been described as one of the most influential newspaper typefaces of all time.

During World War 2 Griffith developed types to meet the US Government's desire that information in every dialect between California and the Chinese coast could be set using Linotype. His own favourite face was Monticello: based on the 1812 typeface Oxford, it was produced for setting *The Papers of Thomas Jefferson*. Griffith retired from his position in 1949 but continued to work for Linotype as a consultant.

Above: Excelsior (1966) and Ionic (1969) specimens from Linotype. (CLR)

Francesco GRIFFO
d.c.1518 I

Renaissance printer and publisher Aldus Manutius commissioned punch-cutter Francesco Griffo of Bologna, who had worked for him on his greek types, to design a roman type to improve upon that of Nicolas Jenson. The resulting roman was first used in Cardinal Bembo's *De Aetna* of 1495. Griffo also cut the roman type for Francesco Colonna's *Hypnerotomachia Poliphili*, which Aldus published in 1499. Griffo's romans were innovative in their use of the calligraphic practice of making capitals shorter than the ascending letters of the lower-case. This improved the colour of the text, resulting in better legibility.

The invention of italic type is generally ascribed to Aldus and Griffo. Their first 'Aldine' italic, based on a script used

Phill GRIMSHAW
1950–98 GB

in the papal chancery, made its debut in a 1501 edition of Virgil's *Opera*. Griffo was to design two other italics, one for the printer Geronimo Soncino for his Petrarch of 1503, and one for himself. Griffo used this when publishing small editions on his own account on his return to his native Bologna after Aldus's death.

Francesco Griffo had a dispute with Aldus, who he claimed had not given him sufficient credit for the types. He died some time around 1518/19. The cause and exact date of his death are not known, but it seems likely that he was hanged for killing his brother-in-law in May 1518 during a fight.

Previous page and above: detail from Aldus Manutius printing of *De Aetna*, photographed for the CLR. (CLR)

Types
Oberon 1986
Hazel 1992
Arriba 1993
Bendigo 1993
Pristina 1994
Shaman 1994
Gravura 1995
ITC Grimshaw Hand 1995
ITC Tempus 1995
ITC Tempus Sans 1995
Scriptease 1995
Zaragoza 1995
Zennor 1995
ITC Braganza 1996
ITC Golden Cockerel Initials
 and Ornaments 1996
 (after Eric Gill)
ITC Kallos 1996
ITC Klepto 1996
ITC Obelisk 1996
ITC Rennie Mackintosh and
 Ornaments 1996
Banco 1997
 (after Roger Excoffon)
ITC Kendo 1997
ITC Noovo 1997
ITC Stained Glass 1997
ITC Regallia 1998
ITC Samuel 1998
ITC Stoclet 1998

Further reading
Patrick Baglee, 'Phill Grimshaw', *U&lc*, vol.25, no.2, 1998

Phill Grimshaw was a modest but irrepressible man whose type designs reflected the latter side of his personality. He studied art under Tony Forster at Bolton College, and on Forster's recommendation applied for entry to the Royal College of Art in London. Accepted there, he studied for a master's degree in design between 1972 and 1975.

His type submissions to Letraset led to a long and productive working relationship and friendship with the company's manager of typographic development, Colin Brignall, who described him as 'one of the best display typeface designers of recent times'. Grimshaw contributed considerably to

Letraset's Fontek library, and later to that of ITC after Brignall became their European type development director. Phill Grimshaw died at the early age of 48 following a long illness.

Above: ITC Kallos specimen, *U&lc,* vol.23, no.1, 1996.; type designs and experimental sketches, *U&lc*, vol.25, no.2, 1998. (both CLR)

Thesis

FF Thesis

AAaAAaAAaAAaAa
AAaAAaAAaAAaAa
AAaAAaAAaAAaAa
AAaAAaAAaAAaAa
AAaAAaAAaAAaAa
AAaAAaAAaAAaAa
AAaAAaAAaAAaAa
AAaAAaAAaAAaAa

TheSans
TheSerif
TheMix

Luc(as) de GROOT
b.1963 NL

Types
Nebulae 1994
Thesis 1994
F MoveMe 1995
JesusLovesYouAll 1995
E Antiqua 2000
SpiegelSans 2001
Sun 2001
Punten 2002
Corpid 2003
Taz 2003
TheAntiqua 2003

Web
lucasfonts.com

Like many of his successful Dutch contemporaries, Lucas de Groot studied type design and typography at the Koninklijke Academie van Beeldende Kunsten in The Hague under Gerrit Noordzij. After qualifying in 1987, a period of freelancing and teaching was followed by four years with the Dutch design group BRS Premsela, working mostly on corporate identities. In 1993 he joined MetaDesign in Berlin, where one of his projects was assisting Erik Spiekermann in the development of FF Meta Plus. Four years later he left to set up his own company, which specializes in typeface and typographic solutions, the Berlin-based FontFabrik.

De Groot, a self-confessed font fanatic, spent five years from 1989 working on the production of his 144 font Thesis project. His own interpolation theory contributed eight weights to each of six styles of three forms, sans, serif and mix, to create one of the largest-ever families of typefaces. The poster designed by de Groot for the FontFont launch of Thesis in 1994 must rate as one of the most informative type specimens ever produced. Thesis has continued to grow, with de Groot adding Antiqua, Typewriter, Mono, Office and Condensed versions.

De Groot's typefaces, now marketed as LucasFonts, appear in newspapers, magazines, corporate identities and advertising campaigns around the world.

Above: cover of FSI Thesis specimen, 1994. (NM)

André GÜRTLER
b.1936 CH

Types
Egyptian 505 1966
Media 1976 (with C Mengelt and E Gschwind)
ITC Avant Garde Oblique 1977
Basilia 1978
Signa 1978
Unica 1980 (with C Mengelt and E Gschwind)

André Gürtler is recognized as a world authority on type and type design. As a writer he has contributed many articles to *Typographische Monatsblätter*.

Born in Basel, Gürtler trained as a typesetter. In 1958, after further training in typography with Emil Ruder, he joined the type-design drawing office of the Monotype Corporation in England. He also worked as a designer at the Deberny & Peignot foundry in France before joining the studio of Adrian Frutiger. From 1965 Gürtler lectured at the Schule für

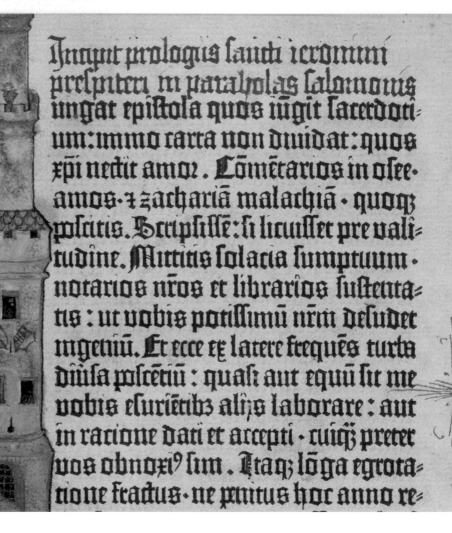

Johann **GUTENBERG**
c.1394–1468 D

Gestaltung in Basel on the history and design of letter forms.

The typeface Unica, designed with Team 77 partners Christian Mengelt and Erich Gschwind, was released by Haas in 1980. Unica is a monoline sans serif combining features from Akzidenz-Grotesk, Helvetica and Univers.

Previous page: detail from *From Helvetica to Haas Unica*, Haas 1977. (CLR)

Types
Mainz Indulgence type 1455
42-line Bible type 1455
Reading
Albert Kapr, *Johann Gutenberg: The Man and his Invention*, Scolar 1996
Blake Morrison, *The Justification of Johann Gutenberg*, Vintage 2001

The German Johann Gensfleisch zur Laden, known as Gutenberg, is generally believed to be the inventor of movable metal type, although there are some who credit the invention to Laurents Coster of Haarlem. The invention, which probably took place between 1440 and 1450, would have involved Gutenberg's bringing together several existing techniques: the screw press, oil-based pigments, the metal-working skills of punch-cutting (developed

for patterning metal) and casting. He was not a typographical innovator in the sense of designing a new style of character. Rather than modifying letter forms for print, he did his best to imitate the lettering of books produced by contemporary scribes.

Gutenberg was born in Mainz, where his father, Friele, was a worker in precious metals, having connections with the episcopal mint there. In 1428 Gutenberg left Mainz, and in 1434 his name begins appearing on documents in Strasbourg, where he became involved in various business ventures and, although little is known of his early life, we can assume that he began work on his invention, for there are records of his borrowing large sums of money

and of purchases of lead, a press and type.

He left Strasbourg, probably in 1444, and is next heard of in Mainz in 1448, where a year later he borrowed 800 guilders for 'work on the books' from Johann Fust, a lawyer. A further loan of 800 guilders proved necessary, however, and at this point Fust became a partner in the proceedings.

The principal works of Gutenberg's Mainz press were the 42-line Bible, probably completed in 1455 – produced in two volumes of 324 and 318 pages respectively – which gets its name from the number of lines to a page, and the Mainz Indulgences of 1454–5. The Bible used type in the style of the German scribes of his day – textura – whilst the Indulgences used textura

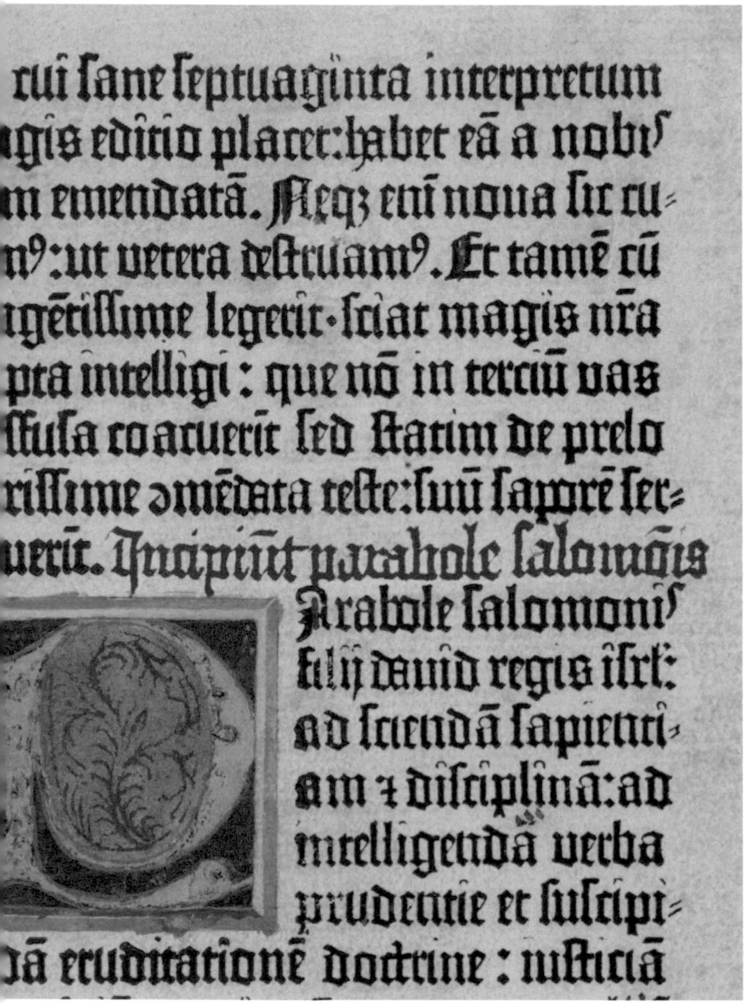

rui sane septuaginta interpretum
agis editio placet:habet eā a nobis
m emendatā. Neq; enī noua sic cu-
n9:ut vetera destruam9. Et tamē cū
tgētissime legerit·sciat magis nr̄a
pta intelligi : que nō in terciū vas
ssusa coacuerit sed statim de prelo
rissime amēdata teste:suū saporē ser-
uerit. Incipiūt parabole salomōgis

Arabole salomonis
filij dauid regis isr̄l:
ad sciendā sapienti-
am 7 disciplinā:ad
intelligēdā verba
prudentie et suscipi-
ā eruditatiōnē doctrine : iusticiā

H

for headings, but a more open, almost cursive script – sometimes referred to as bastarda – for the text. The textura typeface used in the 42-line Bible was later the inspiration for Goudy's Goudy Text.

At some time during 1455 Fust launched proeedings against Gutenberg, accusing him of misappropriating funds that were intended for the printing of the Bible. Fust was successful, and chose to foreclose on Gutenberg and continue the printing business with the aid of Peter Schöffer, his son-in-law, who had worked for the partnership. Amongst the books they produced, using types which must have been essentially Gutenberg's work, were the Mainz Psalters of 1457 and 1459, the Rationale of Durandus and the 1462 Bible.

Mainz became a centre for European printing where others, like Nicolas Jenson, went to learn the trade.

After the loss of his type, presses and money, little is known of Gutenberg's final years, although he is recorded as having received a pension from the prince-archbishop of Mainz from 1465. His invention remained unchanged in its essentials until the Industrial Revolution, and was the first real step in the movement towards universal literacy.

Above: Detail from 42-line Bible, vol.2, folio 1r, 1455. (NLS)

Gareth HAGUE
b.1967 GB

Types
AES 1996
Elephant 1996
Enabler 1996
Text 1996
August 1997
Factory 1997
Granite 1997
Jackdaw 1997
Klute 1997
Metropolitan 1997
Metsys 1997
Sister 1997
Harbour 1998
Intimo 1998
Key 1998
Mantis 1998
Jude 1999
Aminta 2001
Pop 2001
Union 2001
Civility 2002
Perla 2002
Sylvia 2002
Anomoly 2003
Cactus 2003
Vacant 2003
Web
alias.uk.com

Born in Hornchurch, Essex, Gareth Hague studied at Havering Technical College and Bournemouth and Poole College of Art and Design. He met David James in 1990. Working together as David James Associates, they designed record sleeves for bands such as Soul ii Soul, Neneh Cherry and Boy George. Increasingly their designs featured custom-designed typefaces and logos. Projects for independent magazines also combined art-directed photography and custom type design. Alias was formed in 1996 to design and market their typefaces, an ever-increasing collection of style-driven display and text fonts appropriate to the nature of their client base.

Above: Elephant, detail from *A Be Sea* magazine, issue g, 1995. (NM)

Victor HAMMER
1882–1967 A

Types
Hammer Unziale 1921
Samson 1931
Pindar 1933–5
American Uncial 1943
Andromaque Uncial 1958

Victor Hammer was a distinguished printer who devoted a great deal of his life to the design and development of the uncial letter form, which he used to print all his books. His aim was to achieve a letter form which would unify the roman and black-letter traditions.

An Austrian, Victor Hammer was a prominent portraitist and sculptor in Vienna who, in his youth, had been inspired by the work and ideals of William Morris. His first uncial type design was cut in 1921 by A Schuricht and was later produced by the Klingspor foundry at Offenbach under the name Hammer Unziale. Although it was commercially successful, Hammer was not satisfied with this face and resolved to learn the art of punch-cutting himself.

Meanwhile he set up his first printing press in Florence, and in 1929 he moved the press to the Villa Santuccio and called it Stamperia del Santuccio, which became the imprint on all his books. His first book was Milton's *Samson Agonistes*, for which he created his second uncial, Samson, cut by Rudolf Koch's son, Paul. His next uncial, Pindar, was the first type cut by his own hand.

In 1939, fleeing the Nazis, he went to the USA, where he had been offered a post teaching art and lettering in New York. There he started work on American Uncial, his

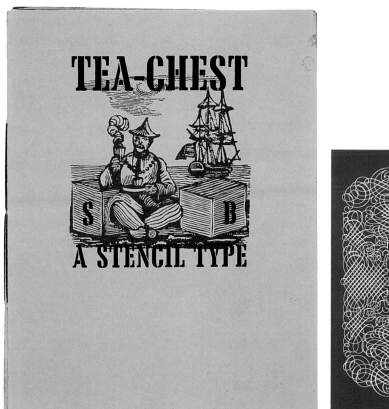

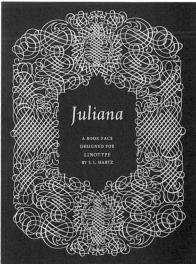

Robert HARLING
b.1910 GB

Sem L HARTZ
b.1912 NL

best-known type; it was not produced commercially until after the war, when Klingspor issued it in both Europe and the USA.

Hammer's last uncial, Andromaque, was cut by the French typefounders Deberny Et Peignot in 1958. It resembles greek cursive letters and shows no evidence of the predominantly medieval character associated with all of his other types.

Hammer's single-minded approach to type design was unusual and highly idiosyncratic. His various attempts at the uncial form were an inspiration to many other leading figures of his generation, including F W Goudy (Friar), S H de Roos (Libra) and G G Lange (Solemnis).

Previous page: Klingspor American Uncial specimen, n.d. (CLR)

Types
Playbill 1938
Chisel 1939
Tea Chest 1939
Writing
The Letterforms and Type Designs of Eric Gill, Eva Svensson 1976

Designer, typographer, publisher and type designer Robert Harling was born in Highbury, London. He was educated in Brighton and London and studied art at the Central School of Arts and Crafts. After earlier work experience at the *Daily Mail* newspaper, he became a freelance designer. His clients included the Post Office and London Transport. In the mid-1930s he became a director of one of London's leading advertising agencies. He was also at that time an adviser to the Sheffield typefoundry Stephenson Blake, designing their promotional

material and developing his three type designs.

A writer of novels, and at one time an adviser to the *Financial Times* and *The Times* newspapers, Harling also edited two significant periodicals. During the 1930s he, along with James Shand as publisher and printer, launched *Typography*. Later in the 1940s they collaborated again to produce *Alphabet Et Image*, a quarterly of typography and graphic arts, which ran for eight issues before being renamed *Image*. *Image* itself ran for eight issues, finishing in 1952.

So broad were Harling's interests that he was also editor of *House and Garden* magazine for many years. Now retired, he lives in Godstone, Surrey.

Above: Stephenson Blake specimen book, n.d. (CLR)

Types
Emergo 1948–53
Juliana 1958
Molé Foliate 1960
Panture 1971

Sem L Hartz was well known as an engraver of stamp and banknote designs before he began designing and cutting types to keep himself busy during the German occupation of the Netherlands during World War 2. He was born in Leiden, where his father taught him art. He continued his education at the Academie voor Bildende Vorming in Amsterdam, where he specialized in copper engraving. Hartz joined the typefoundry of Joh. Enschedé en Zonen in Haarlem as an apprentice, eventually succeeding Jan van Krimpen as chief designer. Although hand punch-cutting had by then almost died out,

aCGgKjkMnR SrUstW

ABCDEFGHIJK abcdefghijklmnop MARCETA lmnopqrstuvwxyz qrstuvwxyz

ABCDEFGHIJK abcdefghijklmnop Braff LMNOPQRSTUVWXYZ qrstuvwxyz

ABCDEFGHIJK abcdefghijklmnop Balthasar LMNOPQRSTUVWXYZ qrstuvwxyz

ABCDEFGHIJK abcdefghijklmnop Mentor Roman LMNOPQRSTUVWXYZ qrstuvwxyz

ABCDEFGHIJK abcdefghijklmnop Mentor Italic LMNOPQRSTUVWXYZ qrstuvwxyz

Michael HARVEY
b.1931 GB

102

he cut his first typeface Emergo by hand onto steel punches without doing initial finished drawings. Emergo, issued by Enschedé, was used by Hartz for his own private press. His next type, Juliana, also a book type, was commissioned by Linotype, and being fairly narrow it proved quite popular in England for paperbacks. Molé Foliate is a redrawing of an 1819 design by the Paris founder Molé (le jeune). Panture is a series of serifed capitals designed for signage. Hartz's other work includes glass-engraving and book illustration. An exhibition of his work was held in The Hague in 1969.

Previous page and above: Linotype Juliana specimen, n.d. (CLR)

Types
Grot R 1964
Zephyr 1964
Stamford 1966
Millbank 1982
Ellington 1990
Studz 1993
Mezz 1994
Andreas 1996
Conga Brava 1996
Strayhorn 1996
Aesop 2000
Moonglow 2000
Unico 2000
Tisdall Script 2001
Braff 2002
Fine Gothic 2002
Marceta 2003
Mentor 2004
Balthasar 2005

Writing
Lettering Design,
   The Bodley Head 1975
*Creative Lettering: Drawing
   and Design*, The Bodley
   Head 1985
*Carving Letters in Stone and
   Wood*, The Bodley Head
   1987
Calligraphy in the Graphic Arts,
   The Bodley Head 1988

*Reynolds Stone: Engraved
   Lettering in Wood*, The Fleece
   Press 1992
Creative Lettering Today,
   A & C Black 1996

Web
finefonts.com

Michael Harvey was an engineering draughtsman when, aged 20, he read Eric Gill's autobiography. Inspired, he spent two periods with Joseph Cribb, Gill's first apprentice, learning to carve letters in stone. In 1955 he joined Reynolds Stone for a six-year period, assisting him in carving inscriptions. Harvey's own inscriptions can be seen in Westminster Abbey, Winchester and Canterbury Cathedrals and the Sainsbury Wing of the National Gallery.

Describing himself as a 'letterer and jazz lover', Harvey has designed over

1,500 book jackets for many English and Dutch publishers, including Methuen, Cambridge University Press, The Bodley Head and B V Uitgeverij de Arbeiderspers. Since 1961 he has combined his carving and design work with teaching and writing. From 1993 to 2001 he ran the letterforms course in the Department of Typography and Typographic Communication at the University of Reading, and he is also the author of several books on the lettering arts.

Michael Harvey's typefaces, of which there are many, have been produced for The Bodley Head, the Tate Gallery, the Ludlow Typograph Company, Monotype, the Dutch Type Library and Adobe. Harvey's choice of nomenclature often reflects his love of jazz.

SYNOPSIS IN 14 POINT

ABCDEFGHIJKLMNOPQRSTUVWXYZ&ÆŒ
abcdefghijklmnopqrstuvwxyzæœ

£1234567890 ‡‡‡F120 G569 .,:;!?"-()[]†§§%/*«»–

ALTERNATIVE CHARACTERS

The bank now recognizes the claim as quite valid and just, so we can expect to receive full and immediate settlement ABCDEFGHIJKLMNOPQRSTUVWXYZ

I have now equalized all my jobs for work excepting those three that are over there ABCDEFGHIJKLMNOPQRSTUVWXYZ

In the vocation of typesetting, dexterity can always be gained by means of quiet, judicious and zealous work ABCDEFGHIJKLMNOPQRSTUVWXYZ ABCDEFGHIJL

The bank now recognizes these claims as valid and just, so we can expect full back payment ABCDEFGHIJKLMNOPQRSTUVWXYZ ABC

Wherever our civilization extends good typographers can expect to be required ABCDEFGHJKMNOPQRSTUWXYZ

Type and quads form even blocks ABDEGHJKMNQRSTUWXYZ

Pierre HAULTIN
d.1589 F

Pierre Haultin, a contemporary of Robert Granjon, was a gifted French punch-cutter. Although he also cut roman and greek types, Haultin was noted for his music types. According to Updike, it is said that 16th-century music printing in France owed its beginnings to Haultin's talents. His invention of notes with fragments of line attached, making a second impression unnecessary, was taken up by Pierre Attaingnant, printer to the king of France for music from 1538 to 1552.

Above: Haultin's English Roman used in the first Bible printed in Scotland, 1576–9. (ECC)

Ashley HAVINDEN
1903–73 GB

Types
Ashley Crawford 1930
Ashley Script 1955
Further reading
Advertising and the Artist. Ashley Havinden, National Galleries of Scotland 2003

Ashley Havinden was director and art director at W S Crawford, the London advertising agency, and also a director of the associated industrial design company Sir William Crawford Et Partners. He was one of the best-known figures in the advertising world in the periods immediately preceding and following World War 2.

Havinden's lettering for a Chrysler advertising campaign so impressed his friend Stanley Morison that Morison suggested that it be cut as a typeface by Monotype. Ashley Crawford was

issued by Monotype in 1930. In 1955 Monotype issued another Havinden type design: Ashley Script is a brush script based on Havinden's own free brush lettering which featured on many of W S Crawford's advertising campaigns from the mid-1930s.

Havinden was appointed Royal Designer for Industry in 1947 and was awarded an OBE in 1951 for services to industrial design.

Above: Sheet from Monotype two-volume loose-leaf specimen book, n.d. (NM)

From 2000 Harvey's collaboration with Andy Benedek (finefonts.com) has resulted in the production of several stunning fonts (some calligraphic), notably the Mentor family of roman and sans-serif typefaces.

Michael Harvey was a member of the Royal Mint Advisory Committee on the Design of Coins, Medals, Seals and Decorations from 1991 to 2004, and was awarded the MBE in 2001 for services to art.

Previous page: FineFonts promotional postcard, n.d. (NM); Above: Monotype Ellington.

103

Introducing "Tribute" —a family of 8 fonts *by* *Frank Heine,* released *by* *Emigre Fonts* (2 0 0 3)

Introducing

Roman, Ligatures, Small Caps, Ordinals; Italic, Ligatures One & Two, Ordinals

P. 1

Stymie Extrabold Condensed (Hess), No. 490

MORE THAN A CENTURY AGO THE Square Serif Types Of Which The members of the Stymie family are the most popular version were first shown in America. After being used for many years, this design of letter fell into disuse, only to be again revived in recent years. These type faces can be distinguished from all others by their monotone weight, the strong, angular and prominent serifs, and by the close fitting of the letters. Strong contrast of color and the white space within the

PRINTERS AND PUBLISHERS Throughout The Entire World appreciate the combination of the Monotype system and the high quality of printing done is a powerful force in $12345

CHARACTERS IN FONTS
A A B C D E F G H I J K K L M N O P
Q R R S T U V W X Y Z &
a a b c d e f g h i j k l m n o p q r s t
t u v w x y z
$ 1 2 3 4 5 6 7 8 9 0 ' ' . , - ' ' : , ! ? ([« ·

FOREST FIRES CAUSE GREAT damage in the far west $67890

COMMERCIAL RATES TO be raised by all railroads

NEW KINTON ARMS to be air-conditioned

Heavy Storm Caused New Flood

Annual Fall Furniture Sale

Government Aid 490

Big Atlantic Cruise

Frank HEINE
1964–2003 D

104

Types
Remedy 1991
Motion 1992
Contrivance 1993
Amplifier 1994
FF Chelsea 1994
FF Instanter 1994
Whole Little Universe 1994
Divine 1995
Feltrinelli 1996
Indecision 1996
Opsmarckt 1996
Dalliance 2000
Tribute 2003

Writing
Frank Heine: Type&c : Personal and Commercial Works 1988–2003, Gmeiner Verlag 2003

Further reading
A Branczyk, J Nachtwey, H Nehl, S Schlaich, J Siebert, 'Frank Heine, U. O. R. G.', *Emotional Digital*, Thames & Hudson 2001

After working with several silk-screen and offset printers, Frank Heine studied at the Staatliche Akademie Bildenden in Stuttgart.

Success as a graphic designer led Heine to found his own design company UORG in 1994. By that time his type designs were already becoming popular. His Remedy font, a playful investigation of the potential of digital type design, issued in 1991, was one of four to be released by Emigre. Finding inspiration for his idiosyncratic letter forms from a variety of historical sources, he also contributed to the T-26 and FSI FontFont libraries. His last font was Tribute, a Renaissance Antiqua based on the types cut by François Guyot, for which he designed the Emigre specimen. Shortly before his premature death in 2003, Gmeiner Verlag published Frank Heine's book, *TypeEtc.*

Above: cover of Emigre Tribute specimen book, 2003. (NM)

Sol HESS
1886–1953 USA

Types
Bruce Old Style No.31 1909
Tourist Gothic 1909
Hess Bold 1910
Hess Old Style 1920–3
Sans Serif Extra Bold,
    Extra Bold Condensed,
    Medium Condensed, Lined
    1930–3
Stymie 1931
Hess Neobold 1933
Twentieth Century 1937–47
Spire 1938
Squareface 1939
Artscript 1940
Stylescript 1940

For 50 years Sol Hess was art director of Lanston Monotype Machinery Co., where he succeeded his friend and collaborator F W Goudy. He started with the company in 1902 after a three-year scholarship course at Pennsylvania Museum School of Industrial Art, and as a type designer there he redrew and readapted all

their typographical materials. His forte was the development of type families, and during his years with Lanston Monotype he carried out commissions for many leading American companies, including Curtis Publishing, Crowell-Collier, Sears Roebuck, Montgomery Ward, Yale University Press and World Publishing Company.

Above: Stymie specimen sheet, Lanston Monotype Co., Philadelphia, c.1962. (SBPL)

WIRELESS <small>BLACK</small>

First Telegraph Transmission <small>BOLD</small>

SPARKS QUALITY RADIO <small>LIGHT</small>

Modulations at 42 KwH <small>BLACK</small>

Airways are jammed by the FCC <small>REGULAR</small>

PROPAGANDA <small>BOLD</small>

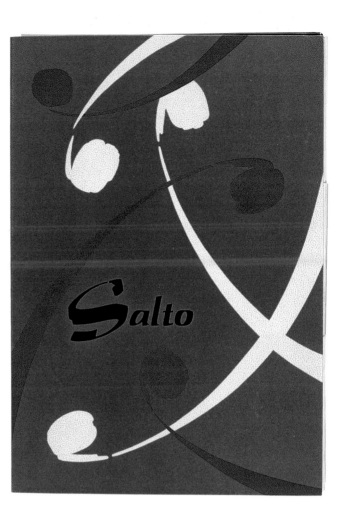

Cyrus HIGHSMITH
b.1973 USA

Types
Benton Sans 1995–2003
  (with Tobias Frere-Jones)
Daley's Gothic 1998
Dispatch 2001
Eggwhite 2001
Occupant Gothic 2001
Relay 2002
Stainless 2002
Prensa 2003
Amira 2004

After graduating with honours from Rhode Island School of Design in 1997, Milwaukee-born Cyrus Highsmith joined the Font Bureau. Now a senior designer there, he concentrates on the development of new type families.

Highsmith's dynamic designs have made a considerable impact on editorial design, featuring in newspapers and magazines across the globe. His type-faces Prensa, a lively serif with a hint of Dwiggins, and Relay, a retro sans, were amongst the winners at Bukva:Raz!, the international type-design competition. He teaches typography in the department of graphic design of his alma mater RISD and lectures and gives workshops across the USA, Mexico and Europe.

Above: specimen of Dispatch, *Font Bureau Retail*, no.24, 2000. (NM)

Karlgeorg HOEFER
1914–2000 D

Types
Salto 1952
Saltino 1953
Monsun 1954
Prima 1957
Permanent 1962
Stereo 1963
Zebra 1963
Elegance 1964
Programm-Grotesk 1970
Bigband 1974
Omnia 1990
San Marco 1990
Notre Dame 1991
Sho 1992
Writing
Das alles mit einer Feder,
  Iserlohn 1950
*Kalligraphie – gestaltete
  Handschrift*, Düsseldorf
  1986

Born in Schlesisch-Drehnow, Germany, Karlgeorg Hoefer trained and worked as a type-setter in Hamburg. After studies in graphic art at the Technische Lehranstalten in Offenbach and some work experience with a printer, he became a teacher of letter-ing. In 1950 he developed the universal Brause 505 pen nib. Hoefer, whose type designs were issued by several prominent German foundries, both lectured and ran calligraphy workshops internationally. His work was exhibited worldwide and he received many awards.

Above: Klingspor Salto specimen cover, n.d. (CLR)

MAGNESIUM
KNOX
ZINC
TOPAZ
MARTINIQUE
KNOX
SERIES

AEGKNQRSWabefgiknorsy134579$&?áêøüßçñ
AEGKNQRSWabefgiknorsy134579$&?áêøüßçñ
AEGKNQRSWabefgiknorsy134579$&?áêøüßçñ
AEGKNQRSWabefgiknorsy134579$&?áêøüßçñ
AEGKNQRSWabefgiknorsy134579$&?áêøüßçñ
AEGKNQRSWabefgiknorsy134579$&?áêøüßçñ
AEGKNQRSWabefgiknorsy134579$&?áêøüßçñ
AEGKNQRSWabefgiknorsy134579$&?áêøüßçñ

Jonathan HOEFLER
b.1970 USA

Types
Champion Gothic 1990
Hoefler Text 1991
Ideal Sans 1991
Leviathan 1991
Mazarin 1991
Ziggurat 1991
HTF Didot 1992
Requiem 1992
Saracen 1992
Acropolis 1993
Knockout 1994
Neutrino 1994
Quantico 1994
Troubadour 1994
Guggenheim 1996
Hoefler Titling 1996
Kapellmeister 1997
Mercury 1997
Chronicle 2002

Further reading
David Earls, 'Jonathan Hoefler',
  Designing Typefaces,
  RotoVision SA 2002

Web
typography.com

Named as one of the 40
most influential designers
in America by *ID* magazine,
self-taught New Yorker

Jonathan Hoefler's type
designs have contributed
to the branding of some
of the world's foremost
publications, corporations
and institutions since the
establishment of the Hoefler
Type Foundry in 1989.
Describing himself as an
'armchair type historian',
Hoefler, aided for inspiration
by his collection of antique
type specimen books, has
created an esoteric library
of original type designs. His
Hoefler Text family of typefaces, designed for Apple
Computer in 1991 and now
part of their operating
system, will be familiar
to every Macintosh user.

In 2002 he was awarded
the Prix Charles Peignot,
ATypI's most prestigious
award, for outstanding
contributions to type design.
His work has been exhibited
internationally and is
included in the permanent
collection of the Cooper-
Hewitt National Design
Museum (Smithsonian
Institute) in New York.
Hoefler is now collaborating
on projects with Tobias Frere-
Jones, who joined him in 1999
at the Hoefler Type Foundry,
renamed in 2004 Hoefler &
Frere-Jones Typography.

Above: detail of Shades series
(showing Cyclone, Knox and
Topaz fonts) designed by
Hoefler with Joshua Darden,
from Hoefler and Frere-Jones,
New typefaces, 2004. (NM)

Cynthia HOLLANDSWORTH BATTY
b.1955 USA

Types
Hiroshige 1986
Vermeer 1986
ITC Tiepolo 1987
  (with Arthur Baker)
Wile Roman 1990
Pompei Capitals 1995
Synthetica 1996
  (with Philip Bouwsma)

Cynthia Hollandsworth Batty
studied at the California
College of Arts and Crafts in
Oakland, California. She was
the manager of type design
and development at Agfa for
many years. As a typeface
designer she has released a
number of typefaces through
her company, AlphaOmega
Typography, and other
foundries. In 1987 she
founded the Typeface Design
Coalition to work for the legal
protection of typeface design
and software in the USA.
Members of the coalition
include Agfa Compugraphic,
Monotype, Linotype, ITC,

Vertical display specimens:
Ein effektvoller graphischer Ent wurf kann wie eine vielflächige Gemme sein. Genauso wie bei e DER EFFEKTIVE GRAFISCHE
Ein effektvoller grafisch wurf kann eine vielfläch nne sein. Ähnlich wie en Diamanten, hänge hönheit und sein Wert A successful graphic

A showing and synopsis of ITC Founder's Caslon

Founder's

Kris **HOLMES**
b.1950 USA

Hewlett-Packard, Bitstream, Adobe and many others. A board member of ATypI, she now works for Simon & Schuster, the publishing division of Viacom.

Previous page: Hiroshige showing from Agfa Monotype Creative Alliance catalogue, 1999. (CLR); Above: from Tiepolo specimen, Berthold Types 170, n.d. (NM)

Types
Leviathan 1979
  (with Charles Bigelow)
Shannon 1982
  (with Janice Prescott)
ITC Isadora 1985
Lucida 1984–95
  (with Charles Bigelow)
Galileo 1987
Sierra 1989
Apple New York 1991
Apple Monaco 1991
Apple Chancery 1994
Kolibri 1994
Writing
'Designing a New Greek Type', *Fine Print on Type*, Lund Humphries 1989

Kris Holmes has been a partner since 1976 in the design studio of Bigelow & Holmes in Santa Monica, California. Born in California in 1950, she studied calligraphy with Lloyd Reynolds and Robert Palladino at Reed College in Oregon and later obtained a BA degree from Harvard University.

With her partner, Charles Bigelow, she created Lucida, an extended family of serif, sans-serif, calligraphic, greek, scientific and linguistic alphabets designed for low-resolution laser printing. She designed several revival typefaces for Rudolf Hell (now part of Linotype) in the 1980s and, in the early 1990s, the 'city' fonts for Apple Computer's operating system. Holmes's lettering and calligraphy have appeared in many publications, such as *Fine Print* and *International Calligraphy Today*.

Above: detail from Berthold type specimen, c.1990. (NM)

Justin **HOWES**
1963–2005 GB

107

Types
ITC Founders Caslon 1998
Writing
Edward Johnston: A catalogue of the Craft Studies Centre collection and archive, Craft Studies Centre 1987
Founder's London, The Friends of St Bride Printing Library 1998
Johnston's Underground Type, Capital Transport 2000

Justin Howes was born in Solihull near Birmingham. He was educated abroad and at Dulwich College and Oxford. An early interest in calligraphy prompted him, at the age of 17, to communicate with Priscilla Johnston about her father Edward. He was later to catalogue Johnston's papers at the Craft Studies Centre in Bath.

Researching Caslon types at Manchester Metropolitan University in 1995, Howes took it upon himself to create

STILL OTHERS CLAIM THAT
language grew out of grunts
of effort, inarticulate chants,
or exclamations of fear or
surprise. Pythagoras and

ΓΙΑ ΟΣΟΥΣ ΔΙΑΒΙΩΝΟΥΝ
σωστά ολόκληρη η ζωή
περνάει γρήγορα, μα για όσους
ασχημονούν και μια νύχτα
είναι ατελείωτη.

В ЧАЩАХ ЮГА ЖИЛБЫЛ
цитрус да, но фальшивый
экземпляръ. Кожна людина
має право на свободу
думки, совісті і релігії.

John **HUDSON**
b.1968 GB

Rian **HUGHES**
b.1963 GB

'no-holds-barred' digital revivals – some were issued by ITC. He re-established the firm of H W Caslon ₨ Co. Ltd, marketing his types through the company's hwcaslon.com website.

His skill as a book designer was considerable, as can be seen in *Founder's London*, produced by the Friends of St Bride Printing Library, an organization he re-established in 1998 to combat threats to the Library's future. He spent some time as the curator of the Type Museum in London before leaving in January 2005 to take up a research position at the Plantin-Moretus Museum. This was not to be, however. Howes died the following month at the early age of 41.

Previous page and above: showing of ITC Founder's Caslon from *Founder's London*, 1998. (NM)

Types
Manticore 1995
Aeneas 1996
  (after Werner Schneider)
Sylfaen 1998
  (with Geraldine Wade)
Helix ISO and ASME 2000
Tír Oghaim 2001
Arabic Typesetting 2002
  (with Mamoun Sakkal and
  Paul Nelson)
Heidelberg Gothic 2002
Helvetica Linotype (Cyrillic,
  Greek and Hebrew) 2003
Adobe Hebrew 2004
Adobe Thai 2004 (with Fiona
  Ross and Tim Holloway)
Constantia 2004
Nyala 2004
  (with Geraldine Wade)
SBL Hebrew 2004
SBL BibLit 2005
SBL Greek 2005
Web
tiro.com

Type designer John Hudson was co-founder in 1994 of Tiro Typeworks in Vancouver. Born in Bristol, he moved to Canada at the age of 10 with his parents. His career in type design, which began in the early 1990s, was encouraged by Gerald Giampa of the Lanston Type Company. Hudson and Ross Mills, as Tiro Typeworks, specialize in the design and development of custom fonts for multilingual computing, publishing and scholarship. Their clients include Microsoft, Adobe, Apple and Linotype Library, as well as smaller technology companies, academic organizations and government. Hudson, who is vice-president of ATypI, writes and lectures on type technology and text encoding issues. To date, he has designed or collaborated on typefaces for the Arabic, Ethiopic, Cyrillic, Greek, Hebrew, Latin, Ogham and Thai scripts.

Above: Constantia. (JH)

Types
FF Identification 1993
FF Revolver 1993
FF CrashBangWallop 1994
FF Knobcheese 1994
FF Outlander 1995
Amorpheus 1997
Blackcurrant 1997
Foonky 1997
Judgement 1997
Lusta 1997
Chascarillo 1998
Quagmire 1998
Regulator 1998
English Grotesque 1999
Novak 2000
Paralucent 2000–3
Mercano Empire 2003
September 2003
Writing
Device, Die Gestalten Verlag
  2002
Web
devicefonts.co.uk

A prolific type designer, Rian Hughes also finds time for illustration, graphic design and cartooning. Introduced to both lettering and Letraset by his architect

father, Hughes studied graphic design at London College of Printing before working in magazine, advertising and record-sleeve design. His exceptional drawing ability led to work as a full-time comic-book artist, where his lettering became a strong element. As a result, he started to create whole alphabets, and in the early 1990s his first commercial fonts were released by FSI FontFont. Although he returned to more general graphic work he realized that his comic-book work had bequeathed him an enormous amount of lettering styles. Enabled by new technology to turn these into fonts, Hughes launched Device Fonts in 1995 with a hundred typefaces.

Above: detail of Device poster for Fontworks, 1997. (NM)

English
Republic
Delightfully
Exhibited
Great Courage
Anniversary
National League
Remarkable
Valedictory Oration
College Diplomas
Beautifully Engraved

Herman **IHLENBURG** 1843–1905 D

Types
Columbus 1892
Bradley 1895
  (after Will Bradley)
Schoeffer Oldstyle 1897
Roundhand 1900

Herman Ihlenburg, who was born in Berlin, trained there with the Trowitzsch Et Son typefoundry. After working with three other European foundries, he emigrated to the USA in 1866, joining the typefounding company of L Johnson Et Co., which, two years later, was to become MacKellar Smiths Et Jordan. In 1892 the company merged to become part of American Type Founders. Ihlenburg's output of more than 80 typefaces over 35 years was prolific – only his most notable are listed here.

Above: Roundhand, from 1923 ATF specimen book. (NM)

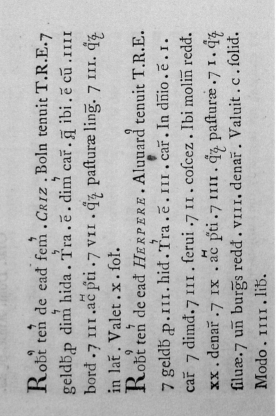

J

Joseph JACKSON
1733–92 GB

Joseph Jackson was acknowledged to be one of the most skilful punch-cutters of his generation. He was born in Old Street, London, and was an apprentice at the foundry of William Caslon I in Chiswell Street. Jackson received no instruction in the art of punch-cutting, as it was carried out in secret at the Chiswell Street foundry. He bored a hole in the wainscot of an adjoining room and took to spying on Caslon. When he and a colleague, Thomas Cottrell, were discharged by Caslon after a dispute about wages, the two set up in business. Jackson, however, on the death of his mother in 1759, joined the navy and did not return to typefounding until the peace of 1763, when he rejoined Cottrell, who now had a foundry in Fetter Lane.

For a time Jackson worked for Cottrell but eventually set up his own business in Cock Lane before moving to larger premises near Fleet Street. Because of his undoubted skill as a punch-cutter the business made rapid progress and William Caslon and his son both acknowledged his supreme craftsmanship. In 1790 the foundry was damaged by a fire in which many moulds and matrices were lost. The shock of this affected Jackson's health and his ability to work. He was fortunate in that his assistant was Vincent Figgins, later to become one of the greatest typefounders of the age, who managed the foundry until Jackson's death in 1792.

Above: Norman Domesday type cut by Joseph Jackson, from *Fry's Pantographia*, Cooper & Wilson 1799. (ECC)

Marcel JACNO
1904–89 F

Types
Film 1934
Scribe 1936
Jacno 1948
Savoie 1949
Chaillot 1951
Molière 1970
Ménilmontant 1973
Corneille 1978
Writing
Anatomie de la lettre, Paris
    1978
Further reading
Robert Ranc, *Jacno, Lettres et
    images*, Paris 1962
Alain Weille, *Jacno*, Paris 1982

The graphic output of award-winning designer Marcel Jacno, who was born in Paris, was considerable. In his early career he designed film posters for Gaumont and Paramount. His typeface Film, the first of several for the type foundry of Deberny ɛt Peignot, was issued in 1934, and in 1937 he designed typographic decorations for the Hall of Graphic Arts at the Paris Expo. He was a designer for Shell, Gauloises, Courvoisier, *France-Soir* and the Théâtre National Populaire, and for the movies, where he designed lettering for screen titles. He taught advertising at the École des Techniques de Publicité in Paris and at the École de L'Union des Arts Décoratifs. Jacno's painting and graphic work have been the subject of many exhibitions.

Above: detail from Jacno, Lettres et images, 1962. (SBPL)

Gustav JAEGER
b.1925 D

Types
Jumbo 1973
Pinocchio 1973
Komet 1976
Semin-Antiqua 1976
Seneca 1977
Becket 1980
Aja 1981
Catull 1982
Cosmos 1982
Delta Jaeger 1983
Jaeger Antiqua 1984
Jaeger Daily News 1985
Jersey 1985
Bellevue 1986
Chasseur 1988
Cornet 1989
Donatus 1990
Prado 1990

Gustav Jaeger, son of a printer, studied at the Hochschule für Gestaltung in Offenbach am Main. An enthusiast for type and typography from an early age, he started his career at the Bauer typefoundry, where he developed type specimens promoting the work of Konrad Bauer and Walter Baum. Encouraged by the former, he designed contemporary 1970s display types for H Berthold AG. He progressed to text types, the first of which, Seneca, was released by Berthold in 1977. Many others followed, highlighting Jaeger's ability to experiment successfully with letter forms for text use, and contributing significantly to the Berthold library. Jaeger's typeface Catull is currently being used in the logotype for the search engine Google.

Above: detail of Berthold Exklusiv Seneca specimen, n.d. (NM)

ABCDEFGHIJKLMNOPQRSTUVWXYZ
ABCDEFGHIJKLMNOPQRSTUVWXYZ
0123456789–1/1(@àçéíòù&§et!?.,fifl

La musique aurait dû être une science hermétique, gardée par des textes d'une interprétation tellement longue & difficile qu'elle aurait certainement découragé le troupeau de gens qui s'en servent avec la désinvolture.

IMAGE DE LETTRES

Alphatier light regular & bold · Expo Sans light regular semibold bold black & italics

semibold bold black & italics

Expo Sans inline & dotscreen

Kinesis light light italic regular italic

semibold semibold italic bold bold

italic black & black italic · TACITUS

Franck JALLEAU
b.1962 F

112

Types
Arin 1986/1990
I N Garamont 1995
Virgile 1995
I N Jalleau 1996
I N Roma 1996
Oxalis 1996
I N Grandjean 1997
I N Perrin 1997
Scripto 1997
Francesco 1998

Parisian Franck Jalleau is considered one of the best contemporary French type designers. He studied typography and lettering under Bernard Arin at the Scriptorium in Toulouse and at the Imprimerie Nationale's Atelier de Création Typographique in Paris under José Mendoza and Ladislas Mandel. Jalleau has designed several types for the Imprimerie Nationale, and has twice won prizes at the Morisawa International Typeface Design Awards, for his fonts Arin and Scripto. His Virgile and Oxalis types were released by the Creative Alliance. He works at the Imprimerie Nationale and teaches at the École Estienne, where he helped establish the Atelier de Création Typographique in 1991.

Above: detail from specimen showing of Oxalis from *Lettres Françaises*, ATypI 1998 (NM)

Mark JAMRA
b.1956 USA

Types
ITC Jamille 1988
Latienne 1991
Kinesis 1997
Alphatier 2001
Tacitus 2002
Expo Sans 2003–5
Web
typeculture.com

Mark Jamra studied architecture at college in the USA before deciding that his future lay in graphic design. After achieving his degree in design and some commercial practice as a designer he did postgraduate work at the Kunstgewerbeschule in Basel. Jamra then joined URW in Hamburg, where he was to establish a design studio before returning to the USA. He is now an associate professor at Maine College of Art and a partner in a design collective in Portland. He developed his typeface Jamille in Hamburg (four and a half years of intensive work) using URW's Ikarus software. Jamille was issued by Dr. Hell GmbH before being licensed and released by ITC in 1987. One recent typeface, Alphatier, a monoline script contrasting considerably with Jamille, explores the limits of textual communication. Jamra lectures and publishes essays on type and typography.

Above: Selection of types by Mark Jamra. (MJ)

Jean JANNON
1580–1658 F

Types
Caractères de l'Université 1621
Garamond/Garamont/
  Garaldus
Further reading
Paul Beaujon, 'The "Garamond" Types', *The Fleuron*, no.5, 1926
Stanley Morison, 'Garamond roman', *A Tally of Types*, Cambridge University Press 1973

The Frenchman Jean Jannon, who trained with Robert Estienne, was a printer and punch-cutter to the Protestant academy at Sedan where he was born. His types there, now known as the Caractères de l'Université, were confiscated on the orders of Cardinal Richelieu and were later placed in the care of the Imprimerie Royale, the French Royal Printing Office, which the cardinal had established in 1640.

Although based very much on Garamond's types, Jannon refined some of the features, particularly the angle of the serifs on the lower-case letters s, m, n, p and r. They were used for the 1642 edition of Cardinal Richelieu's memoirs but thereafter were forgotten until 1825, when they were rediscovered and wrongly attributed to Garamond. In the early years of the last century they were used as the basis for the many Garamond revivals then being issued, and it was not until 1925 that Monotype's Beatrice Warde proved that they were in fact by Jean Jannon with the discovery of his 1621 specimen sheet.

Above: Jannon specimen, 1647. (SBPL)

Enric JARDÍ
b.1964 E

Types
Mayayo 1992
Neeskens 1992
Escher 1993
Deseada 1995
Magothic 1995
Poca 1995
Radiorama 1995
Retòrica 1995
Verdaguera 1995
Peter Sellers 1996
Wilma 1996
Web
type-o-tones.com

Type designer and typographer Enric Jardí is a founder member of the digital typefoundry Type-Ø-Tones based in his home city of Barcelona. Many of his designs are humorous revivals inspired by classic and modernist types. He is also a teacher and director at Eina (Escola de Disseny i Art) in Barcelona.

Above: Neeskens from Type-Ø-Tones 1995/6 catalogue. (NM)

Nicolas JENSON
1420–80 F

Nicolas Jenson was one of the first punch-cutters to create type based on the model of the traditional roman letter in preference to the dark gothic style used in earlier German printed books.

Although known for his work in Venice, Jenson was a Frenchman, born in Sommevoire in the district of Champagne around 1420. He served an apprenticeship in the Paris mint and was promoted to be master of the mint at Tours. Apparently Charles VII sent Jenson to Mainz in 1458 in order that he should discover more about the new invention of printing, but from 1470 until his death he worked in Venice, first as his own master, and then, after the slump of 1473, as head of a syndicate. His roman type was first used in Eusebius's

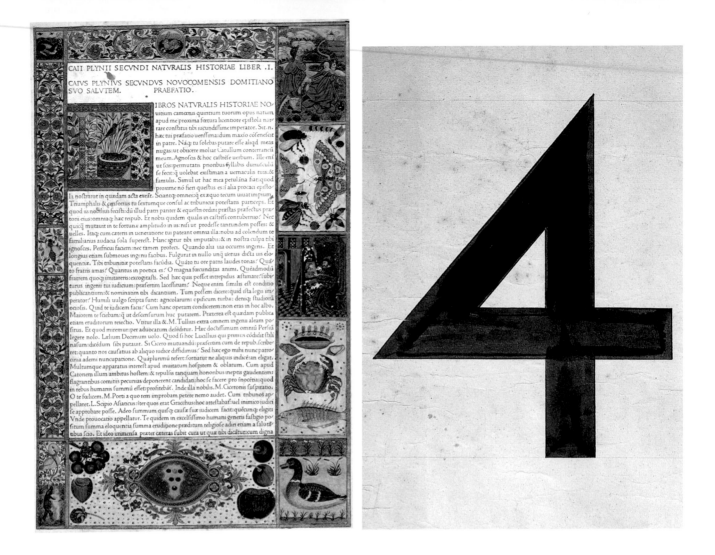

De Praeparatio Evangelica in 1470 and was one of the first to be designed according to typographic ideals and in rejection of manuscript models.

Jenson published regularly until his death in September 1480. Around 155 editions exist known to be printed by him or attributed to his press. Pope Sixtus IX made him a count palatine, probably as a reward for publishing devotional works. He was involved in several partnerships with other Venetian printers. The company of Johannes de Colonia and Nicolas Jenson is mentioned in his will, made shortly before his death. However, in the will Jenson left his punches to another partner, Peter Ugelheimer.

Jenson's roman was influential when a revival

of interest in printing and typography took place in the late 19th and early 20th centuries. Amongst the faces that took Jenson's type as a model were Morris's Golden Type (1890), the Doves Roman of T J Cobden-Sanderson and Emery Walker (1900) and Bruce Rogers's Montaigne (1902).

Above: page showing Jenson's roman type, from Pliny, *Historia naturalis*, Venice 1472. (BL)

Edward JOHNSTON
1872–1944 GB

Types
Cranach Press Italic
Johnston/London Underground Type 1916
Writing
Writing & Illuminating, & Lettering, John Hogg 1906
Further reading
Priscilla Johnston, *Edward Johnston*, Barrie & Jenkins 1976

Born to Scottish parents in Uruguay in 1872, Edward Johnston studied medicine in Edinburgh before coming to London to study art. His discovery of the manuscript collection in the British Library led to a lifelong addiction to lettering. He approached founder William Richard Lethaby to join a lettering class at the Central School of Arts and Crafts but instead was appointed to take the calligraphy class which he began in 1899. Johnston was aware of William Morris's

study of roman letters and he built on this, but in a more practical and inspirational manner.

Eric Gill joined the class in 1901 and it was the start of a long friendship between the two men. Also in 1901, Johnston began teaching at the Royal College of Art, and in 1906 he published what is now regarded as the most influential calligraphy book ever written, *Writing & Illuminating, & Lettering*, to which Gill contributed a chapter entitled 'Inscriptions in Stone'.

Johnston is responsible for the first of the modern chancery italics. Designed for Count Harry Kessler's Cranach Press in Weimar and called Cranach Press Italic, this type was based on the work of the Venetian scribe Tagliente, which

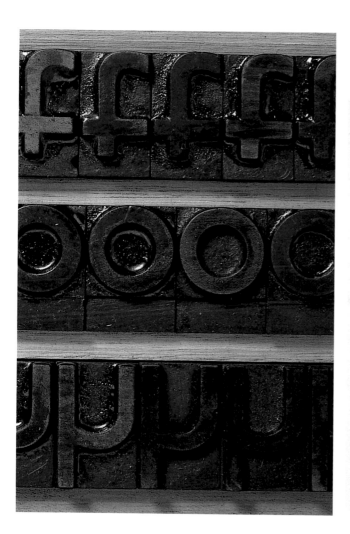

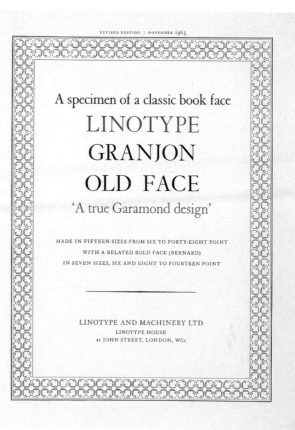

REVISED EDITION : NOVEMBER 1963

A specimen of a classic book face
LINOTYPE
GRANJON
OLD FACE
'A true Garamond design'

MADE IN FIFTEEN SIZES FROM SIX TO FORTY-EIGHT POINT
WITH A RELATED BOLD FACE (BERNARD)
IN SEVEN SIZES, SIX AND EIGHT TO FOURTEEN POINT

LINOTYPE AND MACHINERY LTD
LINOTYPE HOUSE
21 JOHN STREET, LONDON, WC1

George William JONES
1860–1942 GB

appeared in a writing book of 1524.

Johnston was one of the founder editors, with Gerard Meynell and others, of the influential journal *The Imprint*. His involvement there in the development of the typeface Imprint led Meynell to recommend his work to Frank Pick of London Transport. In 1915 Johnston was commissioned by Pick to design what has become his best-known face: Johnston was designed for the exclusive use of London Underground to provide it with one consistent style for all its signs and notices. Johnston's solution was a sans serif based on classical roman forms. Gill helped Johnston in the early stages of the work, receiving 10 per cent of the fee. Later he was to use similar forms for his Gill Sans.

Johnston was working for London Transport as late as 1933 and continued to work until about 1940, when he was forced to stop because of illness. It is hard to overestimate Edward Johnston's influence. Later, remembering his time as his pupil, Gill reported being 'struck as by lightning'; he was not alone.

Previous page: detail from drawing for Johnston type, n.d. (CSM); Above: Johnston wood type as used by London Transport 1916–c.1980. (LTM)

Types
Granjon 1928–31
Venezia 1928
Estienne 1930
Georgian 1934

George W Jones was a renowned printer with a keen interest in early printing and typography. His printing company, based in Gough Square, London, was called the Sign of the Dolphin.

English Linotype made Jones its printing adviser in 1921 to help plan a series of type revivals. It was the first British company to create such a position (Monotype was to follow this example with the appointment of Stanley Morison).

Jones designed Granjon as a rival to Monotype Garamond, naming it in honour of Robert Granjon, the 16th-century punch-cutter. Estienne, which takes its name from a famous Paris printing family, is also based on French types from that period. Venezia was originally cut for the Sign of the Dolphin by Edward Prince; an italic was added by Frederic Goudy in 1925, and it was subsequently issued by Monotype. Georgian is a revival for Linotype of a late 18th-century Scottish type from the Glasgow foundry of Alexander Wilson.

Above: revised edition of Linotype Granjon Old Face specimen, November 1963. (CLR)

115

Heinrich JOST
1889–1948 D

Types
Fraktur 1925
Atrax 1926
Bauer Bodoni 1926
Jost Medieval/Aeterna 1927
Beton 1931–6

Heinrich Jost, although best known as the art director (1923–48) of the Bauer type foundry in Frankfurt, also designed Fraktur for Monotype and Jost Medieval for Ludwig ᴇt Mayer.

Jost was the son of a bookbinder, who trained as a bookseller and later studied book production at the Kunstgewerbeschule in Munich under Paul Renner and Emil Preetorius. After leaving, he worked for a daily paper and various Munich publishers before being invited to Bauer by George Hartmann. Beton, Bauer Bodoni and Atrax were created for Bauer, with Beton

quickly establishing itself as a popular advertising face. Bauer Bodoni is the rival to Benton's ATF Bodoni, which was the model for most other versions. It is one of a number of revivals cut by the foundry.

Above: cover of Bauer specimen, date unknown, photographed for the CLR. (CLR)

Louis JOU
1881–1968 F

Louis Jou, born a Catalan, spent most of his life in Paris, where he worked with other printers before setting up his own press in 1929. He was a master craftsman and a designer of books who excelled in wood-engraving and was skilled enough to cut the punches for his own types. Jou was eventually assisted in the latter by the renowned Parisian punch-cutter Charles Malin. His production of a three-volume edition of Montaigne's *Essais* in 1934 underlined his standing as one of the great designer/printers of the 20th century.

Above: from André Macchia, *Louis Jou*, Gutenberg 1991. (SBPL)

K

Hundertundein
Sätze
zur
Buchgestaltung

Zusammengestellt
von
ALBERT KAPR

ftv

VEB FACHBUCHVERLAG LEIPZIG

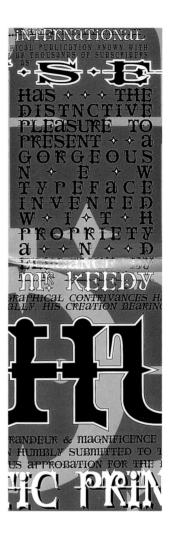

Albert **KAPR**
1918–95 D

Types
Faust 1958
Leipzig 1959
Clarendon 1965
Prillwitz 1971

Writing
*Johannes Gutenberg:
    Tatsachen und Thesen,*
    Insel-Bücherie 1977
The Art of Lettering,
    K G Saur 1983
*Gestalt und Funktion
    der Typografie*
    (with Walter Schiller),
    VEB Fachbuchverlag 1983
*Johann Gutenberg:
    The Man and his Invention,*
    Scolar Press 1996

Albert Kapr was a renowned calligrapher, book designer and type designer. He wrote highly regarded books on these subjects and also on Gutenberg, in whom he had a particular interest.

Kapr started his career as an apprentice compositor in Stuttgart, where he was born. Before and after World War 2 he studied at the Stuttgarter Kunstakademie under F H E Schneidler. In 1951 he became professor at the Hochschule für Graphik und Buchkunst in Leipzig where, from 1956 to 1978, he was head of the Institute for Book Design. He was elected rector of the Hochschule in 1959, and again from 1966 to 1973. From 1964 to 1977 he was art director for the Typoart typefoundry in Dresden.

Above: titlepage set in Leipzig, 1973. (NM)

Jeffery **KEEDY**
b.1955 USA

117

Types
Neo Theo 1989
Keedy Sans 1990
Hard Times 1990
F LushUS 1992

Jeff Keedy, graphic designer, type designer, teacher and writer, lives and works in Los Angeles. Since graduating from Cranbrook Academy of Art he has been an influential figure in the world of graphic design. Clients include the Museum of Contemporary Art, Los Angeles, the Santa Monica Museum of Art and the Pacific Design Center. His best-known type is Keedy Sans, a non-conforming sans serif released by Emigre. Keedy, who contributes to many books and periodicals, now teaches at the California Institute for the Arts.

Above: detail from F LushUS poster for *Fuse*, no.8, FSI 1991. (NM)

abcde

cour
ier.
cour
ier.

A NOTE

This is the first full showing of 'Monotype' Octavian, Series 603–14, a new roman and italic designed by Will Carter and David Kindersley at Cambridge.

The designers, both letter-carvers and one a printer, have set out to give the established pattern a fresh appraisal, with an eye to close fitting, even colour and a generous

Hendrik van den KEERE
c.1540–80 B

118

Hendrik van den Keere of Ghent was the leading Flemish punch-cutter during the mid- to late 16th century, when the Low Countries were the leaders in type design and typefounding. He worked for Christopher Plantin, who was the dominant publisher of the period. The influential roman types that he cut for Plantin were a combination of Flemish black-letter and French roman, showing a large x-height and also offering economy of set. His types have been revived by Fred Smeijers (Renard) and Tobias Frere-Jones (Poynter Old Style).

Above: detail from van den Keere's 7-lines Pica roman type, photographed for the CLR. (CLR)

Howard G KETTLER
1919–99 USA

Types
Courier 1955

Howard G 'Bud' Kettler designed Courier for IBM, probably the best-known and most successful of monospaced typefaces. Kettler started work with IBM in 1952 after running a small-town newspaper and owning a print shop. His long career as a type designer with IBM and its spin-off Lexmark, formed from the company's printer and type-writer business, continued beyond retirement into the 1990s. He designed many typefaces, including a Braille font for the IBM Braille Writer, a project that gave him great satisfaction.

Kettler was loved by his colleagues for both a quirky sense of humour and an even temperament. Eventually given responsiblity for

training by IBM, he produced a type-design tutorial book and organized lectures by the world's leading type designers. These included Adrian Frutiger, with whom Kettler worked closely on fonts for the IBM Selectric Composer.

Above: showing of Apple Computer's TrueType version of Courier.

David KINDERSLEY
1915–95 GB

Types
Octavian 1961
 (with Will Carter)
Kindersley, street name
 alphabet c.1962
MOT Serif c.1962
Itek Bookface 1976

David Kindersley was born in Codicote, Hertfordshire. After early experience of stone-cutting in Paris, he persuaded Eric Gill to take him on as an apprentice at the age of 18. Gill had a profound influence, and Kindersley continued in the Gill studio until 1939 when, at 21, he set up his own workshop in Cambridge.

His many commissions included work on film titles for the Shell Film Unit and, in 1953, the lettering for the American War Cemetery near Cambridge. He also designed lettering for street names and proposed alternative lettering to that designed

ral purpose in mind beyond that of creating a type satisfying to the designers, it soon became clear to some others that it had certain desirable characteristics; so the italic and small caps were added. The latter, after the example of Dr Giovanni Mardersteig, are slightly above the x-height.

Whereas this note is set solid to an 18em measure, the text is set 22 ems and is 2pt leaded.

JANSON

Jock **KINNEIR**
1917–94 GB

Types
Transport 1958–63
Writing
Words and Buildings,
   The Architectural Press 1980

Jock Kinneir studied engraving at Chelsea College of Art, and later lectured there. He worked in the Design Research Unit of the Central Office of Information and in that capacity was involved in the design for the Festival of Britain.

In 1945 he set up on his own, and when he began work on lettering and signage for Gatwick Airport in 1957 he took on Margaret Calvert, one of his former students, to help him. She became a partner in Kinneir Calvert ᴇt Associates in 1966. Together they were to design lettering and signage systems that are used all over Britain and extensively outside it. Following

the Gatwick Airport project, they designed the Transport alphabet and signage for the UK's motorways and roads. They were one of the first British advocates of the idea that sans-serif upper- and lower-case letters are intrinsically more legible for signage systems. Following the success of the Transport alphabet, Kinneir and Calvert were commissioned to produce signage for railways, airports, hospitals, armed services and Tyne ᴇt Wear Metro.

Jock Kinneir was also head of the department of graphic design at the Royal College of Art, London from 1964 until 1969, and he continued to teach there until 1974. He retired in 1979.

Above: directional sign for 'Primary Routes' maquette, c.1963. (SBPL)

by Kinneir and Calvert for the Worboys Committee for use on Britain's roads, but this was not used.

Kindersley developed a system for improving the spacing of all forms of typesetting, particularly text composition. As a result, Letraset awarded him a consultancy, which continued until 1986. His first serious effort in the field of type design, Octavian, co-designed with Will Carter, was released by Monotype in 1961.

David Kindersley's lovingly and painstakingly executed works in marble, stone, slate and wood are superb examples of the letterer's art, many of which may well survive the printed page.

Above: from Stanley Morison, *Tact in Typographical Design, a Type Specimen* [for Octavian], Double Crown Club 1962. (NM)

Nicholas **KIS**
1650–1702 H

Types
Janson (revived 1937)
Ehrhardt (revived 1938)

Nicholas Kis was a Hungarian punch-cutter who worked in Amsterdam from 1680 until 1690, initially learning the art of punch-cutting from Dirk Voskens at the Blaeu typefoundry. Kis's types are some of the greatest in the Dutch old-face style and were used as models for a number of 20th-century developments. Linotype's version of this style, Janson, was created by C H Griffith in 1937 and is based on an original face cut by Kis in 1670–90. The face is named after Anton Janson, a Dutchman who worked in Leipzig, with whom the face has no connection.

Ehrhardt, produced by Monotype in 1938, is another Dutch old-face type similar to Janson and Van Dijck. It is

119

based on a type cut by Kis in 1672 and the name derives from the fact that the original types were held by the Ehrhardt foundry in Leipzig. Since 1919 Kis's original matrices and punches have been held by Stempel typefoundry in Frankfurt, now part of Linotype.

Previous page: from Linotype Janson specimen, 1957.; Above: from Monotype Ehrhardt specimen, n.d. (both CLR)

Max KISMAN
b.1955 NL

Types
Tegentonnen 1988–9
Cattle Brand 1990
FF Cutout 1990
FF Scratch 1990
FF Vortex 1990
Ramblas 1990
FF Fudoni 1991
FF Jacque 1991
F Linear Konstrukt 1991
FF Network 1991
FF Rosetta 1991
SSP Quickstep 1994
Web
hollandfonts.com

Max Kisman, born in Doetinchem, studied at the Rietveld Academy in Amsterdam before setting up in business as a graphic designer. His early and successful exploitation of digital technology in design in the late 1980s led to much acclaim in his native Holland, where he also taught graphic design and typography at several colleges. It was then, too, that he founded the typography magazine *Typ*. After living and working in Barcelona for three years (1989–92) he returned to Holland to become involved in television graphics and interactive media. In 1997 he moved to San Francisco to work as an art director in television. He now lives in California, working for US and Dutch clients and teaching at the College of Arts & Crafts in San Francisco. Kisman has designed typefaces for FontShop International and Neville Brody's digital magazine *Fuse*. His recent work can be viewed at his Holland Fonts website.

Above: spread from FSI FontFont catalogue, n.d. (NM)

Manfred KLEIN
b.1932 D

Types
EF Why Not 1991
FF Carolus Magnus 1991
FF Johannes G 1991
FF Koberger 1991
FF Schoensperger 1991
FF Spontan 1991
A*I FraktKonstruct 1993
A*I FranklySpoken 1993
A*I Fusion 1993
A*I Parma Petit 1993
A*I Quasimodo 1993
A*I Szene 1993
A*I Venezia 1993
A*I BadTimes 1994
A*I ClassiCaps 1994
A*I Fragment 1994
A*I FraktScript 1994
A*I UnciTronica 1994
FF Witches 1994
EF Bloxx 1995
EF Brushable 1995
EF Kleins Sketch 1995
EF Remember I. M. 1995
Web
moorstation.org/typoasis

Manfred Klein, a native of Berlin, trained as both a typesetter and a typographer.

Akira **KOBAYASHI**
b.1960 J

He studied typography under G G Lange at the Meister-schule für Graphik und Buchgewerbe in Berlin. After further studies there he worked as a typographer and creative director for AEG and Ogilvy ɹt Mather, before forming his own company. Now a writer and type designer, he is the author of several publications on verbal and visual communication. Klein is a prolific designer of typefaces. In contrast to his black-letter interpretations, many of his experiments with letter forms are playful and humorous.

Above: A*I Fragment as shown in International Typefounders catalogue, 1995. (NM)

Types
Skid Row 1990
ITC Woodland 1997
FF Acanthus 1998
ITC Luna 1998
ITC Scarborough 1998
ITC Silvermoon 1998
FF Clifford 1999
ITC Magnifico 1999
ITC Vineyard 1999
Calcite Pro 2000
Linotype Conrad 2000
TX Lithium 2001
Avenir Next 2003
  (with Adrian Frutiger)
Optima Nova LT 2003
  (with Hermann Zapf)

Award-winning type designer Akira Kobayashi was born in Niigata, Japan. After studying at the Musashino Art University in Tokyo, he worked in Japan designing and digitizing fonts. After a calligraphy course at the London College of Printing he was employed by TypeBank to create Latin versions of their Japanese fonts. From 1997 until 2001

Kobayashi worked as a freelance type designer contributing to the ITC, FSI FontFont and Linotype libraries. He is currently type director at Linotype, where he is responsible for the aesthetic quality of in-house typefaces and the selection of external submissions.

Above: ITC Luna specimen from *U&lc*, 1998. (NM)

Rudolf **KOCH**
1876–1934 D

Types
Deutsche Schrift 1908–21
Maximilian Antiqua 1913–17
Wilhelm-Klingspor-Schrift
  1920–6
Deutsche Zierschrift 1921
Koch Antiqua/Locarno 1922
Neuland 1922–3
Deutsche Anzeigenschrift
  1923–4
Jessen 1924–30
Wallau 1925–34
Kabel 1927–9
Offenbach 1928
Zeppelin 1929
Marathon 1930–8
Prisma 1931
Claudius 1931–4
Holla 1932
Grotesk-Initialen 1933
Koch Current 1933
Neufraktur 1933–4
Writing
*Das Schreiben als
  Kunstfertigkeit*, Leipzig 1921
Das ABC-Büchlein, Leipzig 1934
Further reading
Warren Chappell, *The Little
  ABC Book of Rudolf Koch*,
  David R Godine 1976
Sebastian Carter, 'Rudolf Koch',

NEULAND
TYPEFOUNDERS
ABCDEFGHIJKLMNOPQRSTUVWXYZABCDEFG 10
HIJKLMNOPQRSTUVWXYZABCDEFGHI 12
JKLMNOPQRSTUVWXYZABCDE 14
FGHIJKLMNOPQRSTUVWX
YZABCDEFGHIJKLMNOP
QRSTUVWXY 30
ZABCDEFGH 42
IJKLMN 54
Stehe auf — und iß!
WOODCUT DESIGN BY RUDOLF KOCH
NEULAND is a black-letter titling, designed by the late Rudolf Koch in 1923. It was used in this country for the Nonesuch Press edition of Genesis, with engravings by Paul Nash. The illustration shown here is from a block-book by Koch, entitled Elia, produced in 1921.
43
MARINA SCRIPT
ROCKWELL BOLD COND.
NEULAND
SANS SERIFS SHADED
PERPETUA
UNION PEARL
PLANTIN
TIMES NEW ROMAN
PLAYBILL
THOROWGOOD'S FAT FACE ITALIC

PARLIAMENT
a small pathway runs
NEDERLAND

Twentieth-Century Type Designers, Lund Humphries 1995
Gerald Cinamon, *Rudolf Koch: Letterer, Type Designer, Teacher*, Oak Knoll Press 2000

The outstanding calligrapher, type designer, typographer and teacher Rudolf Koch was born in Nürnberg in 1876. The son of a sculptor, he was apprenticed in 1892 to a metal foundry in Hanau as an engraver. He attended evening classes at the art school there and left the foundry in 1896 before completing his apprenticeship. After training as an art teacher for a year in Nürnberg, he found work as a designer in Leipzig. There he began experimenting with a broad-nibbed pen and found that he was naturally able to master many calligraphic styles. In 1906, at the age of 30, he joined the Offenbach typefoundry Rudhardsche Gießerei, later to become Klingspor. Within two years, Koch designed his first typeface, the bold black-letter Deutsche Schrift.

After serving in World War 1, Koch began his most creative and productive period. First came Wilhelm-Klingspor-Schrift, the summit of his achievement in the purely black-letter tradition, then Neuland. Jessen, which he cut himself, was a simplified black-letter with romanized capitals, created originally for the great edition of the Gospels printed by Klingspor in 1926. With his design of Kabel and its variants between 1927 and 1929, Koch overcame his personal resistance to the sans-serif letter.

During the mid-1920s, Koch founded the Offenbach Werkstatt, a small class of dedicated students which included Fritz Kredel, Warren Chappell and Berthold Wolpe. In 1930 he was awarded an honorary doctorate by the University of Munich.

Previous page: Klingspor Prisma specimen, n.d. (CLR); Above: Neuland showing from W S Cowell, *A Book of Typefaces*, Ipswich 1952. (NM)

Jan van KRIMPEN
1892–1958 NL

Types
Lutetia 1925
Antigone 1927
Open Roman Capitals 1929
Romanée 1929
Romulus 1931
Cancelleresca Bastarda 1934
Van Dijk 1936
Spectrum 1943–5
Sheldon 1947

Writing
'Typography in Holland', *The Fleuron*, no.7, 1930
On Designing and Devising Type, The Typophiles 1957

Further reading
John Dreyfus, *The Work of Jan van Krimpen*, Sylvan Press 1952

Jan van Krimpen was a skilled calligrapher who believed calligraphy and type design to be essentially different. After studying at the Koninklijke Academie van Beeldende Kunsten in The Hague, van Krimpen, a native of Gouda, worked as a freelance designer and illustrator.

LA MADELEINE
immaculately cut and

ESPOSIZIONE
shaped to resemble the

GESCHICHTE
turrets of the big house

Today Sans Serif

Today Sans Serif

Today Sans Serif

Today Sans Serif

Today Sans Serif

Today Sans Serif

Today Sans Serif

Volker **KÜSTER**
b.1941 D

At the age of 31 he was asked by Joh. Enschedé en Zonen in Haarlem to design a new type. This first van Krimpen type, Lutetia, resulted in him joining Enschedé as one of their house designers. The type was cut by P H Rädisch. Van Krimpen was to stay with the company until his retirement.

His Romanée type was designed to accompany an italic in Enschedé's possession attributed to van Dijck. Stanley Morison, a great admirer of van Krimpen's Lutetia, commissioned him to work on his revival, Van Dijk. Later, Monotype also issued three weights of one of his most original faces, Romulus, originally issued by Enschedé.

Van Krimpen did not confine himself to type design but was also a notable book designer, working for Enschedé and fulfilling commissions from other presses. During the occupation in World War 2 he developed his last type, Spectrum, originally commissioned by Spectrum Publishing Co. but subsequently released by Monotype.

Above: from a Monotype Spectrum specimen, n.d. (CLR)

Types
Neue Luthersche Fraktur 1984
Today Sans Serif 1989

Born in Wernigerode, Germany, and apprenticed as a typesetter, Volker Küster attended the Fachschule Oberschöneweide in Berlin from 1961 to 1964. Küster undertook further studies with Albert Kapr at the Hochschule für Graphik und Buchkunst in Leipzig, where he later went on to tutor in typography and type design from 1969 to 1975. Throughout this period he undertook freelance design work in Leipzig and collaborated with the Typoart foundry in Dresden. He was type director for Scangraphic in Hamburg from 1984 to 1988, for whom he designed the well-known Today Sans Serif family, an informal design with 40 variations, as well

as Neue Luthersche Fraktur, based on the Fraktur designed by Erasmus Luther in 1708. Küster is professor of communications design at the University of Essen.

Above: detail from Scangraphic catalogue, 1990. (NM)

123

L

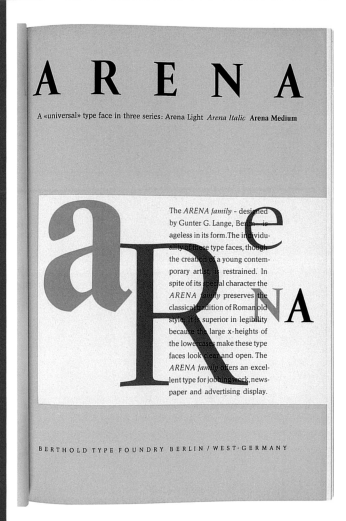

Günter Gerhard **LANGE**
b.1921 D

Types
Arena 1951–9
Derby 1952
Solemnis 1954
Regina 1954
Boulevard 1955
Champion 1957
El Greco 1964
Concorde 1969–78
Concorde Nova 1975
Franklin-Antiqua 1976
Berthold Script 1977
Imago 1978–9
Bodoni Old Face 1983
Whittingham 2001
Further reading
G G L, Typographische
    Gesellschaft München 1983

As artistic director of
H Berthold AG, Günter
Gerhard Lange was responsible for the company's entire
typeface development pro-
gramme from 1961 until 1990.
His meticulous attention to
detail helped create the
Berthold type library's
unsurpassed reputation for
quality and integrity of
production. As well as
designing new typefaces,
Lange supervised Berthold
revivals of several classic
faces, including Akzidenz-
Grotesk, Bodoni, Caslon,
Garamond, Baskerville and
Walbaum. A calligraphic
influence shows itself in
some of his early designs
for Berthold. Derby and
Boulevard are both script
types, as are Champion and
El Greco. His 1954 Solemnis
is an uncial and was part of
the revival of such forms
begun by Victor Hammer.

Born in Frankfurt in 1921,
he studied calligraphy, type
design and the graphic arts at
the Akademie für Graphische
Künste und Buchgewerbe in
Leipzig from 1941 to 1945,
where his tutors included
Georg Belwe. During his
period at the Akademie he
became assistant to Walter

Bodoni Old Face

Probe 011
BERTHOLD
exklusiv

Alessio **LEONARDI**
b.1965 I

Tiemann. After 1945 he freelanced as a painter and graphic designer before moving to Berlin in 1949, where he undertook further studies in painting and drawing at the Hochschule für Bildende Künste.

His career with Berthold commenced in 1950, when he was employed as an artistic freelance. After becoming artistic director in 1960 he was appointed to the main board in 1971. As an ambassador for Berthold he was a charismatic figure, captivating international audiences of designers with his talks on type trends. He retired from the company in 1990 but continued to lecture and teach typography and design. Lange renewed his association with the Berthold name in 2000 by becoming artistic consultant to Berthold Types Ltd of

Chicago, legal successors of H Berthold AG, for whom he designed Whittingham, his rendition of a typeface used in the mid-19th century by Charles Whittingham of the Chiswick Press.

Previous page and above: Arena and Bodoni Old Face specimens for Berthold, n.d. (CLR/NM)

Types
F2F Mekkaso Tomanik 1992
F2F Metamorfosi 1992
F2F Provinciali 1992
FF Priska 1993
FF Cavolfiori 1994
FF Coltello 1994
FF Forchetta 1994
F2F Madame Butterfly 1994
FF Mulinex 1994
FF Baukasten 1995
FF Graffio 1995
FF Letterine 1995
F2F Prototipa Multipla 1995
FF Matto 1996
FF Handwriter 1997
Writing
From the Cow to the Typewriter:
The (true) History of Writing,
BuyMyFonts.com Editions
2004
Web
alessio.de

Alessio Leonardi, who describes himself as artist, typographer, graphic artist and cook, was born in Florence. He studied for his degree at the ISIA (Instituto Superiore per le Industrie

Artistiche) in Urbino before moving to Germany to work with MetaDesign in Berlin and xplicit in Frankfurt. After starting his own company in 1994 he joined forces with Priska Wollein in 1997 to form Berlin-based Leonardi Wollein Visuelle Konzepte. A prolific designer of fonts, only a few of which are named above, Leonardi reflects in his output a love of letter forms and a quirky sense of humour. His type-foundry BuyMyFonts.com, which he set up in 2002, shows his most recent work. As a writer, he has published a book and contributed essays to many publications.

Above: FF Priska specimen, FSI, 1993. (NM)

125

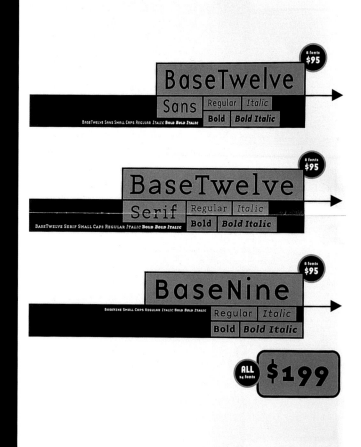

Sebastian LESTER
b.1973 GB

Types
Zoroaster 1995
Equipoize Sans 1996
Equipoize Serif 1996
Cuban 2000
Gimp 2001
Rubber 2001
Scene 2002
Neo Sans 2004
Neo Tech 2004
Soho 2006

A native of London,
Sebastian Lester graduated
with honours from London's
Central Saint Martins College
of Art and Design in 1997.
Before he joined Agfa
Monotype in 2000, Lester had
been designing fonts for the
T-26 (Zoroaster, Equipoize,
Cuban) and Garage Fonts
(Gimp, Rubber) foundries.
   To date Lester has
designed three sans-serif
families for the company,
now renamed Monotype
Imaging: Scene, Neo Sans
and Neo Tech. As part of the

company's custom fonts team
he has worked on projects for
Opel, BG Bank Denmark and
the supermarket chain
Waitrose. He has also helped
develop mastheads for the
Daily Telegraph and *Sunday
Telegraph* newspapers, and
worked on the Barclaycard
logo. His most recent typeface, Soho, was released by
Monotype Imaging in 2006.

Above: Monotype/Faces
promotion of Neo Sans, 2004.
(CLR)

Zuzana LICKO
b.1961 CS

Types
Coarse Resolution 1985
Modula 1985
Lo-Res 1985–2001
Citizen 1986
Matrix 1986
Lunatix 1988
Oblong 1988
Senator 1988
Variex 1988
Elektrix 1989
Triplex 1989
   (italic by John Downer)
Journal 1990
Tall Pack 1990
Totally Gothic and Totally
   Glyphic 1990
Matrix Script 1992
Quartet 1992
Narly 1993
Dogma 1994
Base Nine and Twelve 1995
Modula Round and Ribbed
   1995
Soda Script 1995
Filosofia 1996
Mrs Eaves 1996
Base Monospace 1997
Tarzana 1998
Solex 2000
Fairplex 2002

Writing
*Emigre: Graphic Design
   into the Digital Realm*
   (with Rudy VanderLans
   and Mary E Gray),
   Van Nostrand Reinhold 1993
Web
emigre.com

Zuzana Licko, born in
Bratislava in the former
Czechoslovakia, emigrated
to the USA in 1968. She
graduated in graphic communication from the University
of California at Berkeley in
1984. An early introduction
to computers through her
biomathematician father led
to Licko pioneering digital
type design with the
Macintosh computer. Her
early type designs appeared
in *Emigre* magazine, published by the Emigre design
company, which she formed
with husband and fellow
designer Rudy VanderLans
after leaving college. The

Modula Serif Bold
(Original 1986 design)

Left:
**Original Modula Bold
with diagonal serif**
Right:
**The Remixed
Modula Round Sans**

success and influence of
the magazine created a
demand for these types,
which resulted in the setting
up of Emigre Fonts in 1985
to market those and others
by a new generation of digital
type designers.

Licko's work evolved as
technology improved. Early
bitmap solutions for low-
resolution output were
followed by high-quality new
designs and sensitive revivals
of the work of Bodoni
(Filosofia) and Baskerville
(Mrs Eaves).

Zuzana Licko's design
output continues to be a
major influence on typo-
graphic communication
worldwide.

Previous page: Base poster
from *Emigre*, no.37, 1996.
(NM); Above: detail from
Emigre broadsheet, 1995. (CLR)

Herb **LUBALIN**
1918–81 USA

Types
ITC Avant Garde Gothic 1970
(with Tom Carnase)
ITC Lubalin Graph 1974
(with Tony DiSpigna and
Joe Sundwall)
ITC Serif Gothic 1974 (with Tony
DiSpigna)
Further reading
Gertrude Snyder and Alan
Peckolick, *Herb Lubalin. Art
Director, Graphic Designer
and Typographer*, New York
1985

Herb Lubalin was one of the
most charismatic figures in
design and typography in
America after World War 2,
admired as a prodigious
worker with a vast output.
Most of his design solutions
relied upon typography for
their effect. In the early days
his typefaces, and indeed
those of ITC in general, were
aimed at display advertising
rather than text setting and
became internationally known

through the influential
and stylish magazine *U&lc*,
the house journal of ITC,
which Lubalin not only
designed but also edited.

Born in New York City,
Lubalin graduated from the
Cooper Union School of Art
and Architecture in 1939.
After a spell in advertising
he became art director and
eventually vice-president
and creative director of
Sudler & Hennessey, a
company specializing in
pharmaceutical advertising.

In 1964 Lubalin entered
into partnership with Aaron
Burns. This partnership,
along with Edward
Rondthaler, gave birth to the
concept of ITC, an organization without manufacturing
facilities which became,
through licensing, one of
the world's largest suppliers
of typefaces.

Lubalin also achieved
renown for his work as art
director on the magazines
Eros and *Avant Garde*, which
became famous as much for
their design as for their
content.

Above: *Avant Garde* magazine
cover, from Snyder and
Peckolick, *Herb Lubalin. Art
Director, Graphic Designer
and Typographer*, New York
1985. (NM)

PETIT CANON ROMAIN.

LA différence qu'on remar-
que entre l'homme & la femme,
vient non-seulement de l'éducation, mais aussi de leur nature.

PETIT CANON ITALIQUE.

LA vertu a quelque chose de
plus aimable dans les femmes,
& leurs fautes sont plus dignes de
grace, par la mauvaise éducation
qu'elles reçoivent.

Dans l'enfance, on leur parle
de leurs devoirs sans leur en faire
connoître les vrais principes.

Louis René LUCE
d.1774 F

128

Writing

Essai d'une nouvelle typographie, Barbou 1771

Louis René Luce was the son-in-law of Philippe Grandjean's pupil, Jean Alexandre. After Grandjean died in 1714, Alexandre and Luce completed his work on the Romain du Roi. All three men were royal type-cutters.

Luce contributed his own type designs to the Imprimerie Royale between 1740 and 1770. His types were more elongated and condensed than those of Grandjean. As a result they proved popular for typesetting poetry and became known as Types Poétiques. Luce also designed ornaments. He issued a specimen of these, some of which were to inspire Fournier, in 1740. Ornaments and borders, which Luce intended as an economic replacement for woodcut and engraved decorations, also featured in his *Essaie d'une nouvelle typographie*, printed by Barbou and published in 1771.

Above: Luce type specimen from *Essai d'une nouvelle typographie*, Barbou 1771. (SBPL)

Fargo
Interface
Lexia
Pan

Bruno MAAG
b.1962 CH

Types
Dedica 1986–99
Pan 1989–98
Royalty Anorexic 1989–98
Royalty Average 1989–98
Plume 1997
Interface 2000
Fargo 2004
Web
daltonmaag.com

After working as an apprentice typesetter at the Zürich newspaper *Tages Anzeiger*, and graduating from Schule für Gestaltung in Basel with a degree in typographic design and visual communications, Bruno Maag moved to England to work for Monotype in their type studio. After a year and a half in England, Maag transferred to Monotype Chicago, where he was responsible for their custom typeface department. During this time he re-cut all of *The New*

Yorker magazine's typefaces for use on the Macintosh. After returning to England in 1991 Maag, with Liz Dalton, launched Dalton Maag in London, specializing in all aspects of custom typeface production. Clients include British Telecom, BMW and Hewlett-Packard.

Above: Interface and Pan by Bruno Maag, with Lexia by Ron Carpenter and Fargo by Bruno Maag and Ron Carpenter, all designed for Dalton Maag. (BM)

Martin MAJOOR
b.1960 NL

Types
Serré 1984
FF Scala 1990–8
Ocean 1992
FF Scala Sans 1993–9
Telefont List 1994
Telefont Text 1994
FF Scala Jewel 1996
FF Seria 2000
FF Seria Sans 2000

Martin Majoor has been designing typefaces since the advent of the digital age. Born in Baarn, he studied graphic design at the Kunst Academie in Arnhem. His typeface Scala was originally designed for the Vredenburg Music Centre, for whom he worked as a graphic designer in the late 1980s. The Scala families, published by FSI from 1991 as part of the FontFont library, have achieved international success and many awards. His Seria families, with

exaggerated ascenders and descenders, were designed specifically for literature and poetry texts. The almost vertical italics of Seria are an unusual but successful feature. He produced new typefaces, Telefont List and Telefont Text, for his redesign of the Dutch telephone directories in 1994.

Majoor taught typography and graphic design at the schools of art in Arnhem and Breda from 1990 to 1995. Since 1997 he has worked as type designer and book typographer in Arnhem and Warsaw.

Above: FSI FontFont specimen, 1993. (CLR)

129

IN PRINCIPIO ERA IL
VERBO, E IL VERBO ERA
PRESSO DIO, ED ERA
DIO IL VERBO.

In principio era il Verbo, e il
Verbo era presso Dio, ed era
Dio il Verbo. Era questi in principio presso Dio. Le cose tutte
furono fatte per mezzo di lui, e
senza di lui nulla fu fatto
di quanto esiste.

IN PRINCIPIO ERA IL VERBO,
E IL VERBO ERA PRESSO DIO,
ED ERA DIO IL VERBO.

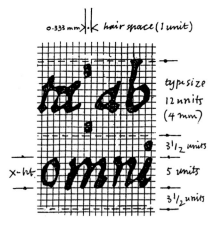

P Scott **MAKELA**
1960–99 USA

130

Types
Carmela 1989
Dead History 1990
Dead History Cyrillic 1990
Writing
Lewis Blackwell, P Scott Makela,
Laurie Haycock Makela,
Whereishere, Laurence King
1998

Born in St Paul, Minnesota,
P Scott Makela studied at
the Cranbrook Academy in
Michigan. An award-winning
designer of film titles, his
idiosyncratic approach to
graphic expression was
reflected in his type designs.
He taught at the Cranbrook
Academy with his wife
and collaborator on many
successful projects, Laurie
Haycock Makela. His early
death cut short an outstanding career.

Above: detail from Emigre type
specimen, 2000. (NM)

Charles **MALIN**
1883–1955 F

Charles Malin, the celebrated
French punch-cutter, worked
for the leading type designers
of his day, including Eric Gill,
Giovanni Mardersteig and
Frederic Warde.

Stanley Morison first
met Malin as a result of his
interest in Frederic Warde's
Arrighi Italic. When Morison
commissioned Gill's
Perpetua, he turned to
Malin to interpret the
drawings rather than use
the pantograph. Only when
he was satisfied with the
result was the type handed
over to the Monotype works
for production.

The designer with
whom Malin had the longest
collaboration was Giovanni
Mardersteig, the German
printer and scholar who
spent the greater part of his
life working in Verona. It was
a fruitful partnership and the
two worked together for
24 years. Malin cut most
of Mardersteig's types and
although Mardersteig
outlived him by more than
20 years he never produced
another type design.

Above: specimen of Zeno, cut
by Malin c.1937, from *The
Officina Bodoni*, British Library
1978. (NM)

Aldus **MANUTIUS**
1450–1515 I

Further reading
Peter Burnhill, *Type Spaces:
In-house Norms in the
Typography of Aldus
Manutius*, Hyphen Press
2004
Martin Davies, *Aldus Manutius:
Printer and Publisher of
Renaissance Venice*, British
Library 1995

The types of the prolific
Renaissance printer and
publisher Aldus Manutius
and his punch-cutter
Francesco Griffo, which
improved upon the earlier
Jenson type, became the
model for the next 250 years.
The invention of italic type
is generally ascribed to Aldus
and Griffo. Their Aldine italic,
based on a chancery hand
and designed to accommo-
date more text on the page,
made its first appearance in
a 1501 edition of Virgil.

Aldus was born in 1450
in the duchy of Sermoneta.

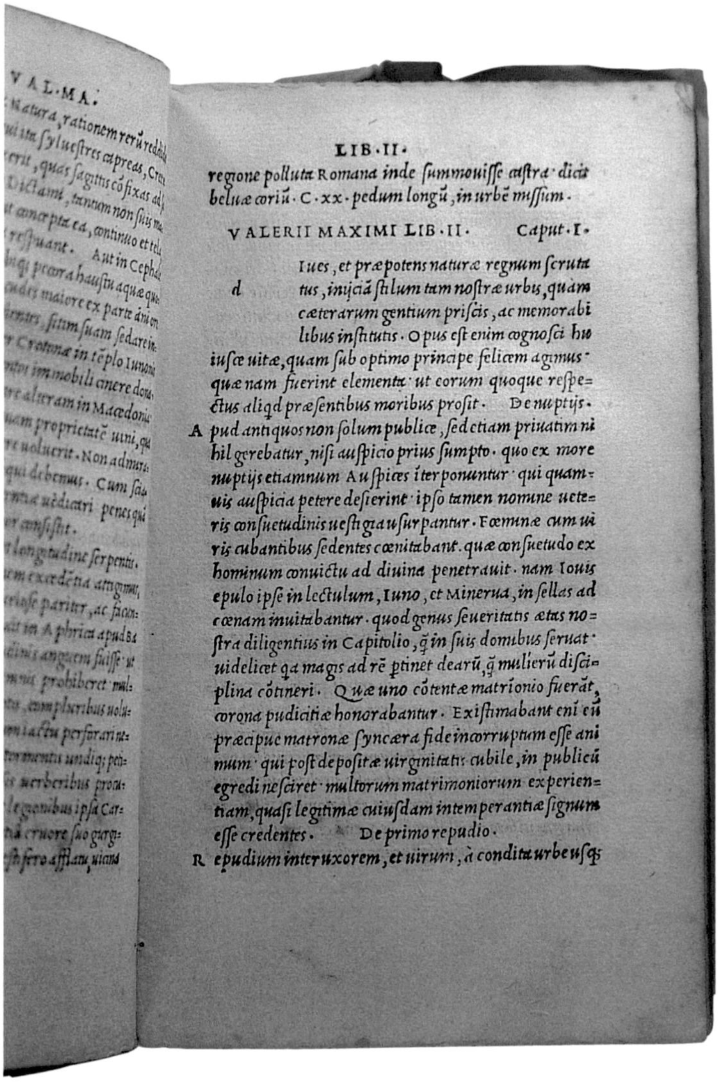

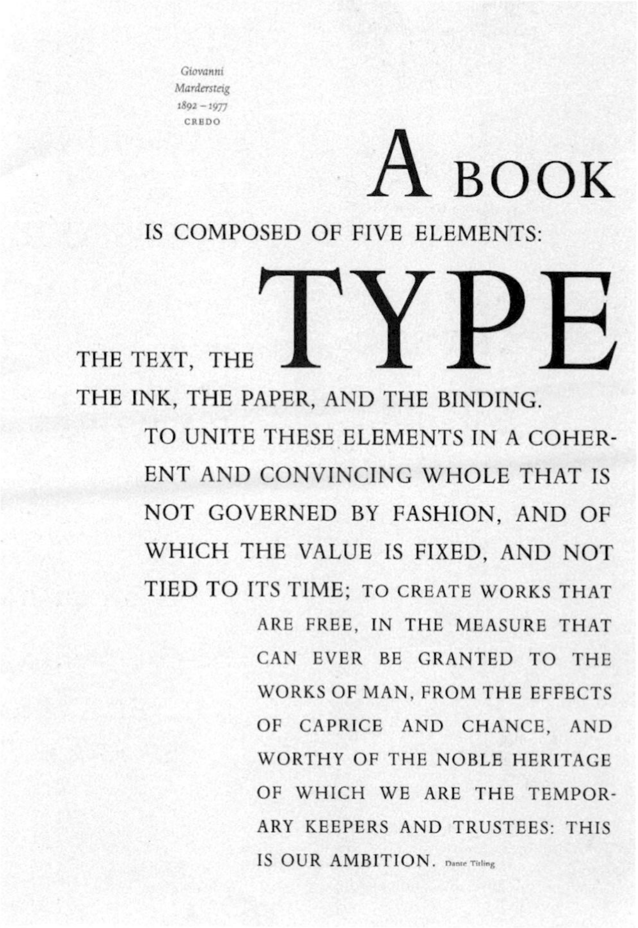

Page from Valerius Maximus, showing Latin text in two columns.

A BOOK

IS COMPOSED OF FIVE ELEMENTS:

TYPE

THE TEXT, THE
THE INK, THE PAPER, AND THE BINDING.
TO UNITE THESE ELEMENTS IN A COHER-
ENT AND CONVINCING WHOLE THAT IS
NOT GOVERNED BY FASHION, AND OF
WHICH THE VALUE IS FIXED, AND NOT
TIED TO ITS TIME; TO CREATE WORKS THAT
ARE FREE, IN THE MEASURE THAT
CAN EVER BE GRANTED TO THE
WORKS OF MAN, FROM THE EFFECTS
OF CAPRICE AND CHANCE, AND
WORTHY OF THE NOBLE HERITAGE
OF WHICH WE ARE THE TEMPOR-
ARY KEEPERS AND TRUSTEES: THIS
IS OUR AMBITION. Dante Titling

Giovanni Mardersteig 1892–1977 CREDO

Hans (or Giovanni) MARDERSTEIG
1892–1977 D

In 1489, aware of a gap in the market, he went to Venice to further his ambition of publishing Greek classics in the original language. His first publication came out in 1484: an edition of the *Galeomyomachia & Musæus' De Herone & Leandro*. Aldus's greek types have been widely criticized, their chief fault being the number of contractions and ligatures they use. His first original roman type did not appear until 1495 in Cardinal Bembo's *De Aetna*, which, as Stanley Morison demonstrated, was the basis for Claude Garamond's types. The type was revised before use in the *Hypnerotomachia Poliphili* of 1499, when a new, larger and lighter upper-case was added. Aldus helped to popularize many works by using an octavo format which made his books cheaper and

more portable. He died in Venice aged 65.

Monotype have produced two faces based on the designs of Aldus and Griffo. Poliphilus, released in 1923, is a facsimile of the type used in the *Hypnerotomachia Poliphili*. Bembo, based on the *De Aetna* types, is considered superior to Poliphilus and has proved to be a popular book typeface.

Previous page: analysis by Peter Burnhill of Griffo's type from *Type Spaces*. (HP); Above: page from one of Manutius's 'Octavo classics', *Exempla quatuor et viginti nuper inventa ante caput de omnibus Valerius Max*, Venice 1502. (CSM)

Types
Griffo 1929
Zeno 1936
Fontana 1936
Dante 1954
Pacioli 1955

Further reading
Hans Schmoller, *Two Titans: Mardersteig & Tschichold*, The Typophiles 1990
John Dreyfus, 'Giovanni Mardersteig's Work as a Type Designer', *Into Print*, British Library 1994
John Dreyfus, 'The Dante Types', *Fine Print on Type*, Lund Humphries 1989
Sebastian Carter, 'Hans (Giovanni) Mardersteig', *Twentieth Century Type Designers*, Lund Humphries 1995

Hans Mardersteig was born in Weimar in 1892. As a young man he edited the art magazine *Genius*, but ill health caused him to leave Germany for Switzerland. There, in 1923, he established

a private press in Montagnola, the Officina Bodoni.

Work by the press includes *The Calligraphic Models of Ludovico Degli Arrighi*, printed for Frederic Warde, using Warde's new Arrighi type. Stanley Morison wrote an introduction – the two shared an interest in the history of types and calligraphy, and maintained a long correspondence.

In 1927 the Officina moved to Verona, and in 1948 Mardersteig extended his operations to include a commercial press, the Stamperia Valdonega. Many of the types used at the Officina were of Mardersteig's design, and were cut by the Paris punch-cutter Charles Malin. Mardersteig continued working until he was 86, but his type designing ceased with Malin's death in 1955.

131

DECORATION AND ITS USES : By EDWARD JOHNSTON

Chapter V : The Choice of Letter forms and the Simple Arrangement of Letters : Formal Writing with the Broad-nibbed Pen (continued).

INSTINCTIVE choice is the decorator's soundest guide : if it be encouraged it will bring us unscathed through all the theories—even through the theories that we ourselves create. But our instincts have been so much disused or abused that Reason must be called to our aid. How many, in these days, who are interested in decoration know what they really like ? It is no passing fancy or doubtful attraction, but it is that which we really like, that matters, and that ought to

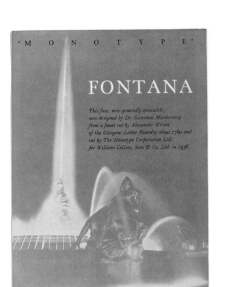

'MONOTYPE'

FONTANA

This face, now generally available, was designed by Dr. Giovanni Mardersteig from a fount cut by Alexander Wilson of the Glasgow Letter Foundry about 1760 and cut by The Monotype Corporation Ltd. for William Collins, Sons & Co., Ltd. in 1936

William MARTIN
d.1815 GB

John Henry MASON
1875–1951 GB

132

Mardersteig's best-known types are Dante and Fontana. The latter was designed for the exclusive use of publishers William Collins of Glasgow and is a revival of a 1760 type cut by Alexander Wilson. Cut by Monotype in 1957, Fontana was not released to the trade until 1961. Dante was designed for the Officina Bodoni in 1954 and later cut for Monotype. It was quickly taken up by other printers and in 1991 was redrawn for digital setting by Ron Carpenter for Monotype. Mardersteig was a scholar of Renaissance printing, in particular the work of Francesco Griffo, and received the Gutenberg Prize in 1968.

Previous page: opening page from Monotype specimen for digital Dante, 1991. (NM); Above: Monotype Fontana specimen, n.d. (CLR)

Types
Bulmer (revived 1928)

William Martin was the brother of Robert Martin, John Baskerville's foreman. He also trained under Baskerville, whose types clearly influenced his own. In 1786 Martin moved from Birmingham to London and became punch-cutter to George Nicol, who, with John Boydell, had set William Bulmer up in business in 1790. The intention was to publish a fine illustrated folio edition of Shakespeare. This, known as the Boydell Shakespeare, appeared in nine volumes between 1792 and 1802 and soon established the reputation of both Bulmer and Martin. Martin's foundry thus became in effect the private foundry of the Shakespeare Press.

Martin's types can be described as the last of the transitional faces, and, although modelled on Baskerville's, they are taller, narrower and more sharply cut. D B Updike has referred to them as 'both delicate and spirited, thoroughly English'. Cut for the exclusive use of William Bulmer's Shakespeare Press in London, they were not used by another printer until John McCreery used them for a specimen of typography, *The Press, a Poem*, in 1803. If Martin issued a specimen sheet no copies have survived, but his types appear on the 1807 specimen of G F Harris, who succeeded McCreery. The current versions of Bulmer are all based on Martin's earlier work of c.1790.

Above: detail from Monotype Bulmer specimen, 1968. (CLR)

Types
Imprint 1913

J H Mason was the editor of the highly influential British journal *The Imprint* and was head of the book production department at the Central School of Arts and Crafts in London, where he taught from 1905.

The Imprint was founded by friends: Gerard Meynell, a director of the Westminster Press, which printed and published the journal; Edward Johnston, who was the lettering editor; and F Ernest Jackson. An advisory board included W R Lethaby and Theodore Low De Vinne.

The typeface used in the journal, Imprint Old Face, was specially cut by Monotype to Mason's brief and was based on Caslon Old Face. Imprint, however,

Now if we are to choose letter forms, the only reasonable course open to us is to do so on the basis of readableness. We will, however, make our basis as wide as possible ; we therefore take readableness to imply not only easy-to-read but pleasant-to-read. If, for the sake of clearness, we here distinguish these qualities, we may also say that, while it is the general function of the craftsman to make a thing legible, it is his particular function as a decorator to make it becoming.

We have discovered then that one of the Uses of Decoration is to make a thing pleasant to read ; but, unless the decorator—like the poet—is "born," he must begin at the beginning and deal first with the more practical side of readableness, that is, with legibility.

There are three things which constitute legibility, namely, simplicity,

Modern & Cool Jazz

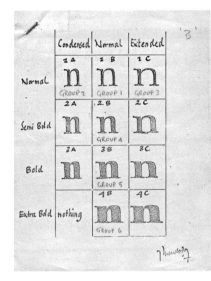

Hans Eduard MEIER
b.1922 CH

designed for mechanical composition and for printing on dry papers, is altogether more regular and precise. It was the first type to be designed specifically for machine composition and was to prove that the new technologies could produce results that rivalled the best hand-composed examples of the past.

The Imprint was not a financial success and after just nine issues it ceased publication in November 1913, albeit with reputation intact. In 1936 Mason became one of the first Royal Designers for Industry. He continued teaching despite deteriorating eyesight and retired in 1941.

Above: detail from *The Imprint*, no.5, 17 May 1913, p.345. (NM)

Types
Syntax 1968
Syntax Phonetic 1980
    (with Charles Bigelow)
Barbedor 1992
ITC Syndor 1992
Oberon 1994
Syntax Letter 1995
Syntax Lapidar 1995
Syntax Serif 1995
ABCSchrift 2002
BasisSchrift 2002
Elysa 2002
ABC Vario 2003
Oberon Serif 2004
Writing
The Development of Script and Type, Syntax Press 1994
Further reading
Sumner Stone, 'Hans Eduard Meier's Syntax-Antiqua', *Fine Print on Type*, Lund Humphries 1989

Hans Eduard Meier was born in 1922 in Horgen, Switzerland, where he trained as a typesetter from 1939 to 1943. He studied graphic arts at the Kunstgewerbeschule in

Zürich before continuing a successful career as a graphic artist. He designed his best-known typeface, Syntax, a humanist sans-serif interpretation of the types of the Renaissance, in 1968.

Although he retired in 1986 from the Kunst-gewerbeschule, where he had taught type design and graphic arts for 36 years, Meier revisited Syntax and, aided by computer technology, expanded the family to include additional weights, small caps and old-style figures. Serif, Letter and Lapidar versions of Syntax followed. He continues to release new typefaces.

Above: page from original Stempel Syntax specimen, n.d. (NM)

José
MENDOZA y Almeida
b.1926 F

133

Types
Pascal 1960
Photina 1971
Fidelio 1980
Sully-Jonquières 1980
ITC Mendoza 1991
Further reading
Sebastian Carter, 'José Mendoza y Almeida', *Twentieth Century Type Designers*, Lund Humphries 1995

French, of Spanish descent, José Mendoza was influenced by his lettering-artist father and designed alphabets from an early age. He was apprenticed as a photo-engraver at Cliché Union in Paris, one of the first companies to adopt Monophoto filmsetting. He worked with Maximilien Vox in the early 1950s. From 1954 to 1959 he was assistant to Roger Excoffon at the Fonderie Olive's Paris office and afterwards became a freelance designer.

MENHART 397

SYNOPSIS IN 10 DIDOT ON 11 POINT

ABCDEFGHIJKLMNOPQRSTUVWXYZ&ÆŒ
abcdefghijklmnopqrstuvwxyzfiflffiffæœ
ABCDEFGHIJKLMNOPQRSTUVWXYZ&ÆŒ
abcdefghijklmnopqrstuvwxyzfiflffiffæœ
1234567890 .,:;!?·"([!)§$*·"§$f))"'!;:;, 1234567890

REGD. TRADE MARK
MONOTYPE

U.A. 378   14D ON 16 PT. 13½ SET

LINE M-1314   U.A. 378

10D ON 11 PT. 9½ SET

When jobs have type sizes fixed quickly the
margins of error widen unless all determining
calculations are based on factual rather than
hypothetical figures. No variation in the total
When jobs have type sizes fixed quickly margins
of error widen unless determining calculations are
ABCDEFGHIJKLMNOPQRSTUVWXYZ ABC

18D ON 20 PT.

When jobs have type sizes fixed quickly margins
of error widen unless determining calculations
are based upon factual rather than hypothetical
When jobs have type sizes fixed quickly margins of
ABCDEFGHIJKLMNOPQRSTUVWXYZ ABCD

DISPLAY MATRICES   LINE T-1896

The art of book design lies mainly in relating size and x-height to the
length and leading of the lines and the type face to the paper surface
He won first prize for keyboard setting and a gold medal for accuracy
ABCDEFGHIJKLMNOPQRSTUVWXYZ *ABCDEFGHIJKLMNOP*

24D ON 30 PT.   DISPLAY MATRICES   LINE T-2536

Oversize blocks may be set jutting into top and side
margins if extra space seems likely to be required
Books were once hand-written on parchment or vellum
ABCDEFGHIJKLMNOPQRSTUVWXYZ *ABCDE*

Oldrich **MENHART**
1897–1962 CS

134   Mendoza's best-known typeface is Photina, released by the Monotype Corporation in 1971. It was only their third typeface designed exclusively for filmsetting, and was intended to work harmoniously with Adrian Frutiger's Univers series. From 1985 to 1990 Mendoza taught type design at the Imprimerie Nationale, Paris, where he influenced and inspired many of today's leading French type designers. His neo-humanist text face ITC Mendoza was released by the International Typeface Corporation in 1991.

Previous page: Mendoza's diagram showing proposed weights for Monotype Photina, c.1970. (MT); Above: cover of *Monotype Newsletter*, no.91, 1972. (CLR)

Types
Menhart Antiqua and Kursive 1936
Menhart 1938
Menhart Roman 1939
Hollar 1939
Figural 1940–62
Victory 1947
Ceska Uncial 1948
Manuscript 1949
Monument 1949
Parlament 1950
Unciala 1953
Grazdanka 1953–5
Triga 1955
Further reading
Paul Hayden Duensing, 'Oldrich Menhart', *Fine Print on Type*, Lund Humphries 1989
Writing
Nauka o písmu, Prague 1954
Tvorba typografického písma, Prague 1957

Oldrich Menhart was born in Prague. The youngest of four sons, he was apprenticed in 1911 as a compositor with the printer Politka in Prague and in his spare time he studied letters in church sepulchres and churchyards.

In 1924 the Czech Institute awarded Menhart a stipend, which enabled him to travel to Antwerp, where he visited the Plantin-Moretus Museum, and then to Paris, where he saw the Imprimerie Nationale. During this trip Menhart made contact with the Bauer foundry. By 1929 he had become dissatisfied with the state printing office in Prague, where he was working, and left to become a freelance calligrapher, author and book designer. In 1930 he produced his first type designs, Codex Antiqua and Kursive, which were strongly influenced by Walter Tiemann and Peter Behrens and which were later produced by the Bauer foundry in 1936 as Menhart Antiqua and Kursive.

Many of his types show a strong calligraphic influence, particularly in the italics, and Manuscript, which is generally regarded as his masterpiece, is based closely on his own handwriting, expressing his belief that 'letters could not be designed until they had been written'. Menhart's last letter forms, the italic swash caps for Figural, were issued in 1962, the year of his death.

Above: Menhart 397 specimen from *Monotype Printing Types*, vol.2, n.d. (NM)

LUDLOW OFFERS
SELECTION OF FA
MAKE FOR BETTE

CONSIDERATE
Numbers Manage

LUDLOW STELLAR BOLD 8pt. to 72pt.

COMMENTS
Often Repeat

LUDLOW KARNAK LIGHT 10pt. to 72pt.

OPERATED
By Men And

LUDLOW KARNAK MEDIUM 10pt. to 72pt.

neue   haas grotesk

wohl durchdacht, ausgewogen
diskret und temperiert,
sachlich, weich und flüssig,
mit ihren ausgefeilten,
harmonisch und logisch
aufgebauten Formen
ist die Schrift
für den täglichen Bedarf
der fortschrittlichen Druckerei

Robert Hunter MIDDLETON
1898–1985 USA

Types
Eusebius 1923–9
Ludlow Black 1924
Cameo 1927
Record Gothic 1927–60
Delphian Open Titling 1928
Stellar 1929
Tempo 1930–42
Karnak 1931–42
Lafayette 1932
Mayfair Cursive 1932
Eden 1934
Mandate 1934
Umbra 1935
Coronet 1937
Stencil 1938
Radiant 1940
Samson 1940
Flair 1941
Admiral Script 1953
Condensed Gothic Outline
    1953
Florentine Cursive 1956
Formal Script 1956
Wave 1962
Further reading
Bruce Beck, *Robert Hunter
    Middleton, the Man and his
    Letters*, Caxton Club 1985

Sebastian Carter, 'Robert
    Hunter Middleton', *Twentieth
    Century Type Designers*,
    Lund Humphries 1995

Born near Glasgow in
Scotland, Robert Hunter
Middleton emigrated to the
USA with his family at the
age of 10. Whilst studying the
printing arts at the Chicago
Art Institute, Middleton was
a student in the class of Ernst
F Detterer.

Detterer and Middleton
started to work together on
the new Eusebius typeface
and subsequently Middleton
was employed by Ludlow to
see it through its production
stages. Middleton stayed
with the foundry and by 1929
he had created matching
bold, italic and open versions
of Eusebius. From then until
his retirement in 1971 he produced nearly a hundred typefaces for Ludlow, including

many of their best-known
sans serif and display types.

Middleton was also
influential in the revival of
interest in the work of
Thomas Bewick (1753–1828),
the celebrated English wood-
engraver, whose work he
printed in his spare time at
his Cherryburn Press.

Above: detail from Ludlow type
catalogue. (PB); detail from
Vincent Steer, *Printing Design
and Layout*, London n.d.,
p.405. (NM)

Max MIEDINGER
1910–80 CH

Types
Pro Arte 1954
Neue Haas Grotesk/Helvetica
    1957–83
Horizontal 1964

Max Miedinger, born in
Zürich, was an in-house
designer with the Haas
foundry in Munchenstein,
Switzerland. His most
famous typeface is Helvetica,
currently one of the most
widely used sans serifs,
which was designed in 1956.

Edouard Hoffman of Haas
had asked Miedinger to adapt
the existing Haas Grotesk to
bring it into line with current
taste. Haas Grotesk had its
origins in the 19th-century
German grotesques like
Berthold's Akzidenz-Grotesk.
The type, which was created
from Miedinger's china-ink
drawings, seemed like a new
design in its own right, rather
than an old one with minor

retouching as had been the original plan. Although designed for the home market, the then-called Neue Haas Grotesk proved popular farther afield. When Stempel AG in Germany released the face in 1961 they called it Helvetica, the traditional Latin name for Switzerland, in order to capitalize on the fashion for Swiss typography. Additional weights were added to the Helvetica family over the years. In 1983 Linotype released a new, more extensive version, Neue Helvetica, in 51 weights.

Previous page: from a late 1950s Haas specimen.; Above: from a Stempel Helvetica specimen, n.d. (both CLR)

Ross MILLS
b.1970 CDN

Types
1530 Garamond 1994
Plantagenet 1996
Academia 1996
Pigiarniq 2001 (with John Hudson)
Euphemia 2004
Plantagenet Cherokee 2004
Plantagenet Novus 2005
Restraint 2005 (with Marian Bantjes)
Web
tiro.com

Ross Mills, who was born in Vancouver, co-founded Tiro Typeworks with John Hudson in 1994. He has designed and produced multilingual typefaces for Microsoft, Apple, Linotype Library and Canadian government departments. His work for the latter, creating alphabets for North American aboriginal languages, has been much acclaimed.

Above: Pigiarniq showing from *Language, Culture, Type*, ATypI Graphis 2002. (PB)

Joseph MOLÉ (le jeune)
active 1797–1820 F

Types
Molé Floriate (revived 1960)

Parisian typefounder Joseph Molé (le jeune) began his career as a painter and designer. In 1819, at the Exposition du Louvre, he exhibited a series of broadsides which, according to D B Updike, made up 'one of the most magnificent typespecimens known'. The result of 27 years of personal labour, the broadsides featured, amongst 206 varieties of type, his roman and italic, which were much influenced by Didot, and a multitude of borders and rules. Molé's foundry became part of the Fonderie Générale of Paris.

Above: detail of Stephenson Blake specimen, n.d. (CLR)

Bernd MÖLLENSTÄDT
b.1943 D

Types
Formata 1984
Signata 1993

Type designer Bernd Möllenstädt studied as a compositor and graphic designer before joining H Berthold AG in 1967. He was responsible for their type-design studio in Munich from 1968 and for all font production from 1976. Formata, a sans serif with humanist characteristics first issued in 1984, has been considerably extended as a family by Möllenstädt since to offer a variety of options including small capitals and old-style figures. Möllenstädt succeeded Günter Gerhard Lange as artistic director of H Berthold AG on the latter's retirement in 1990.

Above: Formata from Berthold Types 128 specimen, n.d. (CLR)

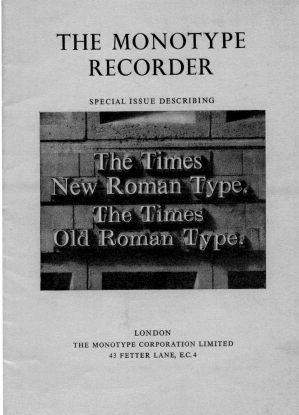

THE MONOTYPE
RECORDER

SPECIAL ISSUE DESCRIBING

The Times
New Roman Type.
The Times
Old Roman Type.

LONDON
THE MONOTYPE CORPORATION LIMITED
43 FETTER LANE, E.C.4

LINOTYPE

Times
roman

TIMES ROMAN WITH ITALIC AND SMALL CAPS
TIMES ROMAN WITH TIMES HEAVY
TIMES HEADING
TIMES HEADING BOLD
TIMES HEADING BOLD CONDENSED
TIMES HEADING LIGHT
TIMES TWO-LINE

TRADE LINOTYPE MARK

Stanley **MORISON**
1889–1967 GB

Types
Times New Roman 1932
Writing
Four Centuries of Fine Printing,
   Ernest Benn 1924
A Tally of Types,
   Cambridge 1953
First Principles of Typography,
   Cambridge University Press
   1936, 2nd ed. 1967
Further reading
James Moran, *Stanley Morison:
   His Typographic
   Achievement*, Lund
   Humphries 1971
Nicolas Barker, *Stanley
   Morison*, Macmillan and
   Harvard University Press
   1972

Stanley Morison, through
his work at Monotype, as
a founder of *The Fleuron*
and as a frequent writer on
type, was one of the most
influential figures in British
typography. He was born
near Wanstead in London.
In 1913 he became editorial
assistant on *The Imprint*.

Like *The Fleuron*, which he
founded with Oliver Simon
in 1919, *The Imprint* was not
a financial success, but both
publications did a great deal
to raise awareness of and an
interest in typography.

Morison then had brief
spells at Pelican Press and
Cloister Press before joining
Monotype in 1923, whilst
also maintaining a long
association with Cambridge
University Press. Monotype
had already begun to revive
historic types but Morison
brought an informed enthusiasm to the work. The revivals
cut during his time at the
Monotype Corporation
eventually covered all
periods of typographic
history. Amongst them were
Baskerville, Bell, Bembo,
Ehrhardt and Fournier.

His interest in types also
embraced contemporary

designs and he commissioned
original faces from Eric Gill
and Jan van Krimpen.

In 1929, responding to
Morison's criticism of *The
Times*'s typography, the
management asked him to
improve it. After experimenting with Perpetua and Plantin
he produced a new face,
which, some now claim,
originated in a specimen
from the archives of Lanston
Monotype in the USA. (If this
is indeed the case Morison
must be at least acknowl-
edged for having recognized
its potential.) It was a
draughtsman from *The Times*,
Victor Lardent, who did the
finished drawings for Times
New Roman, which first appeared in the newspaper on
3 October 1932. A year later
it was made available to the
trade and quickly established
itself as a standard book

typeface. Its popularity
increased from the 1980s,
when it became a core font
on computer software
systems.

Morison also wrote widely
on type, as well as becoming
editor of *The Times Literary
Supplement* in 1945. He was
made a fellow of the British
Academy in 1954 and a Royal
Designer for Industry in 1960.

Above: cover of *The Monotype
Recorder*, 1932.; Linotype
specimen, n.d. (both CLR)

137

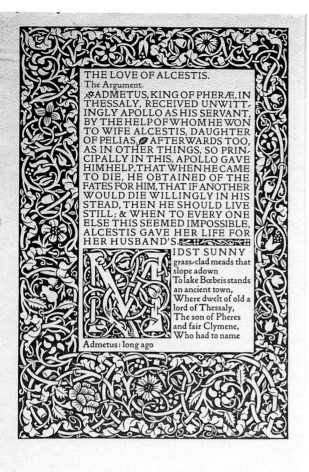

William **MORRIS**
1834–96 GB

Types
Golden Type 1890
Troy 1892
Chaucer 1893
Further reading
William S Peterson, *William Morris: The Ideal Book*, University of California Press 1982

William Morris, notable as a socialist and writer, was a key figure in the Arts and Crafts Movement. His interest in typography at the end of his career was inspired by a lecture on letter forms given to the Arts and Crafts Exhibition Society on 15 November 1888 by Emery Walker.

In 1890 Morris founded the Kelmscott Press, intended as a small private press. He used his own hand presses and types, printing on dampened handmade paper, designing two types for the Press, both cut by Edward Prince. The more influential, Golden Type, drew on his early drawings of Venetian types. Based on Jenson's *Pliny* and a history of Florence printed by Jacobus Rubeus, both from 1476, Golden sparked off interest in Jenson revivals, and Morris's resistance to its commercial use led to foundries cutting their own Jenson-inspired faces. A pre-1900 version was ATF's Nicolas Jenson.

His other face (an informal black-letter) was cut for use in the *Kelmscott Chaucer*, the Press's best-known work. This face came in two sizes known as Troy and Chaucer. The *Kelmscott Chaucer* took four years to produce, the last years of Morris's life, and was completed on 6 May 1896.

Above: page from *The Earthly Paradise*, Kelmscott Press, 1896–7, set in Golden Type, photographed for the CLR. (CLR)

Joseph **MOXON**
1627–91 GB

Writing
Herbert Davis and Harry Carter (eds.), *Mechanick Exercises on the Whole Art of Printing* [1683–4], Oxford University Press 1958

Joseph Moxon, who was born in Yorkshire, was the first English writer on typefounding and a typefounder himself. Originally a maker of mathematical instruments, he issued a type specimen as early as 1669, despite never having been properly taught the art. His letters, however, were of poor quality, and it is for his writing of *Mechanick Exercises* published in London in 1683–4 that he is best remembered.

Above: detail from specimen facsimile of *Mechanick Exercises on the Whole Art of Printing* [1683–4], Oxford University Press 1958. (NM)

Gary **MUNCH**
b.1953 USA

Types
Duomo 1993
Londinium 1993
Nonogram 1993
Pep Rally 1993
Mage 1994
Hieroglyphic 1995
Meter 1995
UrbanSprawl 1995
Chancery Modern 1997
Linotype Ergo 1997
Linotype Finerliner 1997
Linotype Really 2000
Candara 2004
Web
munchfonts.com

Gary Munch offers a variety of type designs through his foundry Munchfonts. Text, display and historical types reflect his considerable skill with letter forms.

His sans-serif text type, Ergo, won First in Text and Overall at the 1997 Linotype-Hell 2nd International Type Design Contest; his Chancery Modern the Judge's Pick in

Linotype Ergo™
Gary Munch, USA

Ergo Regular
Ergo Italic
Ergo Medium
Ergo Medium Italic
Ergo Demi Bold
Ergo Demi Bold Italic
Ergo Bold
Ergo Bold Italic
Ergo Sketch

the 1998 *Serif* magazine Type Design Competition. Really, a serif family of six weights combining transitional, modern and old style features, was an award winner at Linotype's third contest in 1999. Really, with Munch's added greek and Cyrillic versions, was a winner again in the text design category of Bukva:Raz!, the first type design competition of the Association Typographique Internationale. He has also contributed a type design to Microsoft's ClearType project, Candara, a sans serif.

Munch teaches at the University of Bridgeport, Connecticut, and became the president of the Type Directors Club (New York) in 2004.

Above: Ergo showing from Linotype Library's *The Winner Fonts: 2nd International Type Design Contest*, 1998. (NM)

Miles NEWLYN
b.1969 GB

Types
Democratica 1991
Missionary 1991
Sabbath Black 1992
Ferox 1995
Luvbug 1996
Web
newlyn.com

139

The type designs of Miles Newlyn, who studied at London's Central Saint Martins College of Art and Design during the early 1990s, have made a considerable impact on contemporary typographic design. His neo-gothic designs for Emigre (the RIP-busting Missionary took him almost one thousand hours to complete) led to David Carson exclusively licensing seven of his typefaces for *Ray Gun* magazine in the mid-1990s. Newlyn now specializes in designing logotypes and custom typefaces

Robin NICHOLAS
b.1947 GB

Types
Nimrod 1980
Arial 1982
(with Patricia Saunders)
Plantin Headline 1994
Felbridge 2003

Robin Nicholas, who was born in Westerham, Kent, joined Monotype in 1965 after training as an engineering draughtsman. He was made manager of their type drawing office in 1982, and is currently head of typography at Monotype in the UK. He also supervises the company's Custom Fonts service, creating new designs for corporate branding.

Between 1978 and 1980 he designed Nimrod, a group of related roman faces designed for newspaper text, headlines and small ads. Nimrod was widely praised for its readability. In 1982, with Patricia Saunders, he created the

Arial typeface family, a sans-serif typeface for low-resolution laser printers which was chosen by Microsoft as a core operating system font.

Robin Nicholas has supervised the design or revival of many Monotype faces, including Clarion, Bell, Centaur, Janson, Dante, Van Dijck, Walbaum, Bulmer and Pastonchi.

Above: Monotype/Faces promotion of Felbridge, 2004. (CLR)

Gerrit NOORDZIJ
b.1931 NL

Types
Batavian 1980
Dutch Roman 1980
Ruse 2000
Writing
The Stroke of the Pen: Fundamental Aspects of Western Writing, The Hague 1982
De Streek: Theorie van het Schrift, Zaltbommel 1985
De Kind und die Schrift, Munich 1985
Letterletter, Hartley & Marks 2000
Further reading
Mathieu Lommen and Peter Verheul (eds.), *Haagse Letters*, Uitgeverij de Buitenkant 1996

Calligrapher, type designer, teacher and writer Gerrit Noordzij was born in Rotterdam. He trained as a bookbinder and worked as a graphic designer before beginning an outstanding 30-year teaching career in 1960 at the Koninklijke

140

through his company, XEty, which provides typographic branding solutions to major design companies and advertising agencies – his collaboration with Wolf Ollins in particular has led to work for AOL Europe, Honda, the Tate Gallery and others.

Previous page: showing of Ferox.; Above: showing of Luvbug. (both MN)

haec a sapientibus & prudentibus et revelasti ea parvulis etiam Pater quia sic placuit

Eine neue Egyptienne: die PMN Caecilia 45
die PMN Caecilia 55
die PMN Caecilia 75
die PMN Caecilia 85
die PMN Caecilia 46
die PMN Caecilia 56
die PMN Caecilia 76
die PMN Caecilia 86

Peter Matthias NOORDZIJ
b.1961 NL

Types
PMN Caecilia 1991
Web
teff.ne

Peter Matthias Noordzij studied at the Koninklijke Academie van Beeldende Kunsten in The Hague, where he was born, from 1980 to 1985. His courses included lettering under his father, Gerrit. Whilst studying he began work on his PMN Caecilia family, which was issued by Linotype in 1991. He works as a typographer, teaches typography and manages the Enschedé Font Foundry, purveyors of high-quality original typefaces, which he established in 1991.

Above: cover of Linotype PMN Caecilia specimen, 1993. (CLR)

Robert NORTON
1929–2001 GB

Types
Else NPL 1982
Writing
Types Best Remembered/Types Best Forgotten, Parsimony Press 1993

Robert Norton, who was born in London, will be remembered as much as a type businessman as a type designer. After early experiences in publishing, Norton spent time in New York, then Jamaica, returning to the USA to work as a designer with Cambridge University Press in New York. In 1963 he was back in the UK, launching the pioneering display phototypesetting company, Photoscript Ltd. Experience of font production there led him to set up Norton Photosetting Ltd in 1970, a company which manufactured several hundred fonts for BobstGraphic. There, in 1982,

he issued his own design, Else, a transitional type in the Century tradition. After further business ventures into digital type production and manufacturing, he joined Microsoft in Seattle in the early 1990s to develop their TrueType font library. He left in 1997 to return to London, where he founded a small publishing company, Parsimony Press, before his death in 2001. His book *Types Best Remembered/Types Best Forgotten* is witness to his wonderful sense of humour.

Above: Else advertisement from *U&lc*, vol.9, no.2, June 1982. (CLR)

Academie van Beeldende Kunsten in The Hague. His teaching of type design, writing and lettering has made a more than considerable contribution to the unparalleled Dutch impact on contemporary type design. His provocative though sensitive writing on his subject, expounded particularly in *Letterletter*, releases his theories on the structure and nature of letter forms to all typographers. His many typefaces, most unpublished, reflect his theories. Throughout his career he has continued to design books.

Above: showing of Noordzij's unpublished Apex type from *Haagse Letters*, Uitgeverij de Buitenkant 1996. (NM)

141

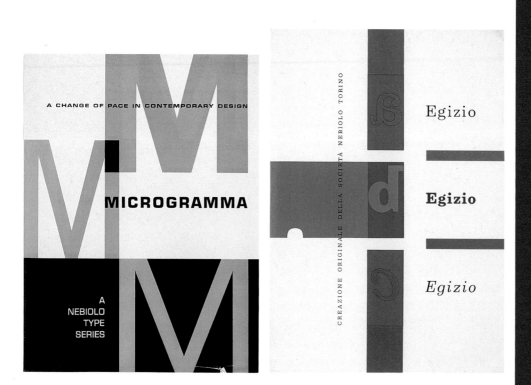

Aldo **NOVARESE**
1920–95 I

Types
Landi Linear 1943
Athenaeum 1945
    (with Alessandro Butti)
Normandia 1946–9
    (with Alessandro Butti)
Augustea 1951
    (with Alessandro Butti)
Microgramma 1952
    (with Alessandro Butti)
Cigno 1954
Fontanesi 1954
Juliet 1955
Ritmo 1955
Egizio 1955–8
Garaldus 1956
Slogan 1957
Recto 1958–61
Estro 1961
Eurostile 1962
Forma 1966
Magister 1966
Metropol 1967
Stop 1971
Sprint 1974
Lapidar 1977
Fenice 1977–80
Novarese 1980
Expert 1983
Colossal 1984
ITC Symbol 1984

ITC Mixage 1985
Arbiter 1989
Writing
Il Segno Alfabeta, Turin 1964
Further reading
S Polano and P Vetta, 'On Aldo
    Novarese', *Emigre*, no.26,
    1993

Born in Pontestura
Monferrato in Piedmont,
Aldo Novarese studied at the
Scuola Arteri Stampatori and
the Scuola Tipografica
Giuseppe Vigliandi Paravia
in Turin. He was to design
most of his types for the
Turin-based Nebiolo foundry,
which he joined at the age of
16 in 1936. He became art
director in 1952, succeeding
Alessandro Butti. Many of the
earlier types he worked on
were designed in a productive
partnership with Butti. These
included Augustea and Microgramma; the latter, with the
addition of a lower-case,

became Eurostile in 1962.
Novarese left Nebiolo in 1975
to pursue a freelance career
and in 1978 he designed the
type that bears his name,
Novarese, for the Haas
foundry. Two years later
Novarese was the first of
his types to be licensed and
issued by ITC. He contributed
further designs to ITC and
several to Berthold. During
a long and productive career
Novarese also devised a
type classification system
and wrote on typography,
contributing to a number
of design and graphics
publications.

Above: cover from *Print in
Britain Type Supplement*,
October 1961; Nebiolo
specimen, n.d. (both CLR)

O

P

FF Olsen™

FACE:

AOPGZ

Morten Rostgaard
OLSEN
b.1964 DK

Types
FF Max 2001
FF Olsen 2001

Graphic designer Morten
Olsen lives and works in
Copenhagen. He studied for
five years at the Danmarks
Designskole. His design company specializes in corporate
and type design. Olsen has
contributed two families to
the FSI FontFont library.
FF Max is a contemporary
sans inspired by Aldo
Novarese's Eurostile, and
FF Olsen is a serif family
with an emphasis on high
legibility. FF Olsen is the
serif type used in this book.

Above: detail from FSI FF Olsen
specimen, 2001. (NM)

Mike PARKER
b.1929 GB

144

Although born in England, Mike Parker has worked for many years in America and until 1981 was director of typography for Mergenthaler Linotype, where he was responsible for adding more than a thousand typefaces to the type library. He had studied architecture and graphic design at Yale, and in 1958–9 worked at the Plantin-Moretus Museum, Antwerp, cataloguing the collection of matrices, moulds and punches. Whilst at Mergenthaler, Parker commissioned original faces from leading designers such as Matthew Carter, Adrian Frutiger and Hermann Zapf, as well as instituting many revivals and expanding the range of non-Latin types. He left Linotype in 1981 and, with Matthew Carter, set up Bitstream Inc., the Cambridge Massachusetts-based digital typefoundry specializing in the development of fonts for desktop-publishing applications. Parker went on to found The Company, a typographical consultancy, in 1987 and Pages Software in 1990.

Above: Mergenthaler Linotype advertisement from *U&lc*, vol.7, no.2, June 1980. (CLR)

Jim PARKINSON
b.1941 USA

Types
El Grande 1993
Poster Black 1993
Showcard Gothic 1993
Generica Condensed 1994
ITC Bodoni 1994 (with others)
Parkinson 1994
Antique Condensed 1995
Jimbo 1995
Showcard Moderne 1995
Diablo 1996
FF Moderne Gothics 1996
Mojo 1996
Industrial Gothic 1997
Comrade 1998
ITC Roswell 1998
Pueblo 1998

Web
typedesign.com

Jim Parkinson was born in Oakland, California, where a lettering-artist neighbour inspired his lifelong love of lettering. After studying at the California College of Arts and Crafts he joined Hallmark Cards in Kansas City as a lettering artist in 1964. Lured back to California by the Summer of Love and the hippy lifestyle, he began his freelance career. He worked for a variety of clients, but a commission to design typefaces for *Rolling Stone* magazine convinced him that his future lay with publishers. He has since designed and 'repaired' mastheads for many magazines and newspapers. After going 'totally digital' in 1990 he has been designing typefaces, mostly display, for The Font Bureau, Agfa Monotype, Adobe, ITC and FSI FontFont. He publishes many of his designs through his company, Parkinson Type Design.

Above: from Faces/Parkinson Type Design promotion, n.d. (CLR)

Bitstream Chianti (continued)

ch ck ct fi fl ff ffi ffl fft gg gy ij I·l sh st tt tz
℄ ℅ Cr LE Ll Mc Mc Qu Rp
Æ ÆR HE IJ L·L Ľ ND NE QU TT TY
ą đ ðę ĵłþ ų ý ž A¢ĐĘŁŠÝŽ£ ₣ abdeilmnorst
¼ ½ ¾ ⅛ ⅜ ⅝ ⅞ ⅓ ⅔ 1234567890¢$

🍇 ℰ ∼ ❦ ❧ ❀ ✳ ⊠ ⌊⌉ ❦

ch ck ct fi fl ff ffi ffl fft gg gy ij I·l sh st tt tz
℄ ℅ Cr LE Ll Mc Mc Qu Rp
Æ ÆR HE IJ L·L Ľ ND NE QU TT TY
ą đ ðę ĵłþ ų ý ž A¢ĐĘŁŠÝŽ£₣ abdeilmnorst
¼ ½ ¾ ⅛ ⅜ ⅝ ⅞ ⅓ ⅔ 1234567890¢$

🍇 ℰ ∼ ❦ ❧ ❀ ✳ ⊠ ⌊ ⌉ ❦

ch ck ct fi fl fr ff ffi ffl fft ij lf l·l of rt sh st tt tz
Cr Qu Rp Æ ÆR HE IJ L·L Ľ ND NE QU TT TY
ą đ ðę ĵłþ ų ý ž A¢ĐĘŁŠÝŽ£₣ abdeilmnorst
¼ ½ ¾ ⅛ ⅜ ⅝ ⅞ ⅓ ⅔ 1234567890¢$

acdefgh͜ij klm͜n͜orstuʋw yz
ABCDEFGHIJKLMNOPQRSTUVW...
1234567890 & äçéñ͜ôù

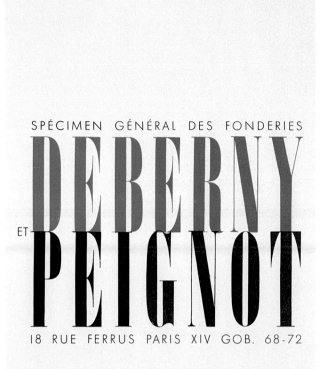

SPÉCIMEN GÉNÉRAL DES FONDERIES

DEBERNY
ET PEIGNOT

18 RUE FERRUS PARIS XIV GOB. 68-72

145

Dennis PASTERNAK
b.1952 USA

Types
Bitstream Chianti 1993
Maiandra GD 1994
ITC Stylus 1995
Baltra GD 2002
Bing 2002
Bisco Condensed 2002
Bartholomé 2003

Web
galapagosdesign.com

Dennis Pasternak was born in Holyoke, Massachusetts. He achieved a Bachelor of Fine Arts degree in design at the Massachusetts College of Art. Pasternak, with over 20 years of experience in type design and production working with leading companies including Compugraphic Corporation, Autologic and Bitstream, reveres and is inspired by the pre-digital era of type design.

In 1994 Pasternak left Bitstream to become a founding partner and principal designer of Galápagos Design Group. Staffed by skilled type designers and type technologists, the Littleton Massachusetts-based Galápagos services the requirements of major typefoundries, software manufacturers, design companies, banks and corporations.

A significant aspect of Pasternak's design philosophy is his belief that for an original type design to rise above the ever-increasing multitude of digital typefaces, its potential market should be carefully and studiously researched.

Above: Chianti showing from Bitstream catalogue, 1997. (NM)

Charles PEIGNOT
1897–1983 F

Charles Peignot, a grandson of the founder, entered the family typefounding business, Peignot ℀ Cie., in 1919. Four years later the company merged with Girard ℀ Cie. (the name of the De Berny foundry from 1914) and became known as Deberny ℀ Peignot.

Within a few years Charles Peignot began to demonstrate the skill that was to make the Deberny ℀ Peignot foundry famed throughout the world. He broadened the range of faces and commissioned leading contemporary artists and designers to create new ones. Faces such as Cassandre's Acier Noir, Bifur and Peignot were produced in the 1920s and 1930s and were rewarded with early success. In 1927 Peignot founded *Arts ℀ Métiers Graphiques*, the forward-looking and influential periodical.

After World War 2, Peignot played an important role in the development and marketing of the new Lumitype photosetting equipment (known in the USA as Photon). Deberny ℀ Peignot acquired the European rights for this equipment and made discs and typefaces for it.

In 1952 Peignot brought in the Swiss designer Adrian Frutiger, then at the beginning of his career as an art director and type designer. The association was a very successful one and amongst the many new typefaces created in this period were Meridien and Univers.

Charles Peignot helped found the Association Typographique Internationale (ATypI) and became its first president in 1957, a position

John **PETERS**
1917–89 GB

Types
Angelus 1953
Castellar 1957
Traveller 1964
Fleet Titling 1967

Son of a UK Member of
Parliament, John Peters
began reading architecture
at Cambridge University in
1936, but after two years he
left the university to join the
RAF. In 1940 he was shot
down over France and
seriously wounded. Despite
this he continued active
service before leaving the
RAF in 1945.

In 1950, after working for
short spells with the Arts
Council and the Shenval
Press, Peters went to
Cambridge University Press.
In 1953, with John Dreyfus,
he created the text typeface
Angelus for a pocket edition
of the Bible which the
University Press never

produced. For Monotype,
where John Dreyfus had
become type director, he
designed the titling fonts
Castellar, Fleet Titling and
Traveller.

Peters set up the Vine
Press in 1956 and designed
and produced some notable
books on a hand press. His
life ended sadly, when the
pain caused by his war injury
became too much for him and
he took his own life in 1989.

Above: Monotype Castellar
specimen, n.d. (CLR)

Alexander **PHEMISTER**
1829–94 GB

Types
Old Style 1860
Franklin Old Style 1863

Born in Edinburgh, Alexander
Phemister showed an early
aptitude for designing letters.
He was apprenticed to the
famous Edinburgh punch-
cutter William Grandison. At
the age of 23, he attracted the
attention of the Edinburgh
typefounders Miller ɛt
Richard, with whom he cut
several series of romans,
including Old Style. As a type,
it was widely admired and
much copied, as it overcame
what was considered archaic
in Caslon. Phemister's work
on body-type faces made
Miller ɛt Richard famous
with English publishers.

In 1861 Phemister emi-
grated to America. He is said
to have worked for two years
with George Bruce ɛt Co., but
it was during this time that

146 that he retained until
he was succeeded by John
Dreyfus in 1968. Deberny
ɛt Peignot continued in
business until 1972, when
it was finally acquired by
the Swiss typefoundry
Haas.

Previous page: titlepage of
Deberny & Peignot specimen
book, 1952. (SBPL)

Text in left specimen image:

Founts of 50 ℔, with Italic.
SOUTH AFRICA.—As you
penetrate into a secluded

Founts of 50 ℔ and upwards.
SCENES IN SOUTH AFRICA.—As
you penetrate into a secluded valley

MILLER & RICHARD.

ART-EDUCATION MAGAZINE

'MONOTYPE'
THIS IS
60 pt.
PLANTIN
SERIES
110

BCDFGHJKS
abcdefghjklmn

QRUVWXZ&
opqrstuvwxyz;

The "family" of this famous design comprises the following series:
'Monotype' Plantin Light 113
'Monotype' Plantin 110
'Monotype' Plantin Bold 194
'Monotype' Plantin Bold Cond. 236
'Monotype' Plantin Titling 438

ABCDEƒ
GHKMN
PORSTZ
UWXYab
cdefghjknp
qrstuwxyz

Here ↑ you see the 36 point italic

THE MONOTYPE CORPORATION LTD
Reg. Office: 55–56 Lincolns Inn Fields, London,
W.C.2. *Head Office and Works:* Salfords, near
Redhill, Surrey. *Reg. Trade Mark:* MONOTYPE

Here is the Light version, Series 113, designed for printing on Antique paper
'MONOTYPE' PLANTIN LIGHT, Series 113, 18 pt.

Joseph W **PHINNEY**
1848–1934 USA

Types
Jenson c.1900

Joseph W Phinney worked for the Dickinson Type Foundry in Boston, where he was responsible for the specimen printing department. When the Dickinson was merged with American Type Founders he continued as a type designer with the new company. During his career he designed many types, including ATF Jenson, which was modelled on Morris's Golden Type.

Above: Jenson Oldstyle No.2, as shown in the 1923 ATF specimen book. (NM)

Frank Hinman **PIERPONT**
1860–1937 USA

Types
Plantin 1913

Although American, Frank Hinman Pierpont spent most of his career working for Monotype as the manager of their Salfords works in Surrey, where he stayed from 1899 until his retirement in 1936. His work lay in adapting existing type designs to suit Monotype machines, but in 1913 he oversaw the design of Plantin. Plantin followed Mason's Imprint as one of the first types to be specifically designed for mechanical composition. Pierpont and Fritz Steltzer, head of the drawing office, worked from a face in the 1905 Plantin-Moretus specimen (although this face was never used by the great Antwerp printer of that name). A large-bodied face, Plantin was designed with ink-spread in mind so that it would print well on smooth and coated papers.

It has been said that Pierpont saw the appointment of Stanley Morison as Monotype typographical adviser as a threat to his own authority, and also that, where conflict did arise between the two men over a revival, it was Pierpont who got his way.

Above: detail from Plantin 'family' (series 110, 113, 194, 236 and 438) specimen sheet, Monotype Corporation, n.d. (CLR)

147

he cut Franklin Old Style, a recut of his 1860 Miller ℞ Richard type, for the Phelps, Dalton ℞ Co. foundry. However, it was with the Dickinson Type Foundry of Boston that he spent the greatest part of his career.

Phemister's influence on type development in the USA was considerable. The bold face cut to accompany his original Old Style became the inspiration for the popular Bookman types issued initially as Antique No.310 by the Bruce foundry, and later by other prominent foundries.

Phemister was one of the few punch-cutters of his time who designed and cut his own alphabets. His workmanship was the very finest. He retired in 1891 when the Dickinson foundry merged with ATF.

Above: Miller & Richard Old Style specimen, 1895. (NM)

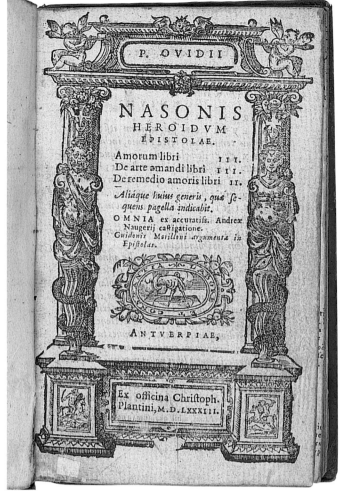

Lucien **PISSARRO**
1863–1944 F

Types
Brook Type 1903
Disteltype 1917

Lucien Pissarro was the eldest son of the painter Camille Pissarro. He came to England from France as a young man and stayed for the rest of his life. He was an outstanding book designer and illustrator, achieved distinction as a wood-engraver and was also a founder member of the Camden Town Group.

In 1894 he founded a private press at Chiswick and named it the Eragny Press after the family home in France. His friend Charles Ricketts allowed him to use Vale Press types for his first books, but in 1903 he designed his own, the Brook Type, named after his house in Hammersmith. This type, a Venetian, shows many of the characteristics of the private-press types of the period and was only available in one size, pica. Eventually, after the closure of the Eragny Press, it came into the possession of Cambridge University Press. Pissarro also designed Disteltype for the use of De Zilverdistel, the Dutch private press founded in 1909.

Above: detail of the Brook Type as shown in T Balston, *Private Press Types*, Cambridge University Press 1951. (CLR)

Christopher **PLANTIN**
d.1589 F

Although Christopher Plantin did not design type, he understood its importance to his publishing business. He purchased type, punches and matrices from, amongst others, Guillaume Le Bé, Robert Granjon and Claude Garamond.

Although he was born in France, it was his work in the Netherlands that made Plantin famous. He began his working life as a bookbinder, first in Caen and then in Paris. In 1548–9 he settled in Antwerp and was soon established as one of the foremost north European publishers. Plantin had an astonishing 21 presses printing books on a wide range of subjects, but his particular interest was publishing. One of his greatest books, produced in the years 1568 to 1573, was the eight-volume Polyglot Bible in Armenian, Hebrew, Greek and Latin.

Plantin set a fashion for engraved titlepages and he and his descendants, despite the added cost to production, led the way in the replacement of wood with copper for this purpose. Peter Paul Rubens, a friend of Plantin's grandson Balthazar Moretus, was among those who were to design engraved illustrations for the Plantin shop. In 1567 Plantin published specimens of his types in the *Index Characterum* (the first book of its kind), and in 1570 he was appointed printer to King Philip II of Spain.

In 1576 Antwerp was sacked by mutineering Spanish soldiers. The effect on Plantin's business was disastrous. He struggled on, but in 1582, with the political situation again becoming

P

difficult, he turned over the business to his sons-in-law and went to Leiden, where he was appointed printer to the university. After almost three years Plantin returned to Antwerp. He died in 1589 but the printing equipment remained in the family until 1875, when it was sold to the city and became the Plantin-Moretus Museum.

Previous page: Plantin titlepage, 1583. (SBPL); Above: MT Plantin.

Albert-Jan POOL
b.1960 NL

Types
URW Imperial 1994
URW Linear 1994
URW Mauritius 1994
FF OCR-F 1995
FF DIN 1995–2001
Writing
Branding with Type
(with Stefan Rögener and
Ursula Packhäuser),
Adobe Press 1995

Amsterdam-born Albert-Jan Pool studied in The Hague at the Koninklijke Academie van Beeldende Kunsten. With some fellow students and type enthusiasts he co-founded the group Letters, which was to produce many of the successful modern Dutch type designers.

Pool was director of type at Scangraphic in Germany for four years from 1987. He followed this with three years as type-design manager at URW in Hamburg where, in 1995, he started his own

company, Dutch Design, which has since become FarbTon Konzept + Design. His contribution to the FSI FontFont library of the successful sans serifs FF OCR-F and FF DIN resulted from an encouraging encounter with Erik Spiekermann at the 1994 ATypI Congress in San Francisco. Pool has taught type design in Kiel and typography in Hamburg.

Above: FF OCR-F promotional postcard, 1995. (NM)

Friedrich POPPL
1923–82 CS

149

Types
Poppl-Antiqua 1967
Poppl-Stretto 1969
Poppl-Exquisit 1970
Poppl-Heavy 1973
Poppl-Pontifex 1977
Poppl-Leporello 1977
Poppl-Residenz 1977
Poppl-Saladin 1979
Poppl-College 1981
Poppl-Nero 1982
Poppl-Laudatio 1983
Further reading
Ed Cleary, 'Friedrich Poppl – a
fine sense of curve', *Baseline*,
no.5, 1984

Born in Soborten, Friedrich Poppl had his early training in calligraphy. After attending the state technical college in Teplitz Schönau and working for two years as a painter and graphic artist, he studied calligraphy from 1950 to 1953 at the Werkkunstschule in Offenbach under Karlgeorg Hoefer, Hans Bohn and Herbert Post. His calligraphy

Berthold
3,75 mm (14 p)

Berthold
4,25 mm (16 p)

Berthold
4,75 mm (18 p)

Berthold
5,30 mm (20 p)

Berthold
6,35 mm (24 p)

Berthold
7,40 mm (28 p)

Berthold
8,50 mm (32 p)

Berthold
9,55 mm (36 p)

Typographe

àbçdéfghijklmñôpqrstüvwxyz0123456&ABCDEFGHIJKLMNOPQRSTUVWXYZ
àbçdéfghijklmñôpqrstüvwxyz0&ABCDEFGHIJKLMNOPQRSTUVWXYZ
àbçdéfghijklmñôprstüvwxyz0123456€&ABCDEFGHIJKLMNQRSTUVYZ
àbçdéfghjklmñôprstüvwxyz0123456789€&ABCDEFGHIJKMNOQRSTUVYZ
àbçdéfghjklmñôprstüvwxyz01234&ABCDEFGHJKMNOQRSUVXYZ
àbçdéfghjkñôprtüyz0123&ABCDEGHJKMNQRSUVXYZ

ANISETTE PETITE THIN, LIGHT, REGULAR, CAPS, DEMI, BOLD, BLACK

ANISETTE THIN, LIGHT, REGULAR, DEMI, BOLD, BLACK & ALTERNATES

AABBCCDDEEFFGGHHIJJKKLLMMNNOOPPQQRRSSTTUUVVWWXV
AABBCCDDEEFFGGHHIJJKKLLMMNNOOPPQQRRSSTTUUVV
AABBCCDDEEFFGGHHIJJKKLLMMNNOOPPQQRRSSTTUU
VVWWXXYYZZ&0123456789€&f£¥&g•••!?,.:;'»)]}←↙aglyrs
AABBCCDDEEFFGGHHIJJKKLLMMNNOOPPQQRRSSTTU
AABBCCDDEEFFGGHHIJJKKLLMMNNOOPPQQRRSSTTU
AABBCCDDEEFFGGHHIJJKKLLMMNNOOPPQQRR

LES BANJOS
5 VILLA DENISE · 23456 DEAUVILLE
UN THÉ GLACÉ, SINON RIEN
& DE LA CONTREBASSE
MAXIMILIEN
VOX

A B C D E
F G H I J K

DAS GRÖSSESTE IST DAS ALPHABET

Jean François PORCHEZ
b.1964 F

Types
FF Angie 1989
Apolline 1993
Angie Sans 1994
Le Monde Journal 1994
Le Monde Sans 1994
Anisette 1995
Parisine 1996
Le Monde Courier 1997
Le Monde Livre 1997
Sitaline 1998
Le Monde Livre Classic 1999
Parisine Plus 1999
Bienvenue 2000
Charente 2000
Ambroise 2001
Anisette Petite 2001
Sabon Next LT 2002

Web
typofonderie.com

Jean François Porchez, who lives and works in Malakoff, a suburb of Paris, was awarded the Prix Charles Peignot by ATypI in 1998. Whilst studying graphic design, Porchez was drawn towards calligraphy and type design. His first venture into the latter, FF Angie, won the Judges' Prize in the Morisawa Awards. Further studies at the Atelier National de Création Typographique followed before he joined Paris design company Dragon Rouge as type director. In 1994, after having type proposals accepted by the newspaper Le Monde, he became a freelance type designer. Porchez launched his own typefoundry in 1996. In 2002 he concluded a major commission from Linotype Library to produce a much-expanded digital version of Jan Tschichold's Sabon. Porchez teaches type design at the École Nationale Supérieure des Arts Décoratifs in Paris.

Above: detail from Anisette specimen, n.d. (JFP)

Herbert POST
1903–78 D

Types
Post Antiqua 1932–5
Post Fraktur 1935
Post Roman 1937
Post Medieval 1951
Dynamik 1952
Post Marcato 1961

Further reading
Angela Dolgner (ed.), *Herbert Post: Schrift, Typographie, Graphik*, Halle 1997

The typefaces of the German type designer Herbert Post were cut and produced by H Berthold AG, Berlin, and were strongly influenced by calligraphy. They were in the tradition of the Offenbach school but still retained the individuality of their creator. Post studied painting and design and also trained as a compositor in local technical schools in Frankfurt and Offenbach before he entered the calligraphy class of Rudolf Koch at Offenbach. Under Koch's direction he was an

150 became well known in the 1960s, when his work was shown in several important exhibitions. He taught in Wiesbaden, at the Werkkunstschule from 1955, then at the Fachhochschule from 1973. All Poppl's typefaces were commissioned by H Berthold AG at the instigation of its artistic director G G Lange. The first, Poppl-Antiqua, was a development from his poster lettering, but it was not until Poppl-Pontifex was released in 1977 that he achieved international recognition as a type designer.

Previous page and above: from Berthold Exklusiv Poppl-Pontifex specimen, c.1982. (NM)

Boston

SIXTEEN LINE ORNAMENTED, No. 1.

ALE

SIXTEEN LINE ORNAMENTED, No. 2.

BUN

AUSTIN LETTER-FOUNDRY,   120, ALDERSGATE STREET.

g

Louis John POUCHÉE
1782–1845 GB

Further reading
Mike Daines, 'Pouchée's lost alphabets', *Eye*, no.15, 1994

In the early 19th century, the London typefoundry of Louis John Pouchée produced ornate and decorative alphabets for printed posters. Originally credited as work from the Victorian period by another foundry, the true source came to light as the result of the discovery of a type catalogue, *Specimens of Stereotype Casting, from the Foundry of L J Pouchée*.

A businessman in London's Holborn area, Pouchée established his typefoundry in Lincoln's Inn Fields in 1818. The decorative letters produced by his highly skilled staff, in the fat-face style of the period, featured flowers, fruit, animals, agricultural implements and Masonic symbols. Pouchée's

typefoundry closed in 1830. The Caslon foundry purchased some of his stock, which was sold at auction. When the Caslon foundry closed, the Monotype Corporation purchased some of the Pouchée stock, including 23 alphabets. These were eventually donated to the University Press in Oxford which, in turn, passed them on to the St Bride Printing Library in the City of London.

In 1994 I M Imprimit, in a collaboration with the St Bride Printing Library, produced *Ornamented Types: Twenty-three alphabets from the foundry of Louis John Pouchée*.

Above: Pouchée types c.1825 as shown in *The Specimen Book of Types Cast by S & T Sharwood*, 1853/4, photographed for the CLR. (CLR)

Thierry
PUYFOULHOUX
b.1961 F

Types
Friz Quadrata Italics 1994
Cicéro 1995
Bebop 1996
Alinéa 1997
Alinéa Sans 1997
ITC Korigan 1997
Présence 1998
Prosalis 1998
Web
presencetypo.com

Type designer and graphic designer Thierry Puyfoulhoux studied calligraphy and typography at the Scriptorium de Toulouse under Bernard Arin and at the Imprimerie Nationale in Paris with José Mendoza. Having spent some time as a graphic designer with the Parisian design company Dragon Rouge, Puyfoulhoux went freelance in 1991 and continues as such today from his base in the French Alps. His first commercially produced typeface designs were

outstanding student. In 1926 Post started a fruitful career as teacher, lettering artist and printer at an art school in Halle. After returning to teach in Offenbach in 1950, he founded the Herbert Post Presse, and from 1956 was director of the Akademie für das Graphische Gewerbe in Munich.

Previous page: detail from Berthold Post Medieval specimen, probe no.3729, n.d.; Above: Post Roman Bold Condensed from Berthold specimen book no.525B, n.d. (both CLR)

Q

Extra Bold
Bold
Demi Italic
Demi
Medium
Book Italic
Book
Light

David QUAY
b.1948 GB

Types
Santa Fe 1983
Quay 1985
Bordeaux 1988
Helicon 1989
Robotik 1989
ITC Quay Sans 1990
Foundry Old Style 1990
Foundry Sans 1991
Foundry Wilson 1993
Foundry Architype 1, 2, 3
   1994–7
Foundry Gridnik 1998
Foundry Journal 1998
Foundry Form Sans and Serif
   1999
Foundry Monoline 2000
Foundry Sterling 2001
Foundry Plek and Flek 2002
Foundry Fabriek 2004

London-born David Quay
studied at Ravensbourne
College of Art Et Design from
1963 to 1968 before beginning
work as a graphic designer
in London, forming his own
company, David Quay
Design, in 1975. In 1983 he
co-founded Quay Et Gray

the italics for Friz Quadrata,
originally created by the
Swiss designer Ernst Friz.
Working with the ITC
Typeface Review Board,
Puyfoulhoux's interpretation
proved a worthy complement
to the existing roman
designs. His uncial-inspired
design Korigan was issued
by ITC three years later.
Several of his typeface
families have been issued
by Creative Alliance.

Previous page: detail of
Présence type showing from
Lettres Françaises, ATypI 1998.
(NM)

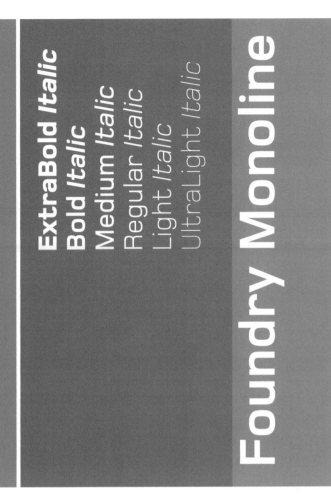

ExtraBold *Italic*
Bold *Italic*
Medium *Italic*
Regular *Italic*
Light *Italic*
UltraLight *Italic*

Foundry Monoline

R

Lettering with Paul Gray and in 1987 set up David Quay Design, contributing type designs to Fontek, ITC, Monotype and Berthold.

Quay's enthusiasm for letter forms resulted in him founding Letter Exchange in 1988. This organization, still active after 16 years, brings fellow enthusiasts together for monthly lectures and discussions. In 1990 he co-founded The Foundry with Freda Sack. Though no longer directly involved, he continues to contribute to The Foundry's type output.

A fellow of the International Society of Typographic Designers since 1992, Quay lectures extensively both in the UK and internationally. He has had a long association with the London College of Printing (now the London College of Communication)

and has been a visiting lecturer at several European design schools. Quay now lives in Amsterdam and works there as an independent type designer and graphic designer. He currently teaches typography at the Akademie Sind Joost in Breda.

Above: showings of Foundry Sans and Foundry Monoline (both with Freda Sack), n.d. (F)

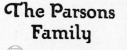

Will **RANSOM**
1878–1955 USA

154

Types
Parsons 1918

Will Ransom started his career in St Louis, Michigan as a printer, studying typography in his spare time. He went to Chicago in 1903 and there started his partnership in the Village Press with Frederic Goudy. The Village Press was one of the first private presses in America and a popular meeting-place for many important figures in the Chicago art world at that time. Two notable visitors there were 'Oz' Cooper and W A Dwiggins.

He designed the typeface Parsons and some ornaments for ATF in 1918 before moving to the University of Oklahoma Press, where he remained for the next 14 years.

Above: Parsons showing from 1923 ATF specimen book. (NM)

Hans **REICHEL**
b.1949 D

Types
Barmeno 1983
FF Dax 1995–2003
FF Schmalhaus 1997
FF Sari 1999

Born in Hagen, Germany, Hans Reichel is a type designer, musician and composer. His first typeface was released by Berthold in 1983. An unconventional sans serif ahead of its time, Barmeno only realized its full potential after the digital revolution. Its successor and near-relative, FF Dax, issued by FSI as a FontFont, is one of the most successful sans serifs of the new millennium. Barmeno was re-released by Reichel and FSI in 1999 as FF Sari, with additional weights and new italics.

Above: page from FSI FontFont Focus No.6 FF Dax specimen, n.d. (NM)

Imre **REINER**
1900–87 H

Types
Meridian 1927–30
Corvinus 1929–34
Gotika 1932
Floride 1939
Matura 1939
Sinfonia/Stradivarius 1945
Reiner Script 1951
Reiner Black 1955
Bazaar 1956
Mercurius 1957
London Script 1957
Pepita 1959
Contact 1968
Writing
Grafika. Modern Design for Advertising and Printing, St Gallen 1947
Schrift im Buch (with his wife Hedwig Reiner), St Gallen 1948
Further reading
Hans Peter Willberg, *Imre Reiner. Die Ziffernbilder*, Stuttgart 1975

Born in Versec, Hungary, Imre Reiner was a painter, sculptor and watercolourist as well as wood-engraver, typographer and type designer. Most of his early type designs were for the Bauer foundry in Stuttgart, for whom Ernst Schneidler had also worked. Schneidler introduced Reiner to type design as his teacher at the Akademie der Bildenden Künste in Stuttgart.

Reflecting his preference for freer and more dynamic letter forms, many of Reiner's typefaces are scripts. These include Matura, Mercurius and Pepita, all of which were issued by Monotype. Pepita is based on Reiner's own handwriting.

After 1931 Reiner lived and worked in Ruvigliana, Switzerland. He wrote widely on typography and design and remained a great believer in the use of ornament.

Above: Monotype specimen, n.d. (CLR)

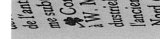

Paul RENNER
1878–1956 D

Types
Futura 1927–30
Futura Black 1948
Topic/Steile Futura 1953–5

Further reading
Chris Burke, *Paul Renner: The Art of Typography*, Hyphen Press 1998

Writing
Typographie als Kunst, Munich 1922
Die Kunst der Typographie, Berlin 1939

Paul Renner, like Jan Tschichold, wanted types that suited the modern age instead of being revivals from an earlier one. In this, his views were similar to those of the Bauhaus movement, whose ideals he shared and influenced without ever being a member.

He established the Meisterschule für Deutschlands Buchdrucker (Advanced School of German Book-printing) in Munich and recruited fellow type designers Georg Trump and Jan Tschichold to teach there. Tschichold was removed from his post and interned by the Nazis for 'subversive typography' in 1933. Renner himself was dismissed under similar circumstances that same year.

His best-known typeface, Futura, is the archetypal geometric sans serif. The original design had a lower-case of experimental characters but these were all abandoned before its release by Bauer in 1927. It has proved the most popular of its type, eclipsing the earlier Erbar, and still retains its popularity today.

Above: cover of Renner's *Die Kunst der Typographie* showing Topic. (CLR)

Charles RICKETTS
1866–1930 GB

Types
Vale Type 1896
King's Fount 1903

An important influence on the private press movement, Charles Ricketts founded the Vale Press in 1895. He was possibly the most significant Art Nouveau book designer, producing some of the most attractive and readable of all the private press books.

Although he admired the early work of William Morris, he preferred Renaissance models, in particular those of Aldus Manutius, to the heavily decorated pages of the Kelmscott Press. Ricketts was less successful as a type designer. Stanley Morison described his Vale Type as 'affected', and his King's Fount as 'thoroughly bad'.

Above: Vale Type. C Ricketts and L Pissarro, *De la Typographie et de l'Harmonie*, 1897. (SBPL)

Tom RICKNER
b.1966 USA

Types
Amanda
Buffalo Gal 1992–4
Hamilton 1993
Eldorado 1993–4 (with others)

Type designer and engineer Tom Rickner was born in Rochester, New York. After graduating from Rochester Institute of Technology in 1988 he moved to California to work with QMS/Imagen Corporation under the direction of Charles Bigelow. His work on the production and hinting of outline fonts for laser printers led to him becoming lead typographer with Apple Computer in 1989. He was involved in the production of Apple's first TrueType fonts.

After two years with Apple he left to work as a freelance with The Font Bureau, where he was involved in a variety of type projects.

Cathedral

MEDIUM

LIGHT

PICTURESQUE VIEWS OF THE CLIFFS OF DOVER

LIGHT

Busloads of Tourists

New Series of the Centaur Types of Bruce Rogers and the Arrighi Italics of Frederic Warde. Cut by Monotype and here first used to print a paper by Alfred W. Pollard

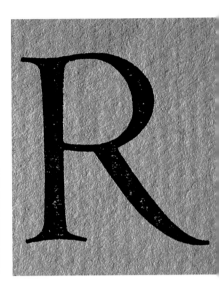

Bruce ROGERS
1870–1957 USA

In 1994 Rickner joined Monotype Typography, later to become Agfa Monotype, where as a specialist in TrueType hinting he worked on the production of Matthew Carter's Georgia, Verdana, Tahoma and Nina types for Microsoft. He also developed custom fonts for Lotus, Hewlett-Packard and Lexmark.

Tom Rickner now utilizes his wide-ranging experience in type design and production as a partner in Ascender Corporation. He lives in Madison, Wisconsin.

Previous page and above: showing of Hamilton from *Font Bureau Type Specimens*, 2nd ed., 1997. (NM)

Types
Montaigne 1902
Centaur 1914
Writing
Paragraphs on Printing, New York 1943
Further reading
Joseph Blumenthal, *Bruce Rogers, a Life in Letters*, W Thomas Taylor 1989
Georgia Mansbridge, *Bruce Rogers: American Typographer*, The Typophiles 1997

Bruce Rogers, one of the most accomplished American book designers, designed the Jenson revival Centaur, regarded by many as one of the finest types produced in the 20th century.

Born in Linnwood, Indiana, Rogers studied at the nearby Purdue College, where he became aware of fine books. His early commercial work was influenced by the work of William Morris's Kelmscott

Press. Rogers moved to Boston, Massachusetts, in 1895 and there met D B Updike, who introduced him to the Riverside Press. He worked there until 1911, establishing his reputation as a designer of fine books.

His first type design was based on the type used by Nicolas Jenson for *De Praeparatio Evangelica* by Eusebius in 1470, and Rogers suggested its use for the Riverside's folio edition of Montaigne's *Essays*, hence its name. It was this experience that made him decide to give up illustration and painting and concentrate on typography.

Rogers returned to the Jenson models 12 years later when asked to design a type for the exclusive use of the Metropolitan Museum in New York. The type was first

used in *The Centaur* (hence its name) by Maurice Guerin, published by the Montague Press in 1915.

Rogers's book designs include Morison's essay on Fra Luca de Pacioli, the late 15th-century Italian mathematician, but his masterpiece is the Oxford Lectern Bible, which took six years to produce, finally being published in 1935.

Above: cover of Monotype Centaur specimen, 1929. (NM); detail, photographed for the CLR. (CLR)

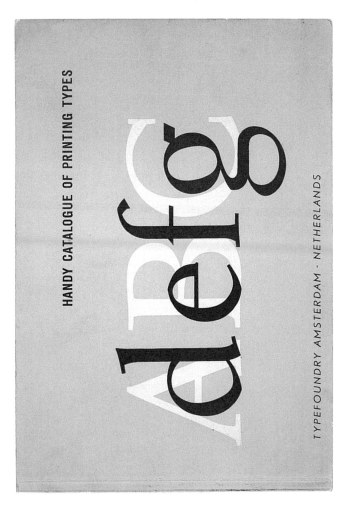

J. F. Rosart's shadowed letter, ca. 1759

J. F. Rosart's lettres fleuragées, ca. 1768

Enschedé's shadowed script, Double Capitale Financier, engraved by J. F. Rosart, 1768

Double Mediaan Fleuragée, engraved by J. F. Rosart, and one of the finest of all lettres fleuragées

Sjoerd Hendrik de ROOS
1877–1962 NL

Types
A Javanese Type 1909
Medieval/Hollandse Medieval
1912
Ella Cursive 1915
Zilver Type 1915
Erasmus Medieval 1923
Grotius 1925
Meidoorn Roman 1927
Egmont 1933
Nobel 1935
Libra 1938
Simplex 1939
De Roos Roman 1947

Sjoerd Hendrik de Roos
was born in Drachten, in
the province of Friesland.
He tried his hand at many
areas of design before set-
tling on type. He joined the
Lettergieterij Amsterdam
(Typefoundry Amsterdam)
as a designer and was later
made its artistic head,
a position he held for
35 years.

De Roos became part of
the revival of interest in

typography then taking place
in Britain and the United
States, and the export of his
types raised the profile of
Dutch printing. He specialized in free adaptations of
historic faces rather than
pure revivals.

His most popular type was
the Egmont family, a light-
faced roman with strikingly
short descenders. His last
type, De Roos Roman, was
designed during the war and
cut on his retirement. It was
much used by printers of
Dutch fine editions.

Above: cover of Typefoundry
Amsterdam specimen book
showing De Roos Roman, n.d.
(CLR)

Jacques-François
ROSART
1714–77 F

Further reading
Fernand Baudin and Netty
Hoeflake, *The Type Specimen
of Jacques-François Rosart,
Brussels 1768*, 2nd ed., Van
Gendt 1973

Punch-cutter and type-
founder Jacques-François
Rosart was born in Namur,
now part of Belgium.
Apparently self-taught, he
started work in Haarlem in
the Netherlands and in 1741
he published his first type
specimens. Although a com-
petitor, he also contributed
many types to the Enschedé
foundry, which was estab-
lished in Haarlem in 1743.
He continued to issue types
and ornaments in the Dutch
style of the day. In 1750 he
issued musical characters
which were the earliest
typographic examples of
round music notes. In 1759
he moved to Brussels and

established a foundry there.
He issued further specimens,
and in 1769 his advertisement
in a Brussels newspaper may
have been the first used to
market a new typeface.
Rosart died in Brussels in
1777 at the age of 62. In 1779
the contents of his foundry
were put up for sale and
acquired by a widow named
Decellier, of Brussels.

Above: reproduction of Rosart
types from *The Fleuron*, no.6,
1926. (NM)

Just van ROSSUM
b.1966 NL

Types
FF Beowolf 1990
  (with Erik van Blokland)
FF Brokenscript 1990
FF Advert 1991
FB Phaistos 1991
  (with David Berlow)
FF Justlefthand 1991
FF Advert Rough 1992
FF BeoSans 1992
F Flixel 1992
FF Instant Types 1992
FF Schulbuch 1992
FF Schulschrift 1992
F WhatYouSee 1994
  (with Erik van Blokland)
LTR Bodoni Bleifrei 2001
  (with Erik van Blokland)
Writing
LettError, Rosbeek 2000
Web
letterror.com

Just van Rossum, partner and collaborator with Erik van Blokland in LettError, was born in Haarlem. He studied at the Koninklijke Academie van Beeldende Kunsten in The Hague, where he was introduced to van Blokland by type-design tutor Gerrit Noordzij. This led to the pair forming *LettError*, initially a college magazine but soon an outlet for the innovative exploitation through computers and programming of digital type technology.

In 1989, after graduating in graphic and typographic design, van Rossum and van Blokland worked at MetaDesign in Berlin for Erik Spiekermann. Spiekermann's association with FontShop and his appreciation of their type design skills led to the release of their fonts through FontShop's FontFont label.

Van Rossum's very varied contribution included FF Instant Types, a collection inspired by labelling, rubber-stamp and stencil lettering, which was an influence on the use of distressed designs in 1990s typography, and FF Schulschrift, developed with children's book publishers, utilizing a 'Scripter' program for automatic character substitution. He made a later similar contribution to the Emigre foundry, Ligature-Maker, which enabled the automatic substitution of ligatures within text using its Mrs Eaves typeface.

Van Rossum's type-design output, combining LettError's understanding of computer codes and scripts with typographic invention, continues to reflect his belief that designers should be their own programmers. In 2000 he received the Charles Nypels Award with van Blokland for their work as LettError.

Above: FF Advert Rough from *FontFont*, no.6, 1992. (CLR);
FF BeoSans spread from *FontZine*, no.3, 1992. (NM)

Adolf RUSCH
15th century D

Adolf Rusch of Strasbourg was the first printer in Germany to design and use a roman type as opposed to the gothic or black-letter types which were commonly used in northern Europe at that time. When a handwritten note, dated 1464, was found in one of Rusch's books (one year before Sweynheym and Pannartz set up their press at Subiaco, near Rome, and started printing using a similar type based on the Renaissance hand), it was thought that his may have been the earliest of roman types. This suggestion, however, was later disproved.

Rusch was associate and successor to the first printer in Strasbourg, Johann Mentelin, reputed to be a careless printer but a smart business man. Rusch was also one of Mentelin's

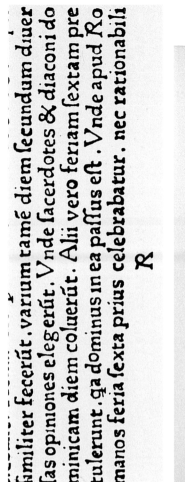

Rudolph **RUZICKA**
1883–1978 CS

sons-in-law, all of whom, like Rusch himself, were printers.

Rusch was sometimes known as the 'R-printer', because of the bizarre form of the 'R' in his roman font. He produced the first printed book with a chapter on medicine, *Opus de universo* by Rabanus Maurus, in 1467.

Previous page and above: details from Isak Collijn, *Adolf Rusch I, Strassburg, Trykaren med det bisaara,* Stockholm 1905. (SBPL)

Types
Fairfield 1939–49
Primer 1951

Rudolph Ruzicka was an engraver and etcher of note, working in wood and copper. He was also an outstandingly versatile typographer, type designer and book designer.

Born in Czechoslovakia (then Bohemia), Ruzicka emigrated to Chicago in 1894. He studied at the Chicago Art Institute and three years later was apprenticed to a wood-engraver. In 1903 he went to New York and, after both working and studying there for seven years, opened his own wood-engraving and print shop in 1910.

Ruzicka worked for Mergenthaler Linotype under Chauncey H Griffith, design-ing Fairfield in 1939 and Primer in 1951. On redesign-ing the *Harvard Business*

Review in 1953, he used Fairfield throughout. During a long association with the printer and historian D B Updike, Ruzicka was responsible for designing many of the annual keepsakes for Updike's Merrymount Press.

Above: paper manufacturer's promotion using specimen of Fairfield, n.d. (NM)

S

C. CORNELII TACITI OPERA

Extra Bold
Bold
Demi
Medium
Book Italic
Book
Light

Foundry Sterling

Bold

Jakob SABON
c.1535–80 F

Punch-cutter and type-founder Jakob Sabon was born in Lyon. In 1563 he assisted in the establishment of Christopher Plantin's typefoundry in Antwerp and whilst employed there completed a set of punches begun by Garamond. He left three years later to work in Frankfurt an der Oder. In 1571 he married the granddaughter of Christian Egenolff and in 1572 took over Egenolff's typefoundry in Frankfurt am Main as sole owner. By producing types by Granjon and Garamond, he enhanced the reputation of the foundry, which was to become one of the most influential of the 17th century.

Above: detail of titling capitals left unfinished by Garamond and completed for Plantin by Jakob Sabon in 1565. (ECC)

Freda SACK
b.1951 GB

Types
Victorian 1976
Paddington 1977
Stratford 1978
   (with Adrian Williams)
Caslon 540 Italic 1981
Jenson Old Style 1982
Proteus 1983
Orlando 1986
Vermont 1987
Ignatius 1987
Foundry Old Style 1990
Foundry Sans 1991
Foundry Wilson 1993
Foundry Architype 1, 2, 3
   1994–7
Foundry Gridnik 1998
Foundry Journal 1998
Foundry Form Sans and Serif
   1999
Foundry Monoline 2000
Foundry Sterling 2001
Foundry Plek and Flek 2002
Foundry Fabriek 2004

Freda Sack studied typo-graphic design at Maidstone College of Art and School of Printing. She began her career in 1972, drawing and stencil-cutting typefaces in the Letraset studio. She later moved to Fonts in London to work on faces for photo-setting and for major type manufacturers. In 1980 she was recruited by TSI, a subsidiary of Letraset, where she became exten-sively involved with the use of Ikarus software in type design and font manufacture.

From 1983 Freda Sack worked freelance, developing typefaces and logotypes for print, television, advertising and corporate identity. She continued to design headline and text faces for type manufacturers, including the text families Stratford and Proteus and numerous display faces.

Since 1989 she has worked with David Quay on a range of type projects. In 1990 they co-founded The Foundry, a

ABC
DEFGHIJKLMNOPQR

partnership specializing in all aspects of type and typography. In April 2001 she set up Foundry Types Ltd to manufacture and market The Foundry typeface library, and to continue to design, develop and implement specially commissioned fonts.

Freda Sack lectures on type design both in the UK and internationally. She is president and a fellow of the International Society of Typographic Designers. She was elected fellow of the Royal Society of Arts in 2000.

Above: showings of Foundry Sterling and Foundry Wilson (both with David Quay), n.d. (F)

Georg SALDEN
b.1930 D

Types
Daphne 1970
Polo 1972
Basta 1972
Brasil 1973
Gordon 1977
Loreley 1977
Tap 1979
Turbo 1983
Salden 1987
Axiom 1994
Votum 1999
Factum 2004

Georg Salden studied at the Folkwang-Werkkunstschule in Essen, where he was born. He worked as a freelance graphic artist before concentrating on type design from 1972 on. Salden formed Georg Salden Typedesign (GST) to distribute his types exclusively through a group of predominantly Berthold typesetters. Supplied both in headline and text formats, GST types offered members an edge in a highly competitive

market. Salden, whose best-known typeface is the distinctive sans serif Polo, continues to expand his collection of typefaces, now available as digital fonts to all users.

Above: *Page* magazine cover using Salden's Polo types, April 1994. (NM)

Rosemary SASSOON
b.1931 GB

Types
Sassoon Primary 1990
Sassoon Infant 1995
Sassoon Sans 1995
Writing
Creating Letterforms,
    Thames & Hudson 1992
Computers and Typography,
    Intellect 2003

The author of many books on aspects of lettering and handwriting, Rosemary Sassoon first trained as a classical scribe, and much of her early work concerned the devising of methods for teaching lettering. She diversified into studying handwriting and was awarded a PhD by the University of Reading for her work on children learning to write. This educational work led to research into what kind of letters children find easiest to read. As a result of this she began to develop a family of typefaces first for

161

STUVWXYZabcdefgh
ijklmnopqrstuvwxyz
1234567890&?;:)($]

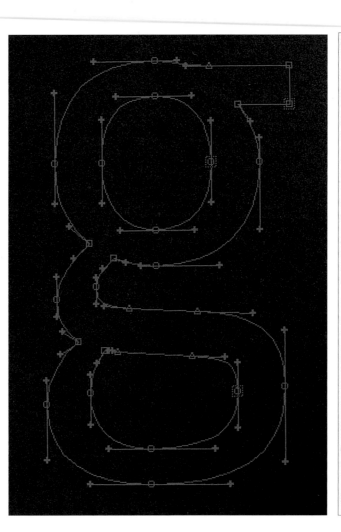

DI
IJ
C
U

162 reading and then for bridging the gap between reading and writing.

Her work has always been that of a designer directed at perceived needs, and she feels strongly that type designers have a responsibility to research and consider the specific requirements of various groups of readers and writers.

Previous page and above: detail of Sassoon Primary specimen sheet, Linotype, 1989. (CLR)

Ole SCHÄFER
b.1970 D

Types
FF Scribble 1995
FF Info 1996–2000
 (with Erik Spiekermann)
FF Dotty 1997
ITC Officina Sans 1997
 (with Erik Spiekermann)
FF Meta Condensed 1998
 (with Erik Spiekermann)
FF Fago 2000
FF Govan 2001
 (with Erik Spiekermann)
FF Zine 2001
FF Turmino 2002
Web
primetype.com

Ole Schäfer, who studied graphic design at the Fachhochschule Bielefeld, worked at MetaDesign from 1995 to 1999. During that time, first as a type designer then as type director, he contributed considerably to MetaDesign's corporate type projects and to the FSI FontFont library. He has expressed his enthusiasm

for the sans serif with several successful interpretations and continues to do so as an independent designer since leaving MetaDesign. He markets his own and other designers' types through his foundry, Primetype, which he set up in 2003.

Above: detail from FF Fago specimen, from FSI *FontFont Focus*, no.3, n.d. (NM)

Werner SCHNEIDER
b.1935 D

Types
Schneider-Antiqua 1987
Schneider Libretto 1995
Vialog 2002 (with Helmut
 Ness)
Senatus 2003

The award-winning type designer Werner Schneider was born in Marburg. He studied under Friedrich Poppl at the Werkkunstschule Wiesbaden from 1954 to 1958. Schneider worked as Poppl's teaching assistant for a year before starting as a designer. In 1973 he began his long career with the Fachhochschule Wiesbaden as professor of communication design.

Schneider considers himself a designer whose speciality is letter forms. In 1987, under the supervision of artistic director Günter Gerhard Lange, with whom he shared a commitment to

F H Ernst **SCHNEIDLER**
1882–1956 D

Types
Deutsch Römisch 1926
Kontrast 1930
Grafik 1934
Schneidler Medieval 1936
Schneidler Old Style 1936
Legend 1937
Zentenar Book and Fraktur
  1937
Amalthea 1956

Born in Berlin, Friedrich
Hermann Ernst Schneidler
worked for the Bauer foundry
in Stuttgart and designed a
number of elegant typefaces
in the years leading up to
World War 2.

He taught at the Staatliche
Akademie der Bildenden
Künste in Stuttgart from 1921
to 1949, where he had an
important influence on many
young designers who were
to become distinguished type
designers in later years,
including Imre Reiner and
Georg Trump. He also ran

a private press in Stuttgart,
the Juniperus Presse, from
1921 to 1925.

His best-known typefaces
are Schneidler Medieval and
the distinctive script Legend,
issued in 1936 and 1937
respectively, both cut by the
Bauer foundry. Amalthea, the
italic of Schneidler Medieval,
was not issued until the year
of his death in 1956.

Above: Bauer specimen of
Schneidler Medieval, n.d. (CLR)

Peter **SCHÖFFER**
c.1425–c.1503 D

The printer and typefounder
Peter Schöffer was born in
Gernsheim, Germany. After
studying at the university
in Erfurt he worked as a
calligrapher at the Sorbonne
in Paris. Moving to Mainz,
Schöffer worked for the
partnership of Gutenberg
and Johann Fust, learning from
the former the secrets of the
new art of typefounding. He
married the daughter of Fust,
and after Fust had taken over
the business, became his
partner, designing and casting
type. As Fust and Schöffer
they published the Mainz
Psalter of 1457. Schöffer fell
heir to the business when
Fust died of the plague in
Paris in 1466. He continued
a long and productive life,
printing his last book in 1502.

Above: detail of vernacular type
from Schöffer, Mainz, 1485,
photographed for the CLR. (CLR)

163

the highest quality, he
contributed his text typeface
family Schneider-Antiqua
to the Berthold library.
A second text family,
Schneider Libretto, was
issued by Berthold in 1995.
Berthold Types released
Schneider's roman titling
font Senatus in 2003. In
2002 Linotype released
Vialog, a reworking by
Schneider of a sans-serif
information and signage
type which he had developed
for the German Federal
Transportation ministry
in 1988.

Above: detail of page showing
Schneider-Antiqua from
Berthold Exklusiv specimen,
1990. (NM)

WEALTHY SOCIALITE
DISPLAY BLACK

Bohemian Neighbor
DISPLAY REGULAR ITALIC SWASH

Brick
DISPLAY LIGHT

VERY UNUSUAL ARCHITECTURE
DISPLAY REGULAR SMALL CAPS

$9,532/month is almost worth it for the location
DISPLAY MEDIUM

Cocktail Hour
DISPLAY MEDIUM ITALIC

TONIC SPILLED ALL OVER THE SOFABED
DISPLAY BLACK SMALL CAPS

Noticeable
DISPLAY BOLD

FABULOUS SKYLINE VIEW
DISPLAY MEDIUM ITALIC

FIREPLACE
DISPLAY LIGHT

Christian **SCHWARTZ**
b.1977 USA

Types
Casa Latino 2000 (with Andy Cruz and Ken Barber)
Pennsylvania 2000
Amplitude 2001–3
FF Bau 2001–4 (with Erik Spiekermann)
Simian 2001
Los Feliz 2002
Luxury 2002 (with Dino Sanchez)
FF Unit 2003–4 (with Erik Spiekermann)
Neutraface 2003–4
Farnham 2004
FF Oxide 2005
Local Gothic 2005

Web
orangeitalic.com

Like many of his peers, Christian Schwartz, who was born in New Hampshire, developed an affinity with letter forms from an early age.

After graduating from Carnegie Mellon University in Pittsburgh in 1999, he spent three months under Erik Spiekermann at MetaDesign in Berlin before joining the design staff at Font Bureau in Boston.

Schwartz founded multi-disciplined design company Orange Italic with designer Dino Sanchez at the end of 2000. He left Font Bureau in 2001 to focus on this venture. He has contributed to many other leading digital type-foundries including FSI, Emigre and House Industries, and has received several awards for his work.

From his base in New York City, Schwartz provides custom type solutions for a variety of clients while continuing to produce innovative commercial typefaces.

Above: Font Bureau specimen of Schwartz's Farnham, inspired by the work of Johann Michael Fleischmann featured in this book. (NM)

Nick **SHINN**
b.1952 CDN

Types
Gryphon 1980
Shinn Sans 1987
FF Fontesque 1994
FF Merlin 1997
FF Oneleigh 1999
FF Fontesque Sans 2001
Artefact
Beaufort
Bodoni Egyptian
Handsome
Walbaum News
Worldwide
Paradigm

Web
shinntype.com

Nick Shinn, who was born in London, studied fine art at Leeds Polytechnic before moving to Toronto in 1976 to begin his career as an art director in advertising. In 1989, embracing the new technology, he formed his own studio. His enthusiasm for letter forms applied to reading has resulted in the creation of a variety of type designs which feature regularly in newspapers, magazines and advertising campaigns around the world. Describing himself as a 'generalist', Shinn, who has contributed types to, amongst others, the Creative Alliance and the FSI FontFont libraries, also markets directly through his ShinnType foundry.

Above: cover of FF Fontesque specimen designed by Shinn, n.d. (NM)

164

Arnhem

OurType SALES
Baron de Gieylaan 41 b-9840 De Pinte Belgium
telephone +32 (0) 9 220 26 20 fax +32 (0) 9 220 34 45
www.ourtype.com · www.ourtype.be

Robert SLIMBACH
b.1956 USA

Types
ITC Slimbach 1987
ITC Giovanni 1988
Adobe Garamond 1989
Utopia 1989
Minion 1990
Myriad 1992
  (with Carol Twombly)
Poetica 1992
Caflisch Script 1993
Sanvito 1993
Adobe Jenson 1996
Cronos 1997
Kepler 1997
Warnock 2000
Brioso 2002
Further reading
'Robert Slimbach – A Type
  Designer at the Heart of
  Technology', *Baseline*, no.20,
  1995

Robert Slimbach, who was
born in Evanston, Illinois,
received his training and
early experience of type
design in the drawing office
of Autologic in California. In
1987, after two years of self-
employment, which saw him
contribute ITC Slimbach
and ITC Giovanni to the
International Typeface
Corporation, he joined
Adobe Systems. Since then,
he has been designing and
developing typefaces for the
Adobe Originals program.
Slimbach's typefaces offer
type users a rich palette of
designs, mostly for text use,
based on his enthusiasm for
classic letter forms. One
exception to the latter is
his rendition into a font of
renowned Swiss typographer
Max Caflisch's handwriting.
In 1991 he received the Prix
Charles Peignot from the
Association Typographique
Internationale for excellence
in type design.

Above: showing from Adobe
Original Minion Multiple
Master Typeface specimen
book, 1992. (NM)

Fred SMEIJERS
b.1961 NL

Types
Renard 1992
FF Quadraat 1992–7
DTL Nobel 1993
  (with Andrea Fuchs)
FF Quadraat Sans 1997–2000
Fresco 1998
Arnhem 1998–2002
Monitor 2000
Sansa 2005
Writing
*Counterpunch: Making Type
  in the Sixteenth Century,
  Designing Typefaces Now*,
  Hyphen Press 1996
Type Now, Hyphen Press 2003
Web
ourtype.com

Although he trained as a
graphic designer and still
practises as such, Fred
Smeijers is noted for the
success of his type designs.
He describes himself as
a 'new traditionalist', and
his designs are determined
by his appreciation and
understanding both of past
production methods and
of contemporary type
technology. His enthusiasm
for and skill at punch-cutting
contrast considerably with
his role as a typographic
consultant to product manufacturers. His best-known
typeface is FF Quadraat,
originally released as a serif;
the addition to the family of
a sans version with headliner
and display weights has
expanded its flexibility.
Smeijers, who has written
two books on his craft, also
teaches, lectures and gives
workshops. A native of
Eindhoven, he now lives and
works in Antwerp, and is a
professor at the Hochschule
für Grafik und Buchkunst at
Leipzig.

Above: OurType specimen of
Arnhem, 2003. (CLR)

165

robust enough
to be used
in headline

The FF Meta characteristics

Jason SMITH
b.1971 GB

Types
FS Ingrid 2000
FS Rome 2000
FS Albert 2002
FS Sophie 2003
FS Clerkenwell 2004
FS Rigsby 2005
Web
fontsmith.com

Born in Lisburn, Northern Ireland, Jason Smith studied calligraphy, lettering and signwriting at Reigate School of Art and Design in Surrey. After six months' work experience at Monotype, which was local to his college, Smith, whose main interest had been graphic design, decided that his future lay in typography and type design. After graduation he worked with David Quay at The Foundry, learning more about his chosen craft. Smith then spent some time with Bruno Maag, becoming familiar with computers and with digitizing. A period of freelancing as a lettering artist and type designer followed before he launched Fontsmith to focus on type design. Although a specialist in custom work for large corporates, Fontsmith is creating an interesting library of commercially available designs with a particularly humanist edge. Custom clients include Channel 4 and the Post Office.

Above: detail from digital specimen of FS Albert. (JS)

Erik SPIEKERMANN
b.1947 D

Types
Berliner Grotesk 1979
LoType 1980
ITC Officina 1990
    (with Just van Rossum)
ITC Officina Sans 1990–7
    (with Ole Schäfer)
FF Meta 1991–2003
F Grid 1992
FF Info 1996–2000
    (with Ole Schäfer)
FF Meta Condensed 1998
    (with Ole Schäfer)
FF Govan 2001
    (with Ole Schäfer)
FF Unit 2003–4
    (with Christian Schwartz)
Writing
Ursache & Wirkung:
    ein typografischer Roman,
    Erlangen 1982
Rhyme & Reason:
    A Typographic Novel,
    H Berthold AG 1987
Studentenfutter,
    Nürnberg 1989
Stop Stealing Sheep & Find Out
    How Type Works (with E M
    Ginger), Adobe Press 1993

Further reading
David Earls, 'Erik Spiekermann',
Designing Typefaces,
RotoVision SA 2002
Web
spiekermann.com

An early introduction to type at the age of 12 began Erik Spiekermann's typographic career. His home-based letterpress printing business, where he set the metal type, helped finance his studies in art history and English at the Freie Universität, Berlin. In 1973 he moved to London, where he worked with design companies, taught at the London College of Printing and became a popular figure amongst the city's typomaniacs.

His long association with H Berthold AG and Günter Gerhard Lange began around that time when he persuaded the company to revive their

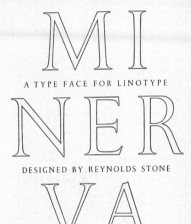

A TYPE FACE FOR LINOTYPE

MINERVA

DESIGNED BY REYNOLDS STONE

Johannes (d.1470) & Wendelin de **SPIRA** D

Johannes de Spira, a goldsmith from Mainz in Germany, was the first printer in Venice. His first book, printed in 1469, was *Epistolae ad Familiares* by Cicero. De Spira and his brother Wendelin successfully claimed their roman type an invention and obtained protection against plagiarism for five years. Some attribute the de Spira type to Nicolas Jenson. In 1470 the brothers printed St Augustine's *De Civitate Dei*, the first book to have page folios (numbers). Johannes died that year and the plagiarism agreement was rescinded.

Above: detail from Donatus, *Commentarius in Terentium*, printed by de Spira, showing the first type used in Venice, 1472. (ECC)

Reynolds **STONE** 1909–79 GB

Types
Minerva 1954
Janet 1965
Writing
A Book of Lettering,
London 1935
Further reading
Reynolds Stone 1909–1979,
Victoria & Albert Museum
1982

Named after his ancestor, the painter Sir Joshua Reynolds, Reynolds Stone is primarily known for his wood-engravings, which are characterized by the use of a white line on a black background. He also cut memorials to Winston Churchill and T S Eliot in Westminster Abbey.

Stone's lettering was greatly influenced by the *cancelleresca* style of the 16th-century Italian writing masters, and by the work of Eric Gill, whose pupil he

classic Berthold types for photosetting. He drew the new versions under the supervision of Lange, an invaluable experience which laid the foundation for his career in type design. When he co-founded MetaDesign in 1979 his understanding of the role of type in corporate branding and communication contributed an important ingredient to the company's success.

In 1989, with the start of the digital revolution in type design and distribution, Spiekermann's vision and insight led to the creation of the mail-order digital type retailer FontShop. He combined the output of his young team of predominantly Dutch designers working at MetaDesign with that of established figures in the world of type to launch

FontFont, FontShop's exclusive type library. FontFont's issue in 1991 of Spiekermann's sans serif, Meta, which has become a worldwide bestseller, established the label as one of the most exciting and influential in contemporary typographic communication.

Now independent after leaving MetaDesign in 2000, Erik Spiekermann spreads his typographic gospel internationally through consultancy work, lectures and a continued association with FontShop International.

Previous page: detail from FSI *FontFont Focus*, no.4, FF Meta specimen, n.d.; Above: detail from LoType specimen, MetaDesign, 1980. (both NM)

is an art in which violent revolutions can scarcely, in the nature of things, hope to be successful. A type of revolutionary novelty may be extremely beautiful in itself; but, for the creatures of habit that we are, its very novelty tends to make it illegible...

TYPOGRAPHY FOR THE TWENTIETH-CENTURY READER, ALDOUS HUXLEY 1928

Designed by Sumner Stone

Silica Extra Light
ABCDEFGHIJKLMNOPQRSTUVWXYZ
abcdefghijklmnopqrstuvwxyz1234567890
Writing is dead in Europe; and even when

Silica Light
ABCDEFGHIJKLMNOPQRSTUVWXYZ
abcdefghijklmnopqrstuvwxyz1234567890
it flourished, it was never such a finely

Silica Regular
ABCDEFGHIJKLMNOPQRSTUVWXYZ
abcdefghijklmnopqrstuvwxyz1234567890
subtle art as among the Chinese. Our

Silica Semibold
**ABCDEFGHIJKLMNOPQRSTUVWXYZ
abcdefghijklmnopqrstuvwxyz1234567890
alphabet has only six and twenty letters**

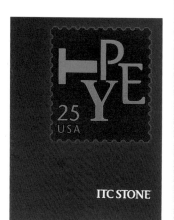

ITC STONE

Sumner STONE
b.1945 USA

was for a brief spell. He was encouraged to take up engraving, and from 1934 he concentrated on woodcutting. In 1935, *A Book of Lettering* was published.

Stone's Minerva typeface was commissioned by Linotype as a display accompaniment to Gill's typeface Pilgrim. In addition to Minerva, Stone designed Janet (named after his wife) for his own use.

Previous page: Linotype Minerva specimen, n.d. (CLR)

Types
Stone Family 1987
Stone Print 1991–2
Silica 1993
Cycles 1993–7
ITC Bodoni 1994 (with others)
Arepo 1995
Scripps College Old Style 1997
  (after F W Goudy)
Lectern Bible Initials 1998
Basalt 1998–2003
SFPL 1999–2003
Magma 2004
ITC Stone Humanist Sans 2005
Munc 2005

Writing
On Stone. The Art and Use of Typography on the Personal Computer, Bedford Arts 1991
Font: Sumner Stone, Calligraphy and Type Design in a Digital Age, Ditchling Museum and the Edward Johnston Foundation 2000

Web
stonetypefoundry.com

Sumner Stone was born in Venice, Florida, and studied calligraphy with Lloyd

Reynolds in Oregon before joining Hallmark Cards in Kansas City as type designer. In 1972 he started his own studio for lettering and design in Sonoma, California and studied mathematics there at the State University. Spells as director of typography at Autologic and Camex in Boston followed between 1979 and 1984 before he was appointed to the same role at Adobe Systems in California. There he supervised the development of the Adobe Originals typeface collection and contributed his own Stone type family, or 'type clan' as he calls it, consisting of 18 weights of roman, sans-serif and informal fonts. A humanist sans version was added in 2005.

After leaving Adobe he launched the Stone Type Foundry Inc. in Palo Alto

in 1990. The foundry's first project was a new typeface for the text of *Print* magazine. *Print* started using Stone Print in 1991. In 1998 the San Francisco Public Library held the first large restrospective exhibition of Stone's work.

Now relocated to a walnut farm in northern California, foundry and farm continue to produce both typefaces and walnuts.

Above: ITC Stone specimen, 1989. (CLR); Silica specimen, 1994. (NM)

NotFür Lang Texts &
EYE DOMMAGE EDGES
Refuse WEAR Glasses
Mramor**Text**Tylko**Dla**_Tękstuw_
Bardzo_Krotkich_

WgVAaRr&Tyffi
Spiritually cultivated
WgYy&123AaEeRrMmNn
Make This Ear NEW TESTAMENT

agit. ut buana diuinis tribuát auctoritaté:cú pocius buerint. Que nüc sane omittamus. ne nihil apud istos materia, spedat. Ea igr queramus restimonia. q̃bus ill aut certe non repugnare. Sibillas plurimi et maximi greco4: Aristoricus: et Appollodorus: Erithreus:n nestella. Hi omes ṕcipuam et nobilem preter ceteras, memorát. Appollodorus q̃dé ut de ciui ac populari fi ucro ená legatos Erithreos a senatu eé missos refert. 1 mína Romã deportarent.et ea consules Curio et Oc̃ quod túc erat curance Quinto Catulo restituti: poned de súmo & conditore rerú deo huiusmói uersus reuer

Frantisek STORM
b.1966 CS

Types
Alcoholica 1993
Bahnhof 1993
Mramor 1994
Negro 1994
DynaGrotesk 1995
ITC Malstock 1996
ITC Tyfa 1998
ITC Biblon 2000
Web
stormtype.com

Frantisek Storm graduated from the School of Book and Type Design at the Academy of Applied Arts in his home city of Prague in 1991, and works as a freelance graphic designer, typographer and type designer. He markets his typefaces, many of them revivals from the rich Czech tradition in type design, through the Storm Type Foundry which he set up in 1993. Storm's revival of Tyfa, a design by fellow Czech Josef Tyfa from the 1950s, was issued by ITC in 1998. ITC, who had previously issued Storm's sign-painting-influenced sans serif Malstock in 1996, also released Biblon, which won an award of excellence in the third Type Directors Club design competition in 2000.

Above: Mramor and Biblon specimens from Storm Type Foundry, *Typokatalog*, no.4, 2001. (NM)

Conrad SWEYNHEYM & Arnold PANNARTZ
15th century D

Types
Subiaco (revived 1902)

The first press to be set up in Italy was at the Benedictine monastery, Santa Scholastica, at Subiaco, near Rome, where two Germans, Conrad Sweynheym and Arnold Pannartz, began printing in 1465 using a type considered by some to be the first example of roman type in use. It became known as the Subiaco type. Although strongly influenced by the *scrittura umanistica* then in favour with Italian scholars, it does bear gothic traces. Having printed three books at Subiaco, including St Augustine's *De Civitate Dei*, the press was moved in 1467 to Rome, where the type was modified to become much more of a roman. Because the new type was associated with Rome it was called 'roman', the name still used to the present day. The partnership was dissolved in 1473 following financial problems.

A revival of the Subiaco type, which is now in the possession of Cambridge University Press, was cut by Edward Prince for the Ashendene Press in 1902.

Above: detail of Sweynheym and Pannartz 'Subiaco' type, 1465, photographed for the CLR. (CLR)

T

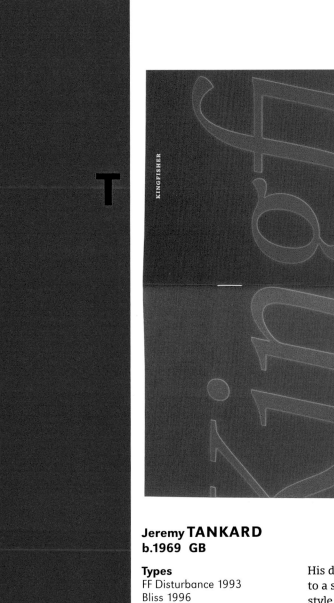

Jeremy **TANKARD**
b.1969 GB

Types
FF Disturbance 1993
Bliss 1996
Alchemy 1998
Blue Island 1998
The Shire Types 1998
Enigma 1999
Shaker 2000
Aspect 2002
Kingfisher 2005
Writing
TypeBookOne, Jeremy Tankard
    Typography 2005
Further reading
David Earls, 'Jeremy Tankard',
    Designing Typefaces,
    RotoVision SA 2002
Web
typography.net

Jeremy Tankard completed
his design education at the
Royal College of Art in 1992,
graduating in graphic design.
After working for six years
with major design companies
creating typographic
solutions for international
brands, he established Jeremy
Tankard Typography in 1998.

His design output is witness
to a successful flexibility of
style. The disciplined sans
serif Bliss, his ode to
Johnston and Gill, contrasts
considerably with unicase
products FF Disturbance and
The Shire Types, the neo-
black-letter Alchemy and his
upright script Aspect. His
dynamic serif type Enigma
and its companion sans serif
Shaker currently feature in
the typography of a variety
of publications.

Above: cover of Kingfisher
specimen, 2005. (CLR)

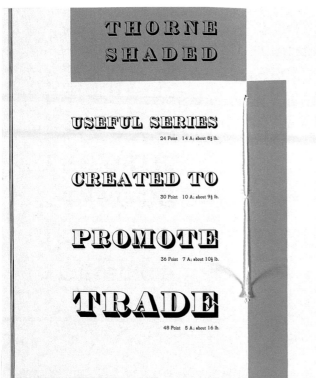

Above: Stephenson Blake specimen for Thorne Shaded, n.d. (CLR)

SYNOPSIS

ABCDEF
GHIJKL
MNOPQR
STUVWX
YZ&£123
4567890
.,:;!?'-

Northampton £12345

Robert THORNE
1754–1820 GB

Types
Thorne Shaded c.1810

In the first half of the 19th century London was at the forefront of typographical innovation, and of the London foundries none was more prominent than that of Robert Thorne.

In 1794 Thorne acquired the London foundry of the late Thomas Cottrell in Nevil's Court. Thorne moved the foundry to No.11 Barbican and disposed of most of the Cottrell stock in favour of types resembling those of Jackson and Figgins. His specimen book of 1798 shows a series of types which excelled those of all his competitors for lightness and uniformity. He also produced some fat-face jobbing letters which were unique for their boldness. Their introduction is judged to have entirely changed the appearance of posters of the period.

In 1802 the foundry moved to a former brewery in Fann Street, Alder's Gate, and became known as the Fann Street Foundry. It was at this time that Thorne produced his 'improved printing types', which were the first recorded examples of 'modern' faces, with strong vertical colour and fine, horizontal, bracketed serifs. They were an immediate success, and his style was followed by nearly all typefounders.

In the next ten years the foundry added many new faces. His fat-face display types were particularly admired abroad, and in 1818 Thorne received a commission from the Imprimerie Royale in Paris for cutting fat faces of this kind. The fat faces were peculiarly English and have been described by Stanley Morison as the ugliest letters ever cut. Thorne continued working until his death in 1820, when the foundry was purchased by William Thorowgood.

William THOROWGOOD
d.1877 GB

Types
Thorowgood c.1820

After Robert Thorne's death in 1820, his Fann Street Foundry was put up for auction and was purchased by William Thorowgood with the proceeds, it was said, of a lucky draw in a state lottery. Thorowgood came from Staffordshire and had no previous connection with typefounding. Despite this disadvantage he very quickly established himself. Within a few months he brought out his first specimen book, which for the most part consisted of the stock as Robert Thorne left it. During the next seven years he introduced greek, hebrew and Russian faces as well as three frakturs.

In 1828 Thorowgood purchased the Fry foundry

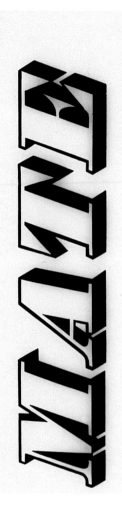

THOROWGOOD & Co. LONDON.

GEBR. KLINGSPOR
TYPEFOUNDERS
OFFENBACH A.M.(GERMANY)
presents

Tiemann Old Face
designed by Walter Tiemann

Linotype
Modern

The PRACTICAL text type
for up-to-date letterpress
and offset publications

in Type Street (now Moore Street) and made many important additions to the stock, including numerous oriental and learned faces as well as book fonts, blacks, titling and flowers. In 1838 Robert Besley became a partner in the firm and when Thorowgood retired in 1849 the company was renamed R Besley Et Co.

Previous page: 5-lines Pica No.3 from 1825 specimen book. (SBPL); Above: detail of 8-lines Pica italic shaded. Photographed for the CLR. (CLR)

Walter **TIEMANN**
1876–1951 D

Types
Tiemann Medieval 1909
Tiemann 1923
Orpheus 1928
Daphnis 1931
Offizin 1952

Walter Tiemann was one of the most important book and type designers of his generation. In 1906, with his friend Carl Ernst Poeschel, he founded the first private press in Germany, the Janus Press. Over 30 years he produced 16 typefaces for the Klingspor foundry in Offenbach, where he was chief outside designer during the time that Rudolf Koch was resident type designer. For many years he lectured at the Leipziger Akademie, now Hochschule für Graphik und Buchkunst, and in 1920 became its director.

Above: Klingspor specimen sheet of Tiemann, n.d. (CLR)

Walter **TRACY**
1914–95 GB

Types
Jubilee 1954
Adsans 1959
Maximus 1967
Linotype Modern 1969
Times Europa 1972
Telegraph Newface Bold 1989
(with Shelley Winter)

Writing
Letters of Credit, a View of Type Design, Gordon Fraser 1986
The Typographic Scene, Gordon Fraser 1988

Walter Tracy trained as a compositor with William Clowes but soon moved on to typography with the Barnard Press and Notley Advertising. In 1947, as a freelance designer, he was recruited by James Shand to work part-time with Robert Harling on the influential publishing venture Art Et Technics, which produced the journal *Alphabet Et Image*.

His first involvement with Linotype came when he was

engaged to write and design *Linotype Matrix*, the English Linotype Company's typographical journal. In 1948 he joined the staff of Linotype as manager of the typeface development programme. During 30 years with Linotype he developed types for newspaper text and classified advertising work and was also responsible for the first major typeface development programme for the composition of Arabic in electronic systems.

His outstanding work earned him the appointment as Royal Designer for Industry in 1973. In later years, after retirement, he pursued his special interest in the design of Arabic typefaces, designing six before his death in 1995.

Above: Linotype Modern specimen, 1970. (CLR)

THE BOY PRINTER OF ISHPEMING

It is graduation day in the little brown schoolhouse on Baltimore Street in Lynn, Massachusetts, just outside Boston. Miss Parrot is the teacher — a dear! You are six years old; next month you will be seven. The blackboard is covered with chalk drawings: sailboats, steamboats, ferryboats, trains of cars, houses, people and animals. You are the artist. Your mamma, with other mammas, is sitting on the platform, proud of her Willie — who is probably plenty proud of himself.

Lynn is a shoe town. This is 1875.

3

Joseph D **TREACY**
b.1955 USA

Types
TF Bryn Mawr 1980–4
TF Star 1984–5
TF Habitat 1986–90
TF Forever 1986–91
TF Hotelmoderne 1986–91
TF Crossword 1990
TF Ardent 1992
TF Avian 1992
TF Akimbo 1993
Web
treacyfaces.com

Joe Treacy was born in Virginia and studied fine and applied arts before beginning an award-winning career in graphic design and packaging. In 1980–4, focusing on lettering and type design, he designed and developed Bryn Mawr as a proprietary font for the Linotype Company. Four years later Treacy launched Treacyfaces Inc. to create original corporate typefaces and to make Bryn Mawr and his new type designs available worldwide.

His output over 20 years, which he markets through his website, treacyfaces.com, shows Treacy to be a prolific designer of successful types in a wide variety of styles.

Above: cover of Treacyfaces type catalogue, 1996. (CLR)

George F **TRENHOLM**
1886–1958 USA

Types
Trenholm Oldstyle 1927
Georgian Cursive 1934
Egmont Decorative Initials 1936
Nova Script 1937
Waverley 1940
Cornell 1948

Type designer, calligrapher and printer George Trenholm was born in Cambridge, Massachusetts. His typeface designs were mostly for Intertype Corporation to whom he was a consultant, although his first issued type, Trenholm Oldstyle, was for the Chicago foundry of Barnhard Bros & Spindler. His calligraphic skills came to the fore in his designs for the Trenholm Cursive and Shaded Capitals fonts. Those same skills are evident in his Egmont Decorative Initials, which he designed for Intertype to complement

the foundry's own cut of S H de Roos's Egmont family. He is best remembered for his Intertype family, Cornell, an original roman family of distinctive character. He died in Weston, Massachusetts, in 1958.

Above: page set in Waverley from *Will Bradley. His Chapbook*, The Typophiles 1955. (NM)

173

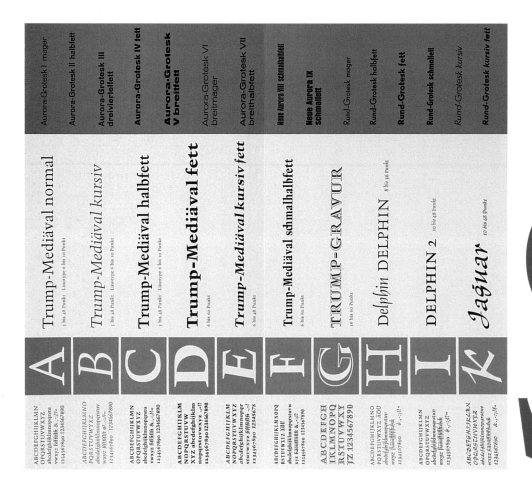

Above: type specimen from
C E Weber, Stuttgart, n.d. (CLR)

Georg **TRUMP**
1896–1985 D

Types
City 1931
Trump Deutsch 1935
Schadow Antiqua 1945–58
Trump Medieval 1948–61
Amati 1953
Delphin I and II 1951–5
Forum I and II 1951
Codex 1954–6
Palomba 1954
Signum 1955
Time-Script 1955–7
Trump-Gravur 1960
Jaguar 1964
Mauritius 1964–8
Further reading
Sebastian Carter, 'Georg
Trump', *Twentieth Century
Type Designers*, Lund
Humphries 1995

Georg Trump, artist, type
designer and graphic artist,
designed the majority of his
types for the Weber foundry
in Stuttgart. Trump's early
designs, City and Trump
Deutsch, were all issued
by the Berlin foundry
H Berthold AG.

While a student at
Stuttgart's Staatliche
Kunstgewerbeschule Trump
studied under F H Ernst
Schneidler. In 1929 Trump
became a lecturer alongside
Jan Tschichold at the Meisterschule für Deutschlands
Buchdrucker in Munich at
the invitation of director Paul
Renner. Trump left the school
in 1931 to become director of
the Höheren grafischen
Fachschule in Berlin but
in 1934 was to return as
director, after both
Tschichold and Renner were
dismissed by the Nazis for
'subversive' typography. It
was at this time that Trump
began working for Weber.

Trump had fought in
World War 1 and was called
up again in 1939. In 1945 he
was badly wounded and in
1953 he retired from teaching
as a result of his injuries but

continued to design type.
Although Georg Trump
created successful types in
a variety of styles, the highly
condensed Signum, issued by
Weber in 1955, was his only
sans serif. His major work is
considered to be the old-face
type family, Trump Medieval.

Above: type specimen from
C E Weber, Stuttgart, n.d. (CLR)

Jan **TSCHICHOLD**
1902–74 D

Types
Transito 1929
Saskia 1931
Zeus 1931
Sabon 1964–7
Writing
'Die neue Gestaltung' and
'Elementare Typographie',
*Typographische
Mitteilungen*, 1925
Die neue Typographie,
Berlin 1928
Typographische Gestaltung,
Basel 1935
Meisterbuch der Schrift,
Ravensberg 1952
*Ausgewählte Aufsätze über
Fragen der Gestalt des
Buches und der Typographie*,
Birkhäuser 1975
*The Form of the Book: Essays on
the Morality of Good Design*,
Harley & Marks 1991
Further reading
Ruari McLean, *Jan Tschichold:
Typographer*, Lund
Humphries 1975
Hans Schmoller, *Two Titans,
Mardersteig and Tschichold:
A Study in Contrasts*, The
Typophiles 1990

Schriftschneider Sabon

Schriftschneider Sabon

Schriftschneider Sabon

Schriftschneider Sabon

Schriftschneider Sabon

Schriftschneider Sabon

Schriftschneider Sabon

SCHRIFTSCHNEIDER SABON

Antiqua	Grad	kg	a	A
5921	14 p	8	92	28
5922	16 p	9	84	26
5923	20 p	12	72	22
5924	24 p	14	54	18
5925	28 p	16	48	14
5926	36 p	18	32	10
5927	48 p	24	24	8

Paul Barnes, *Jan Tschichold: Reflections and Reappraisals*, Typoscope 1995

Jan Tschichold, son of a sign-painter and lettering artist, was born in Leipzig. From 1919 he studied calligraphy, typography and engraving in Leipzig and Dresden. After visiting the Bauhaus exhibition at Weimar in 1923 he became an avid exponent of the 'new typography', which advocated asymmetric layouts and sans-serif typefaces.

Tschichold was given a teaching post in Leipzig by Walter Tiemann, the director of the Leipziger Akademie. He stayed there until 1926. The first of his controversial writings, 'Elementare Typographie', appeared in the trade journal *Typographische Mitteilungen* in 1925.

From 1926 to 1933 Tschichold taught at the Meisterschule für Deutschland Buchdrucker in Munich founded by Paul Renner. Both men were forced out of their posts by the Nazis, and Tschichold emigrated to Basel.

Tschichold's *Die neue Typographie*, aimed at the whole of the printing trade, was written in Munich in 1928. In 1935, in Basel, he published *Typographische Gestaltung*, but his chief work in Switzerland was book design. He worked for Penguin Books in London between 1946 and 1949, drawing up rigorous guidelines for all Penguin typography and creating a new design for the standard Penguin paperback.

Tschichold designed Sabon in the 1960s for German printers who wanted a Garamond-derived type that could be set in foundry type, on Monotype or Linotype machines, and would always look the same on the page. The resulting design, a remarkable success, was named after the Lyon punch-cutter Jakob Sabon, said to have brought the Garamond matrices to Frankfurt.

In 1954 the American Institute of Graphic Arts, New York presented Tschichold with its Gold Medal, and in 1965 the Royal Society of Arts made him the first Honorary Royal Designer for Industry. Tschichold died in Switzerland in 1974.

Previous page: MT Sabon.; Above: Stempel specimen of Sabon, n.d. (CLR)

Carol TWOMBLY
b.1959 USA

Types

Mirarae 1984
FB Californian 1987
 (with David Berlow)
Charlemagne 1989
Lithos 1989
Trajan 1989
Adobe Caslon 1990
Myriad 1992
 (with Robert Slimbach)
Viva 1993
Nueva 1994
Chaparral 1997

Further reading

Sebastian Carter, 'Carol Twombly', *Twentieth Century Type Designers*, Lund Humphries 1995

175

Carol Twombly studied design at the Rhode Island School of Design, where she became interested in type design and typography. She received an MS from Stanford University in the graduate programme of digital typography under Charles Bigelow, and later joined the Bigelow & Holmes Studio. In the Morisawa

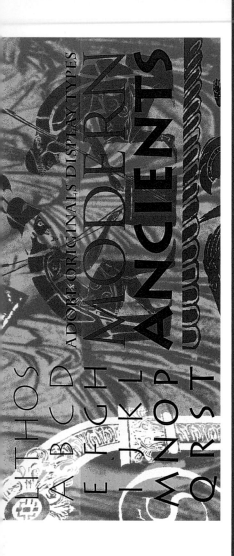

Typeface Design Competition in 1984 she won first prize for Mirarae, a latin design which has since been licensed and released.

Carol Twombly, a member of the Adobe type studio since 1988, has designed many successful display and text typefaces for the Adobe Originals library. In 1994 she was the first woman to receive from ATypI the Prix Charles Peignot for outstanding contributions to type design.

Previous page and above: poster for Adobe Originals display types by Twombly, 1990. (CLR)

U

DTL
para
dox
LETTERPROEF

Gerard UNGER
b.1942 NL

Types
Markeur 1972
M.O.L. 1975
Demos 1976
Praxis 1977
Hollander 1983
Flora 1984
Swift 1985
Amerigo 1986
Oranda 1987
Cyrano 1989
Argo 1991
F Decoder 1992
Gulliver 1993
Swift 2.0 1995
Capitolium 1998
Paradox 1999
Coranto 2000
Vesta 2001
Big Vesta 2003
Writing
Dutch Landscape with Letters
   (with Marjan Unger),
   Utrecht 1989
Terwijl je leest,
   Amsterdam 1997
Further reading
Robin Kinross, 'Technology,
   Aesthetics and Type', *Eye*,
   no.3, 1991

abcdefghijklmno
abcdefghijklmnop
abcdefghijklmno
ARGO
BY GERARD UNGER

abcdefghijklmnop
abcdefghijklmno
abcdefghijklmno · Light
abcdefghijklmno · Light Italic
abcdefghijklmno · Regular
abcdefghijklmno · Regular Italic
abcdefghijklmno · Medium
abcdefghijklmno · Medium Italic
abcdefghijklmn · Bold
abcdefghijklmn · Bold Italic
abcdefghijklmn · Black
abcdefghijklmn · Black Italic

Unger-Fraktur

Aa Bb Cc Dd
Ee Ff Gg Hh
Ii Jj Kk Ll
Mm Nn Oo Pp
Qq Rr Sſ Tt
Uu Vv Ww Xx
Yy Zz

Johann Friedrich UNGER
1753–1804 D

Sebastian Carter, 'Gerard Unger', *Twentieth Century Type Designers*, Lund Humphries 1995

Web
gerardunger.com

The award-winning designer Gerard Unger, who was born in Arnhem, studied at the Gerrit Rietveld Academie in Amsterdam from 1963 to 1967. He worked at Total Design under Wim Crouwel and later at Joh. Enschedé en Zonen before becoming a freelance designer and typographic consultant. He has designed stamps, coins, magazines, newspapers, books, logos, corporate identities, annual reports and a number of typefaces. Recent projects include a new typeface for Dutch road signs and typography for the city of Rome's orientation and information system.

Unger, a visiting professor at the University of Reading's Department of Typography and Graphic Communication, also teaches part-time at the Rietveld Academie. He lectures at home and abroad, about his own work, type design, the reading process, newspaper design and related subjects. Unger is also an expert on the history of Dutch chocolate letters – chocolate alphabets are a traditional part of the St Nicholas Day celebrations in the Netherlands.

Above: DTL specimens for Paradox, April 2002, and Argo, 1993. (NM)

Types
Unger-Fraktur 1794 (revived 1926)

Berlin-born Johann Friedrich Unger enjoyed the distinction of holding the sole agency for Didot types in Germany, and as a printer he was therefore the first in Germany to use the Didot roman, but it is for his attempts to reform the fraktur that he is chiefly remembered.

After training as a wood-cut artist and printer, Johann Friedrich Unger set up his own printing business in Berlin in 1780. At that time German printing had fallen into decline, partly as a result of the closure of the Luther foundry at Frankfurt, which had done so much to secure the popularity of the Garamond and Granjon designs in the previous two centuries. Within ten years Unger had added a foundry to his printing business, using some of the matrices which he had acquired from the Luther foundry and also from his friend Firmin Didot in Paris.

In 1793 Unger published his ideas on simplifying and reforming fraktur, *Probe einer neuen Art deutscher Lettern, erfunden und in Stahl geschnitten von J F Unger*. His aim was to bring to fraktur the lightness and delicacy of roman lettering. At first he commissioned Firmin Didot to re-cut the face; but without success. Finally he decided to learn how to cut type himself and eventually, with his second attempt in 1794, produced a satisfactory result.

Above: showing of Unger-Fraktur. (NM)

Les USHERWOOD
1932–83 GB

Types
Caxton 1981
Flange 1981
Lynton 1981
Marbrook 1983
ITC Usherwood 1984

A graduate from the Beckenham School of Art in Kent, Englishman Les Usherwood emigrated to Toronto in 1957 after working as a lettering artist on magazines. With the advent of photo-type and Letraset Instant Lettering he realized he could apply his lettering skills to producing exclusive alphabets for the advertising market. In 1968 he launched his company, Typsettra, as his vehicle. With the addition to the company of the Berthold Diatronic System offering high-quality text-setting services, Usherwood managed to achieve the complex task of creating fonts of his own alphabets for output. His distinctive designs became popular and were soon eagerly acquired for licensing worldwide by companies like Letraset, Berthold and ITC. The calligraphic Caxton is perhaps his best-known font. He was working on a typeface that he called Saxony for ITC before his early death in 1983. In his memory ITC renamed the typeface Usherwood.

Above: showing of Caxton from *Baseline*, no.4, 1981. (NM)

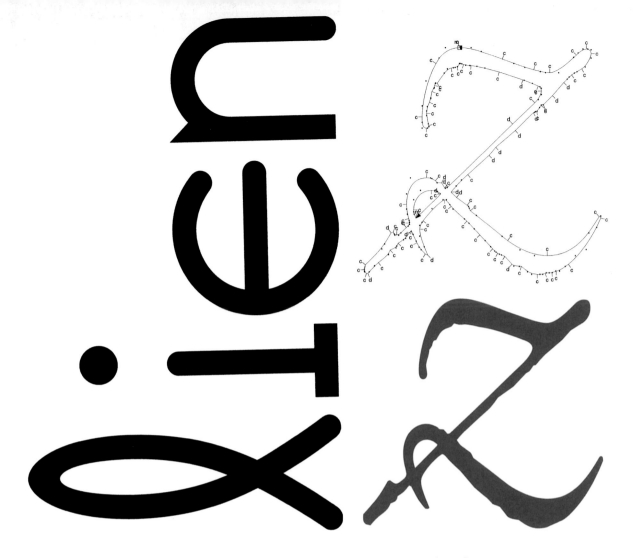

Rudy **VANDERLANS**
b.1955 NL

Types
Oblong 1988
Variex 1988
Suburban 1993
Writing
Emigre: Graphic Design into the Digital Realm (with Zuzana Licko and Mary E Gray), Van Nostrand Reinhold 1993
Web
emigre.com

Born in The Hague, Rudy VanderLans studied at the Koninklijke Academie van Beeldende Kunsten there from 1974 until 1979. After work experience with Total Design, Vorm Vijf and Tel Design he took time off in 1980 to travel around the USA. He was accepted as a graduate student at the University of California, where he studied photography. There he met fellow student Zuzana Licko whom he married in 1983, the year he began work as a designer at the *San Francisco Chronicle*.

In 1984 VanderLans launched the arts magazine *Emigre* with two fellow Dutchmen. That year saw the introduction of the Macintosh computer, which was to become a major influence on both VanderLans and Licko. In 1987 they started working together as Emigre Graphics. The demand created by the frequent use of Licko's typefaces in *Emigre* led to the launch of Emigre Fonts. In 1989, when the duo decided to focus on type design and manufacturing and publishing, the magazine became a graphic design journal.

VanderLans continues to publish *Emigre* magazine and to support the development of the Emigre Font library.

Above: detail of Suburban showing from Emigre catalogue, 1997. (NM))

Jovica **VELJOVIC**
b.1954 YU

Types
ITC Veljovic 1984
ITC Esprit 1985
ITC Gamma 1986
Ex Ponto 1995
Silentium Pro 2001

Jovica Veljovic, who now lives in Germany, was born in Suvi Do in the former Yugoslavia. He received an MA degree in calligraphy and lettering from the Academy of Applied Arts in Belgrade. This he followed with a period of research before returning to the academy to teach typography in 1987.

Between 1984 and 1986 the International Typeface Corporation released three typefaces by Veljovic. All three are serifs designed for display and text use.

Veljovic was appointed a professor of lettering at the Fachhochschule in Hamburg in 1992, teaching type design, calligraphy and typography. He contributed the beautiful Ex Ponto, based on his own handwriting, to the Adobe Originals collection in 1995. A recent release, again for Adobe, is Silentium Pro, his first in the OpenType format.

Amongst many awards received by Veljovic is the coveted Prix Charles Peignot received from ATypI in 1985 for excellence in calligraphy and type design.

Above: outline showing the large number of Bezier points needed to create the contours of Veljovic's Ex Ponto font, from Adobe Ex Ponto specimen, April 1995. (NM)

Walbaum

Justus Erich Walbaum was born in Steinbach, Brunswick in 1768. A clergyman's son, he was apprenticed at an early age to a confectioner but later became an engraver and caster of metals. Finally he turned to letter-cutting and learned to make typefounders' matrices and tools. In his thirtieth year he started his own type foundry at Goslar, and five years later he moved to Weimar, where he remained until 1856.

During his lifetime his types were celebrated and admired. But, through the change in taste in the mid-nineteenth century away from the "classical", his importance was forgotten almost immediately after his death. It is only recently, with the return to popularity of the "modern" letter, that the intrinsic value of his Antiqua has been recognized. Its slight and almost imperceptible irregularities provide an interest and human quality that is often lacking in other nineteenth-century faces.

Walbaum's types, the original matrices of which are still extant in Germany, were so faithful to those of Firmin Didot that their elegance may be said to be characteristically French. Carefully modelled and cut, they are particularly suitable for certain kinds of bookwork and display. The italic is beautifully legible and reminiscent of both Didot's and Bodoni's designs.

'Monotype' Walbaum (Series 574) was cut in 1954. It is surprisingly versatile for a "modern" face, and it appears best on a smooth-surfaced paper. To do it full justice, it needs to be leaded, especially in the smaller sizes where it is eminently readable. Its related bold face, Walbaum Medium (Series 575) can be used in combination with Series 574 or on occasions as a text face on its own.

Justus Erich WALBAUM
1768–1839 D

Types
Walbaum 1803–28
(revived from 1933)

Justus Erich Walbaum was a German punch-cutter who had his own letter foundry, first based in Goslar and later in Weimar. His faces were neo-classical, derived from the Didot roman.

Walbaum, the son of a clergyman, was born in Steinbach, near Brunswick. He was apprenticed to a confectioner and reputedly taught himself engraving by making his own confectionary moulds, using chisels he had made from sword blades. When he was free to leave the pastry shop he got a job engraving music types for the Brunswick firm of Spehr.

Walbaum purchased the typefoundry of Ernst Wilhelm Kircher in Goslar in 1793. In 1802, just before Goslar was incorporated into Prussia, Walbaum left for Weimar. The foundry he set up there was extremely successful and the types he cut, modelled closely on those of Firmin Didot, were much admired.

In 1836 Walbaum sold the business to F A Brockhaus in Leipzig – in 1918 many of his matrices were purchased by H Berthold AG in Berlin.

Walbaum was introduced into England in 1925 by the Curwen Press, which had purchased the types from Berthold. The Monotype Corporation issued Walbaum in 1933. Under the direction of Günter Gerhard Lange, Berthold issued Walbaum Buch and Walbaum Standard between 1975 and 1979.

Above: Monotype Walbaum specimen, n.d. (CLR)

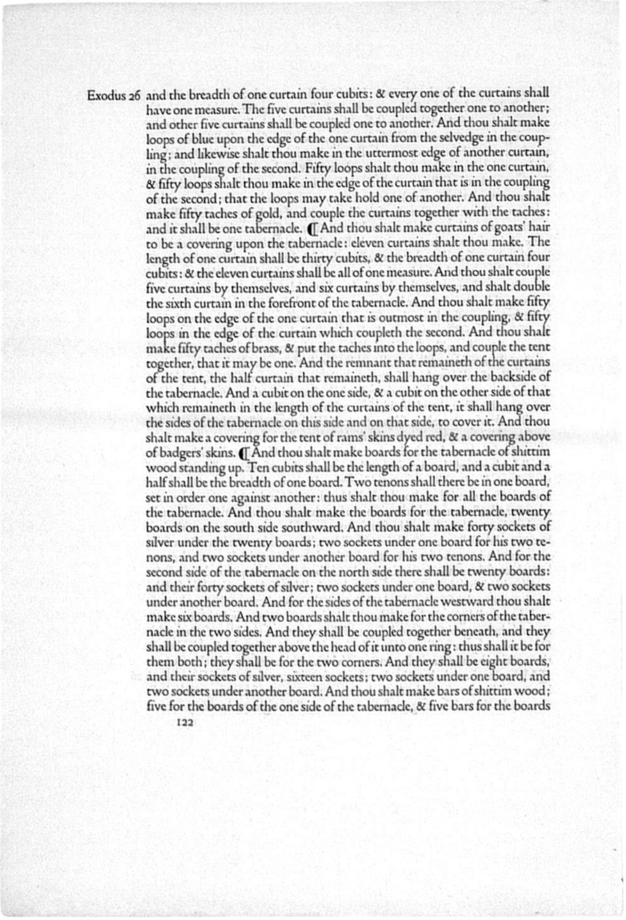

Exodus 26 and the breadth of one curtain four cubits: & every one of the curtains shall have one measure. The five curtains shall be coupled together one to another; and other five curtains shall be coupled one to another. And thou shalt make loops of blue upon the edge of the one curtain from the selvedge in the coupling; and likewise shalt thou make in the uttermost edge of another curtain, in the coupling of the second. Fifty loops shalt thou make in the one curtain, & fifty loops shalt thou make in the edge of the curtain that is in the coupling of the second; that the loops may take hold one of another. And thou shalt make fifty taches of gold, and couple the curtains together with the taches: and it shall be one tabernacle. ¶ And thou shalt make curtains of goats' hair to be a covering upon the tabernacle: eleven curtains shalt thou make. The length of one curtain shall be thirty cubits, & the breadth of one curtain four cubits: & the eleven curtains shall be all of one measure. And thou shalt couple five curtains by themselves, and six curtains by themselves, and shalt double the sixth curtain in the forefront of the tabernacle. And thou shalt make fifty loops on the edge of the one curtain that is outmost in the coupling, & fifty loops in the edge of the curtain which coupleth the second. And thou shalt make fifty taches of brass, & put the taches into the loops, and couple the tent together, that it may be one. And the remnant that remaineth of the curtains of the tent, the half curtain that remaineth, shall hang over the backside of the tabernacle. And a cubit on the one side, & a cubit on the other side of that which remaineth in the length of the curtains of the tent, it shall hang over the sides of the tabernacle on this side and on that side, to cover it. And thou shalt make a covering for the tent of rams' skins dyed red, & a covering above of badgers' skins. ¶ And thou shalt make boards for the tabernacle of shittim wood standing up. Ten cubits shall be the length of a board, and a cubit and a half shall be the breadth of one board. Two tenons shall there be in one board, set in order one against another: thus shalt thou make for all the boards of the tabernacle. And thou shalt make the boards for the tabernacle, twenty boards on the south side southward. And thou shalt make forty sockets of silver under the twenty boards; two sockets under one board for his two tenons, and two sockets under another board for his two tenons. And for the second side of the tabernacle on the north side there shall be twenty boards: and their forty sockets of silver; two sockets under one board, & two sockets under another board. And for the sides of the tabernacle westward thou shalt make six boards. And two boards shalt thou make for the corners of the tabernacle in the two sides. And they shall be coupled together beneath, and they shall be coupled together above the head of it unto one ring: thus shall it be for them both; they shall be for the two corners. And they shall be eight boards, and their sockets of silver, sixteen sockets; two sockets under one board, and two sockets under another board. And thou shalt make bars of shittim wood; five for the boards of the one side of the tabernacle, & five bars for the boards

122

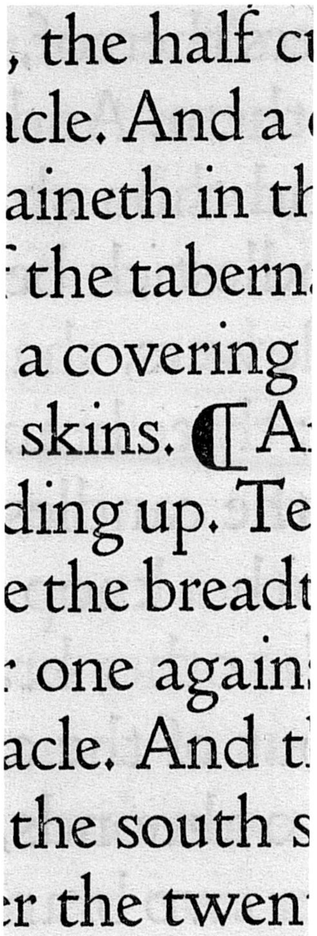

, the half c
cle. And a
aineth in t
the tabern
a covering
skins. ¶ A
ding up. Te
e the bread
one again
acle. And t
the south
r the twen

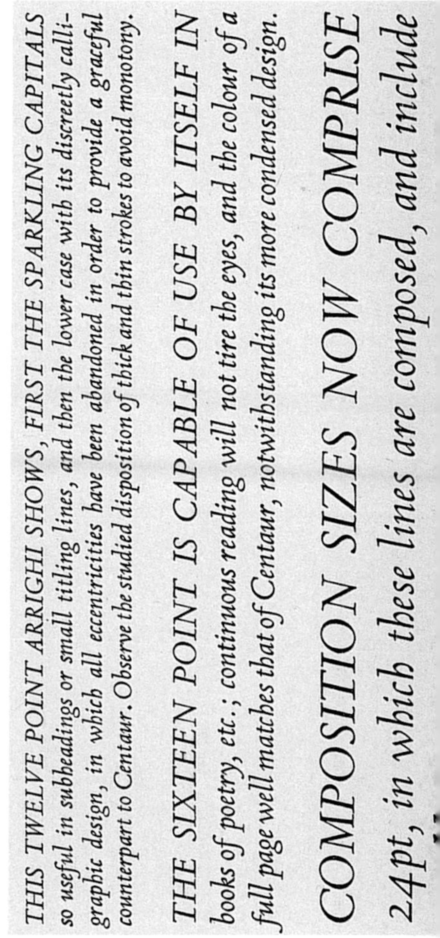

THIS TWELVE POINT ARRIGHI SHOWS, FIRST THE SPARKLING CAPITALS
so useful in subheadings or small titling lines, and then the lower case with its discreetly calligraphic design, in which all eccentricities have been abandoned in order to provide a graceful
counterpart to Centaur. Observe the studied disposition of thick and thin strokes to avoid monotony.
THE SIXTEEN POINT IS CAPABLE OF USE BY ITSELF IN
books of poetry, etc.; continuous reading will not tire the eyes, and the colour of a
full page well matches that of Centaur, notwithstanding its more condensed design.
COMPOSITION SIZES NOW COMPRISE
24pt, in which these lines are composed, and include

Emery **WALKER**
1851–1933 GB

Types
Doves Roman 1900
(with T J Cobden-Sanderson)
Subiaco Type 1901
Cranach Press Roman 1913
Ashendene Press Type
Eragny Press Type
Vale Press Type

Emery Walker trained as a letterer, engraver and printer in his native London. His involvement with printing and its allied trades led to his now famous lecture on typography to the Arts and Crafts Exhibition Society, which he delivered on 15 November 1888, and at which William Morris was present, and was inspired to start the Kelmscott Press. Walker was one of the most active participants in the typographic revival of the time.

Having rejected the chance to run the Kelmscott Press with Sydney Cockerell on Morris's death in 1896, Walker set up the Doves Press in 1901 in partnership with Thomas J Cobden-Sanderson, a bookbinder who had worked with Morris. Like other private presses of that time, the Doves Press modelled its type on a Jenson cut, in this case one used in his edition of Pliny of 1476. It was cut by Morris's punchcutter Edward Prince and was used in the press's first work, the five-volume Doves Bible. Unfortunately each partner claimed authorship, and in 1912, as a result of this dispute, Cobden-Sanderson threw the matrices and type over Hammersmith Bridge into the Thames. Emery Walker had left the partnership in 1908.

After this, Emery Walker acted as an adviser for the Ashendene, Eragny and Vale presses and for the Cranach Press in Weimar. He sat on many committees and helped instigate the teaching of printing at the Central College of Arts and Crafts.

In 1927 Walker became president of the Arts and Crafts Exhibition Society. He was on the governing bodies of three art schools, was knighted in 1930, and elected an honorary fellow of Jesus College, Cambridge in 1933.

Above: page and type detail from the Doves Bible, 1903. (CLR)

Frederic **WARDE**
1894–1939 USA

Types
Arrighi 1925, 1929
Further reading
Herbert H Johnson, 'Notes on Frederic Warde and the True Story of his Arrighi Type', *Fine Print on Type*, Lund Humphries 1989

Frederic Warde was born in Wells, Minnesota. In 1918 he met Beatrice Becker, whom he later married. Through her mother he got his first job, with the MacMillan Company, which he left for the printing house of William E Rudge, with whom he was to maintain a connection for much of his life. In 1922 he was appointed director of printing at Princeton University Press. His work was chiefly book design, and he established a reputation as an uncompromising perfectionist.

It was during this period that he married Beatrice,

A MONSIGNORE ALIOTTI

[*di Roma, ottobre 1542*]

Monsignore,

La vostra Signoria mi manda a dire che io dipinga, et non dubiti di niente. Io rispondo, che si dipinge col ciervello et non con le mani; et chi non può avere il ciervello seco, si vitupera: però fin che la cosa mia non si acconcia, non fo cosa buona. La retificagione dell'ultimo contratto non viene; e per vigore dell'altro fatto presente Clemente, sono ogni dì lapidato come se havessi crocifixo Cristo. Io dico che detto contratto non intesi che fussi recitato presente papa Clemente, come ne ebbi poi la copia: et questo fu, che mandandomi il dì medesimo Clemente a Firenze, Gianmaria da Modena, imbasciadore fu col notaio, et fecielo distendere a suo modo; in modo che quand'io tornai, e che io lo riscossi, vi trovai su più mille ducati che

Corporate A A A
Corporate *A A A*
Corporate S S S
Corporate *S S S*
Corporate E E E
Corporate *E E E*

Kurt WEIDEMANN
b.1922 D

Types
Biblica 1979
ITC Weidemann 1983
Corporate ASE 1985–90
Writing
Wo der Buchstabe das Wort führt, Stuttgart 1995
Wortarmut, Karlsruhe 1995
Further reading
Yvonne Schwemer-Sheddin, 'The aesthetics of technology. Kurt Weidemann's Corporate ASE', *Type & Typographers*, Architecture Design and Technology Press 1991

then working at the ATF Library in New Jersey. In 1925 they left America for Europe, going first to France, where they met Stanley Morison, and then with him to England. Whilst in England Frederic and Beatrice (she under the name of Paul Beaujon) wrote for *The Fleuron*.

In 1925 Frederic designed Arrighi, an italic inspired by a type used by Arrighi in his 1524 *Coryciana*. Cut by Charles Plumet in Paris, it first appeared in Robert Bridges's poetry book *The Tapestry*. Warde twice revised this first Arrighi italic: the second variant, named Vicenza, appeared in Plato's *Crito*, printed for Warde at the Officina Bodoni; the third was adapted for Monotype in 1929 to accompany Bruce Rogers's Centaur.

After its cutting, Frederic separated from Beatrice and returned to America hoping to find financial stability, but the stock market crash worked against him. He resumed work with William E Rudge as a book designer until Rudge's death. Similar positions followed, including a partnership in a publishing company and a production management role with the Oxford University Press in New York before his death in 1939.

Previous page: from Monotype Arrighi specimen, 1929.; Above: specimen of Vicenza as used at the Officina Bodoni, tipped in (p.125) to *The Fleuron*, no.7, 1930 (1970 reprint). (both NM)

The award-winning typographer, graphic designer, author and teacher Kurt Weidemann was born in Eichemedien, Germany (now part of Poland). Weidemann trained as a typesetter in Lübeck (1950–2) before studying graphics and typography at the Staatliche Akademie der Bildenden Künste in Stuttgart (1953–5).

On leaving he began his freelance career as a graphic designer, advertising consultant and copywriter. His clients included many high-profile German companies; in 1987 he became corporate identity consultant to Daimler-Benz AG.

Weidemann's first published typeface was Biblica, commissioned by the German Bible Society for a new edition of the Bible. Weidemann succeeded in producing a highly legible typeface with a narrow set width and a relatively large x-height. Biblica, expanded from three to four weights, was licensed and issued by the International Typeface Corporation as ITC Weidemann in 1983.

Between 1985 and 1990 Weidemann developed a trinity of corporate typefaces

Antiqua

Antiqua

rifenlose

rifenlose

yptienne

yptienne

ABCDEFGHIJKLMNO
PQRSTUVWXYZ
1234567890

Emil Rudolf **WEISS**
1875–1943 D

for Daimler-Benz AG. Corporate ASE (Antiqua, Sans Serif and Egyptian) followed in the footsteps of Sumner Stone's Stone family and Otl Aicher's Rotis in offering compatibility of style.

Weidemann, who was a professor at his alma mater in Stuttgart for 20 years (1965–85), also taught at art schools in Koblenz and Karlsruhe.

Above: showing of Weidemann's Corporate types. (NM)

Types
Weiss Fraktur 1909
Weiss Antiqua 1926–31
Memphis 1929
Weiss Gotisch 1936
Weiss Rundgotisch 1937

The German Emil Rudolf Weiss's work embraced calligraphy, typography and type design, including roman and fraktur types. He designed hundreds of books, including many for the leading German publishers of the day.

He studied painting at the Julian in Paris, where one of his fellow students was Toulouse-Lautrec. His first ambition in life, however, was to be a poet and in 1894 he sent some poems to the literary magazine *Pan*, edited by Otto Julius Bierbaum. Weiss's particularly fine writing hand impressed Bierbaum so much that

he asked Weiss to prepare a page of letters for publication in *Pan*. These letters appeared, and were the forerunner of a long and distinguished association with design, typography and calligraphy.

Like many German artists of his generation, Weiss greatly admired the work and ideals of William Morris. But unlike Morris he did not eschew the mechanical methods of reproduction available at the time and he mainly studied the typefaces of the 18th-century masters.

In 1902 Weiss was commissioned by the Bauer foundry to design a roman typeface, a fraktur and some ornaments. Weiss Fraktur was issued by the Bauer foundry in 1913 but Weiss Antiqua was not completed

until 1931. His Memphis, the earliest modern revival of the egyptian, was issued by Stempel in 1929.

As a calligrapher Weiss had few equals, and his etched titlepages for several limited editions of the Marees Gesellschaft *Sappho* are regarded as supreme examples of book art.

Above: cover of Linotype Memphis specimen, date unknown, photographed for the CLR. (CLR); showing of Weiss Antiqua from *Type*, SGM Books 1949. (CD)

ENGRAVERS ROMAN

H. BERTHOLD AG

Admark Regular
Admark Italic
Admark Medium
Admark Medium Italic
Admark Bold
Admark Bold Italic
ABCD *abc* 1234 QRS890ghij CT870 *EFG567abcdef*

Congress Sans 45
Congress Sans 46
Congress Sans 55
Congress Sans 56
Congress Sans 65
Congress Sans 66
Congress Sans 75
Congress Sans 76
ABCD abcd 1234 *QRSTU* efghijklmnop CT6089

Bulldog Regular
Bulldog Italic
Bulldog Medium
Bulldog Medium Italic
Bulldog Bold
Bulldog Bold Italic
ABCDE abcde 12345 *FGH678abcdefghi* WXYZ&qrstu CT871

Eurocrat Regular
Eurocrat Italic
Eurocrat Medium
Eurocrat Medium Italic
Eurocrat Bold
Eurocrat Bold Italic
ABCD abcd 1234 QRSTUV890qrst *EFG567efghijk* CT1094

ABC123abc DEF4 *12345&* Column Book *Column Book Italic* *Column Book Italic Swash* Column Medium **Column Bold** *ABCdefghijklmrst* CT6090

Mercurius Light
Mercurius Light Italic
Mercurius Medium
Mercurius Medium Italic
Mercurius Black
Mercurius Black Italic
ABCDE abcdef 1234 **FGH567890ghi** CT873

Robert WIEBKING
1870–1927 D

184

Types
Engravers' Roman 1899
Artcraft 1912
Invitation Text 1914
Advertisers Gothic 1917
Munder Venezian (Laclede
 Oldstyle) 1922

Robert Wiebking was born in Schwelem, Germany, but emigrated to the USA in 1881. After serving an apprenticeship with the Chicago engraver C H Hanson, Wiebking eventually established himself as an independent engraver of punches and matrices for many major North American foundries. He worked with Bruce Rogers on the development of Centaur and cut many of Goudy's typefaces before 1926.

As a designer he is best known for his Engravers' Roman, which was issued by Barnhart Bros & Spindler in 1899. His work on Centaur inspired his most elegant design, Munder Venezian, originally issued by the Laclede Type Foundry as Laclede Oldstyle. Stephenson Blake copied the roman, releasing it as Verona in 1923.

Above: detail of Engravers' Roman page from *Berthold Types*, 1985. (NM)

Adrian WILLIAMS
b.1950 GB

Types
Worcester Round 1974
Raleigh 1977
Seagull 1978
Stratford 1978
 (with Freda Sack)
Claridge 1979
Congress 1980
Trieste 1983
Monkton 1986
Eurocrat 1987
Poseidon 1987
Mercurius 1988
Bulldog 1990
Column 1992
Congress Sans 1992
Web
clubtype.co.uk

Adrian Williams trained at Hornsey School of Art. His first job in 1969 was drawing photosetting fonts from manufacturers' drawings but he soon set up in business on his own and began designing his own typefaces.

In 1985 he formed a new company, Club Type, to meet the demand for quality typefaces on dedicated typesetting systems. Since the advent of PostScript, Williams has marketed his Club Type fonts through various distributors. His designs include many successful revivals as well as novel original serif and sans-serif typefaces for text and display.

Above: detail from Club Type leaflet, 1993. (NM)

SCOTCH DRINK

Gie him strong drink until he wink,
   That's sinking in despair:
An' liquor guid to fire his bluid,
   That's preſt wi' grief an' care:
There let him bowse, and deep carouse,
   Wi' bumpers flowing o'er,
Till he forgets his loves or debts,
   An' minds his griefs no more.

SOLOMON'S PROVERBS, XXXI. 6, 7.

From Poems, Chiefly in the Scottish Dialeƈt
by Robert Burns 1786

Set in Foundry Wilson
Presented on Burns Night 25th January 1993

Quoufque tandem abutere, Catilina, pa-
tientia noſtra? quamdiu nos etiam furor
iſte tuus eludet? quem ad finem fefe ef-
frenata jaƈtabit audacia? nihilne te noc-
turnum præſidium palatii, nihil urbis vi-
giliæ, nihil timor populi, nihil confenfus

Alexander WILSON
1714–84 GB

Types
Great Primer Greek 1757
Double Pica Roman 1768

Alexander Wilson was born in St Andrews, Scotland, but, on completing his education, left for London in 1737. After visiting a London letter foundry with his friend and fellow Scot John Baine, they returned to their home town to set up one of their own in 1742. This foundry, which later moved to Glasgow, ended the dependence of Scottish printers on types brought in from London and the Netherlands; indeed it was soon to become a serious rival to London foundries. Whilst Alexander Wilson ran the foundry (originally in partnership with Baine) it produced types which were influenced by the work of Caslon and Baskerville.

How many of the types offered by the Wilson foundry were cut by Wilson himself is not known. Only one roman and a greek can be firmly attributed to him, but both types are highly acclaimed. Notable punch-cutters to work for the Wilson foundry included Richard Austin, who cut a modern face for them, and Johann Christian Bauer, who was later to start his own foundry in Frankfurt. The influential Miller ɛt Richard foundry in Edinburgh was started by an ex-manager of the Wilson foundry.

After being made the first professor of practical astronomy at Glasgow University, Wilson handed over the running of the foundry to his son Andrew and grandson Alexander. They ran the company until

it went bankrupt in 1845, at which point the younger Alexander sold the stock to various foundries, including Caslon and possibly Figgins.

English Roman No.1, a Wilson foundry type, served as the model for Fontana, designed for Collins of Glasgow by Hans Mardersteig in 1936. As is obvious from its name, it was a Wilson cut which inspired The Foundry's Freda Sack and David Quay to create Foundry Wilson, issued in 1993.

Above: detail of Foundry Wilson specimen, 1993. (NM); showing of Wilson's 1788 specimen of English Roman from Monotype Fontana specimen, n.d. (CLR)

Cornel WINDLIN
b.1964 CH

Types
F Moonbase Alpha 1991
FF Dot Matrix 1994
  (with Stephan Müller)
FF Magda 1995
FF Screen Matrix 1995
  (with Stephan Müller)
FF Luggagetag 1997
Autoscape 1998
Water Tower 1998
Supermax 1999
Web
lineto.com

Cornel Windlin was born in Küsnacht, Switzerland. He studied at the Schule für Gestaltung in Lucerne before moving to London, where he worked with Neville Brody. After a spell as art director of *The Face* magazine from 1991 he returned to Switzerland in 1993 to work on his own. Windlin now works between Zürich and Berlin as designer/ art director. He shares a fascination for typography in public spaces with Stephan

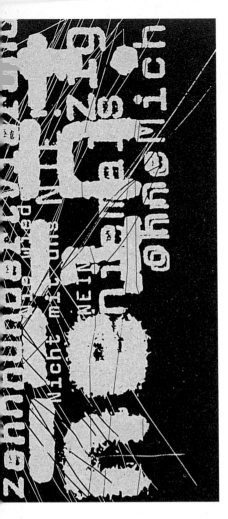

Macho man gives beauty counter a wide berth

TB tests for 5,000 pupils as outbreak reaches 24

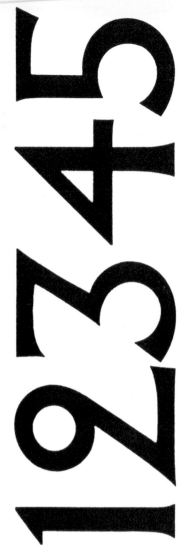

Müller, and their type-design activities reflect this. Their Lineto label, named after a PostScript code, is the marketing vehicle for these activities, incorporating an international network of designers with shared interests and concerns.

Previous page and above: FF Magda promotional postcard, 1993. (NM)

Shelley WINTER
b.1959 GB

Types
Pegasus Bold 1980
   (with Matthew Carter for
   Berthold Wolpe)
New Johnston Signage Light
   1988
Sun Life Engraved 1988
Telegraph Newface Bold 1989
   (with Walter Tracy)
Telegraph Newface Roman
   1990

Shelley Winter has been an independent type consultant since 1981. She has carried out commissions for major international companies and has worked with some of the leading figures in type design. Her career started in the type development department of Linotype in 1977, where she worked with Walter Tracy in the development of Arabic and Cyrillic typefaces. After leaving Linotype she collaborated with Tracy on Telegraph Newface Bold, the headline

face for the *Daily Telegraph*, and later, by herself, developed Telegraph Newface Roman.

With Matthew Carter she collaborated on the development of foreign characters for his Galliard series, and with Berthold Wolpe and Matthew Carter she worked on Pegasus Bold for the Berthold Wolpe 75th birthday tribute at the Victoria & Albert Museum in 1980.

Above: roman and bold weight headlines from the *Daily Telegraph*, 5 April 2005. (PB)

Berthold WOLPE
1905–89 D

Types
Albertus 1932–40
Hyperion 1932
Tempest Titling 1935
Sachsenwald 1938
Pegasus 1938–9
Decorata 1955
LTB Italic 1973
Further reading
*Berthold Wolpe. A
   Retrospective Survey*,
   Victoria & Albert Museum
   and Faber & Faber 1980
Sebastian Carter, 'Berthold
   Wolpe', *Twentieth Century
   Type Designers*, Lund
   Humphries 1995

Berthold Wolpe, born in Offenbach near Frankfurt, spent most of his working life in England. From 1941 to 1975 he designed book jackets for Faber & Faber, creating as many as 1,500 designs. His best-known type is Albertus, which was commissioned by Stanley Morison for Monotype after an encounter between

ALBERTUS
Series 481

THE MONOTYPE CORPORATION LIMITED

WYNKYN de Worde
d.1535 F

the two on Wolpe's visit to England in 1932. He was also a teacher of lettering at both Camberwell College of Art and the Royal College of Art, London.

As a young man Wolpe was apprenticed to a firm of metal-workers, where he learnt his engraving skills. His interest in inscriptional lettering and calligraphy led him to study at the Kunstgewerbeschule in Offenbach under Rudolf Koch. He became Koch's assistant and then a teacher in his own right in 1929.

Koch's son, Paul, cut Wolpe's first type, Hyperion, in 1932 for the Bauer foundry, but it was not made available to the trade until after World War 2. Albertus was issued in 1932 and for a time became the most ubiquitous display typeface in Britain.

In 1935, with Koch's death and the rise of Nazism, Wolpe returned to England to stay. Before joining Faber, he worked with the Fanfare Press for whom he designed Tempest Titling, cut by Monotype. Pegasus was another Morison commission, cut by Monotype in 1938. Wolpe also designed a romanized black-letter called Sachsenwald in 1938; a set of foliated capitals called Decorata for the Westerham Press in 1955; and in 1973 an italic for London Transport.

Wolpe was appointed a Royal Designer for Industry in 1959. He received an honorary doctorate from the Royal College of Art in 1968, and was awarded an OBE in 1983.

Previous page: from *Monotype Newsletter*, no.84, 1968.; Above: Monotype specimen, n.d. (both CLR)

When William Caxton died in 1491 his types were passed to his foreman, Wynkyn de Worde, who had originally come from Wörth in Alsace. He continued to use them until about 1493, when he developed a type of his own, which was probably formed on a French model. Wynkyn de Worde, who printed more than seven hundred books, also printed music with movable type for the first time. He was the first English printer to print on English-made paper, and until his death in 1535 he concentrated on producing cheaper books in a smaller format.

Above: detail from page of *The descrypcyon of Englande*, 1515. (SBPL)

Z

Eine zweckmäßige, vernünftige Schrift

Bei der Entwicklung der Melior, die nach Entwürfen von Hermann Zapf in unserem Hause geschnitten wurde, hat vom ersten Federstrich an eine ganz klare Konzeption bestanden. Es sollte eine Antiqua geschaffen werden, die weitgehend allen Erfordernissen gerecht wird, die an eine vielseitig verwendbare, also echte Gebrauchsschrift zu stellen sind. Sie mußte gut lesbar sein und wurde daher offen und klar gehalten. Um jeder Auflagenhöhe gewachsen zu sein, wurde sie sehr widerstandsfähig angelegt. Sie mußte sich für alle Druckverfahren eignen, auf jeder Papierqualität gut stehen und sie mußte in allen Garnituren prägefest sein. Diese Anforderungen der Praxis erfüllt die Melior nun in geradezu hervorragender Weise durch ihre kräftige Strichstärke in allen Buchstabenteilen und durch die leicht abgerundeten Endungen. Die Berücksichtigung aller dieser Überlegungen im technischen Bereich brachte wie von selbst die vielseitige Verwendungsmöglichkeit mit sich.

Hermann ZAPF
b.1918 D

Types
Gilgenart 1938–41
Alkor 1939–40
Novalis 1946
Michelangelo 1950
Palatino 1950
Sistina 1950
Melior 1952
Saphir 1953
Aldus 1954
Kompact 1954
Optima 1958
Hunt Roman 1962
Medici Script 1969
Venture Script 1969
Orion 1974
Comenius 1976
ITC Zapf Book 1976
Marconi 1976
ITC Zapf Chancery 1979
ITC Zapf International 1979
Edison 1978
Vario 1982
Aurelia 1983
URW Antiqua 1984–95
URW Grotesk 1985–94
Zapf Renaissance 1987
Zapfino 1998
Optima Nova 2003
    (with Akira Kobayashi)

Writing
Pen and Graver,
    Museum Books 1952
Manuale Typographicum,
    Frankfurt am Main 1954
About Alphabets,
    The Typophiles 1960;
    revised ed., MIT Press 1970
*Hermann Zapf and his Design
    Philosophy*, STA Chicago 1987

Further reading
Sebastian Carter, 'Hermann
    Zapf', *Twentieth Century
    Type Designers*, Lund
    Humphries 1995

Hermann Zapf was born in Nürnberg. An outstanding calligrapher, book designer and teacher, Zapf is also a notable writer on his subjects. In 1935, as an apprentice to the printers Karl Ulrich Et Co., an exhibition of the work of Rudolf Koch drew him to calligraphy. He taught himself, using books by Koch and Edward Johnston. Zapf then worked for Paul Koch in Frankfurt, where he was introduced to the Stempel foundry and began creating types for them, assisted by head punch-cutter August Rosenberger. He designed his first type for Stempel, a fraktur black-letter named Gilgenart, in 1938. In 1939 he was conscripted by the German military, eventually serving as a cartographer.

On his return to civilian life, Zapf took over the design at Stempel, and, although he resigned in 1956, this was a particularly productive period for him. Zapf's types of this time include the Renaissance-inspired Palatino, which was much admired and quickly issued by other foundries.

In 1958 he designed Optima, inspired by inscriptional lettering he had seen in Florence. The much-expanded Optima Nova, a collaboration

der Schaffung identischer Linotype-Matrizen für die Garnituren Antiqua, Kursiv und halb-
fett ist die Melior zu einer geradezu idealen Schrift für die Zeitung geworden. Hier werden
ihre technischen Vorzüge auch bei den Handsatztypen in großen Graden besonders geschützt.
Die vierte Garnitur—die Schmalfette Melior—verdankt ihr Entstehen den Stoßseufzern der
Redakteure nach kräftigen Überschriften für schmale Zeitungskolumnen und nach werbe-
wirksamen Auszeichnungen für den knappen Anzeigenraum. D. Stempel AG Frankfurt/M.

MELIOR

Diotima

d

D. STEMPEL AG
Schriftgießerei und Messinglinienfabrik
Frankfurt am Main Süd

Gudrun ZAPF-VON HESSE
b.1918 D

Types
Smaragd 1953
Ariadne 1954
Diotima 1954
Shakespeare 1968
Nofret 1986
Carmina 1987
Alcuin 1991
Christiana 1991

Further reading
Paul Hayden Duensing,
    'Diotima of Gudrun Zapf-von
    Hesse', *Fine Print on Type*,
    Lund Humphries 1989

between Zapf and Akira Kobayashi, was issued by Linotype Library in 2003.

Hermann Zapf, with over two hundred typefaces to his credit, has contributed to the libraries of most established manufacturers. He has embraced technology, designing new types for each generation of development as well as overseeing the transfer of his older designs to new systems. In 1977 he was made professor of typographic computer programming at the Rochester Institute of Technology, New York. He is married to type designer and lettering artist Gudrun Zapf-von Hesse. The sans-serif type used in this book is Zapf's URW Grotesk.

Previous page: Stempel specimen for Michelangelo, Palatino and Sistina, n.d.; Above: Linotype Melior specimen, n.d. (both CLR)

Gudrun Zapf-von Hesse is a calligrapher, type designer and teacher who started her career as a specialist in hand binding after studying under Otto Dorfner at Weimar. She taught herself lettering from the books of Edward Johnston and Rudolf Koch but later took instruction with Johannes Boehland at the Meisterschule für das grafische Gewerbe in Berlin. In 1946 she became an instructor in calligraphy at the Städelschule in Frankfurt am Main. She has designed a variety of typefaces which reflect her calligraphic skills. Those originally issued by Stempel include Diotima, a light roman, Smaragd, a set of outline capitals with hair-line serifs, and Ariadne, a set of flowing italic initials. Later work includes Nofret and Christiana for Berthold, Carmina for Bitstream and Alcuin for URW.

Above: Stempel specimen of Diotima, n.d. (CLR)

FURTHER READING

Jeremy Aynsley, *Graphic Design in Germany 1890–1945*, Thames & Hudson, London 2000

Phil Baines and Andrew Haslam, *Type & Typography*, 2nd ed., Laurence King, London 2005

John D Berry (ed.), *Language Culture Type: International Type Design in the Age of Unicode*, Association Typographique Internationale /Graphis, New York 2002

Charles Bigelow, Paul Hayden Duensing and Linnea Gentry (eds.), *Fine Print on Type*, Lund Humphries, London 1989

Lewis Blackwell, *20th-Century Type*, Laurence King, London 1992

Robert Bringhurst, *The Elements of Typographic Style*, Hartley & Marks, Vancouver 1992

Sebastian Carter, *Twentieth Century Type Designers*, revised ed., Lund Humphries 1995

Warren Chappell, *A Short History of the Printed Word*, André Deutsch, London 1972

James Craig and Bruce Barton, *Thirty Centuries of Graphic Design*, Watson Guptill, New York 1987

John Dreyfus, *Into Print. Selected Writings on Printing History, Typography and Book Production*, British Library, London 1994

David Earls, *Designing Typefaces*, RotoVision SA, Brighton 2002

Friedrich Friedl, Nicolaus Ott and Bernard Stein (eds.), *Typography: When Who How*, Könemann, Cologne 1998

W Pincus Jaspert, W Turner Berry and A F Johnson, *The Encyclopaedia of Typefaces*, Blandford Press, Dorset 1970

Albert Kapr, *The Art of Lettering*, K G Sauer, Munich 1983

Manfred Klein, Yvonne Schwemer-Scheddin and Erik Spiekermann, *Type and Typographers*, Architecture Design and Technology Press, London 1991

Simon Loxley, Type: *The Secret History of Letters*, I B Taurus, London 2004

Mathieu Lommen and Peter Verheul, *Haagse Letters*, Uitgeverij de Buitenkant, Amsterdam 1996

Mac McGrew, *American Metal Typefaces of the Twentieth Century*, Oak Knoll Press, New Castle DE 1993

Ruari McLean, *Manual of Typography*, Thames & Hudson, London 1980

Ruari McLean (ed.), *Typographers on Type*, Lund Humphries, London 1995

Douglas C McMurtrie, *The Book: The Story of Printing and Bookmaking*, Oxford University Press, New York 1943

Stanley Morison, *A Tally of Types*, revised ed., Syndics of the Cambridge University Press, London 1973

Alexander Nesbitt, *The History and Technique of Lettering*, Dover Publications, New York 1957

Erik Spiekermann and E M Ginger, *Stop Stealing Sheep & Find Out How Type Works*, Adobe Press, Mountain View 1993

S H Steinberg, *Five Hundred Years of Printing*, Penguin, Harmondsworth 1955

James Sutton and Alan Bartram, *An Atlas of Typeforms*, Lund Humphries, London 1968

Walter Tracy, *Letters of Credit: A View of Type Design*, Gordon Fraser, London 1986

Walter Tracy, *The Typographic Scene*, Gordon Fraser, London 1998

Jan Tschichold, *Treasury of Alphabets and Lettering*, Lund Humphries, London 1992

Daniel Berkeley Updike, *Printing Types: Their History, Forms and Use*, 3rd ed., Oak Knoll Press, New Castle DE 2001

Lawrence W Wallis, *Modern Encyclopedia of Typefaces 1960–90*, Lund Humphries, London 1990

INDEX

193

196

COUNTRY CODES

A Austria
B Belgium
CDN Canada
CH Switzerland
CS Czechoslovakia
D Germany
DK Denmark
E Spain
F France
GB Great Britain
H Hungary
I Italy
J Japan
NL Netherlands
P Portugal
S Sweden
USA United States of America
USSR Soviet Union
YU Yugoslavia
ZA South Africa

ABBREVIATIONS

ATF American Type Founders Inc.
ATypl Association Typographique Internationale
D&AD Design & Art Direction
DTL Dutch Type Library
FF FontFont
FSI FontShop International
ITC International Typeface Corporation
U&lc Upper and Lower Case Magazine
URW Unternehmensberatung Rubow Weber

PICTURE SOURCES

The images used in this book came from the following sources (their initials are in brackets after the captions), to whom we are very grateful:
BL British Library © British Library; BM Bruno Maag; CD Catherine Dixon; CLR Central Lettering Record at Central Saint Martins College of Art & Design; CSM Central Saint Martins College of Art & Design Museum & Study Collection; DTL Dutch Type Library; ECC Edward Clark Collection, Napier University, Edinburgh; F The Foundry; HP Hyphen Press; JFP Jean François Porchez; JH John Hudson; JS Jason Smith; LTM London Transport Museum; MG Michael Gills; MJ Mark Jamra; MN Miles Newlyn; MT Monotype; NC Nick Cooke; NM Neil Macmillan; PB Phil Baines; SBPL St Bride Printing Library, London; NU © Napier University Department of PMPC/Licensed via www.scran.ac.uk; NLS National Library of Scotland

COPYRIGHT CREDITS

We are grateful to the following for permission to reproduce the images in this book:
Aicher courtesy Florian Aicher; Arrighi courtesy Edward Clark Collection, Napier University, Edinburgh; Augereau, Benguiat, DiSpigna, Grimshaw, Hollandsworth Batty, Kobayashi, Lester, Nicholas © Monotype Imaging; Austin, Blumenthal, Calvert, Carpenter, Detterer, van Dijck, Gill, Havinden, Hess, Kis [2], Krimpen, Mardersteig, Martin, Morison, Munch, Peters, Pierpont, Reiner, Rogers, S Stone [1], Walbaum, Warde, Wilson [2], Wolpe © Monotype Corporation; Baker courtesy URW++ Design & Development; Balius, Ev Blokland [2], Bloemsma, Kisman, Leonardi, Majoor, Olsen, Pool, Reichel, van Rossum, Schäfer, Spiekermann [1], Windlin courtesy FontShop International; Barnbrook courtesy Jonathan Barnbrook; Bauer, Baum, Caflisch, Crous-Vidal, Jost, Schneidler courtesy fundición tipográfica Bauer/Neufville Digital; Bayer, Behrens, G Noordzij © DACS 2005; Belwe, Berndal, J Burke, Cassandre, Chappell, Cochin, Dair, Diethelm, Dwiggins, Eckmann, Erbar, Excoffon, Frutiger, Ganeau, Garamond, Griffith, Gürtler, Hammer, Hartz, Hoefer, Jones, Kis [1], Koch, Meier, Mendoza, Menhart, Miedinger, PM Noordzij, Parker, Peignot, Ruzicka, Sassoon, R Stone, Tiemann, Tracy, Trump, Tschichold, Weiss [1], Zapf, Zapf von-Hesse © Linotype Library GmbH; Benton [2], Berlow, Pv Blokland, Frere-Jones [2], Highsmith, Rickner, Schwartz © The Font Bureau, Inc.; Bilak courtesy Peter Bilak; FE Blokland, Brand, G Unger courtesy Dutch Type Library; Ev Blokland [1] LettError; Boge courtesy Garrett Boge; Bosma, Carnase courtesy World Typeface Center Inc.; Boton [1], Gerstner, Holmes, Jaeger, Lange, Möllenstädt, Poppl, Post, Schneider, Wiebking courtesy Berthold Types; Boton [2] © International Typeface Corporation; Brignall, Usherwood © Bradbourne Publishing Ltd 2006; Brody © Fontworks UK Ltd; Bronkhorst courtesy Mark van Bronkhorst; C Burke courtesy Chris Burke; M Carter courtesy Matthew Carter; Connare courtesy Vincent Connare; Cooke courtesy Nick Cooke; Quay, Sack, Wilson [1] courtesy The Foundry/Foundry Types Ltd www.foundrytypes.co.uk; Deck, di Sciullo, courtesy Research Studios; F-A Didot, F Didot [2] © Napier University, Department of PMPC/Licensed via www.scran.ac.uk; Downer [1] courtesy John Downer; Downer [2], Fella, Heine, Licko, Makela, VanderLans courtesy Emigre Inc.; Fairbank courtesy Pennyroyal Press; Farey courtesy Times Newspapers Limitied/Dave Farey; Feliciano © Feliciano Type Foundry; Forsberg courtesy Castcraft Software Inc.; Frere-Jones [1], Hoefler © Hoefler & Frere Jones; Gills courtesy Michael Gills; Griffo © Peter Burnhill 2003, reproduced with permission, from Peter Burnhill, *Type spaces* (Hyphen Press); de Groot courtesy Lucas de Groot; Gutenberg courtesy National Library of Scotland; Hague courtesy Alias; Harvey courtesy Michael Harvey; Howes courtesy of Friends of St Bride Library; Hudson courtesy John Hudson; Hughes courtesy Rian Hughes; Jamra courtesy Mark Jamra; Enric Jardí courtesy Enric Jardí; Jenson, Malin © British Library; Keedy courtesy Jeffery Keedy; Klein © International TypeFounders, Inc.; Küster © Scangraphic Fonts; Lubalin courtesy of The Herb Lubalin Study Center of Design and Typography at The Cooper Union School of Art; Maag courtesy Bruno Maag; Mills courtesy Ross Mills, Newlyn courtesy Miles Newlyn; Parkinson © Parkinson Type Design; Pasternak © Bitstream Inc.; Porchez courtesy Jean François Porchez; Shinn courtesy Nick Shinn; Slimbach, Twombly, Veljovic © 1990–1995 Adobe Systems Incorporated. All rights reserved. Adobe, Charlemagne, Ex Ponto, Lithos, Minion and Trajan are registered trademarks of Adobe Systems Incorporated in the United States and other countries; Smeijers courtesy OurType; Smith courtesy Jason Smith; Spiekermann [2] courtesy Erik Spiekermann; S Stone [2] courtesy Sumner Stone; Storm courtesy Storm Type Foundry; Tankard courtesy Jeremy Tankard; Treacy courtesy Joseph D Treacy; Williams – Admark, Bulldog, Congress and Eurocrat are registered trade marks of Adrian Williams Deisgn Ltd, UK. Column is a trade mark of Adrian Williams Design Ltd, UK. The name Mercurius is a registered trade mark of Monotype Imaging, used under licence to Adrian Williams Design Ltd, UK.

IMPRINT

Published in North America by Yale University Press
P.O. Box 209040
New Haven
CT 06520-9040
U.S.A.
www.yalebooks.com

Copyright © text 2006
Neil Macmillan

This book was simultaneously published in London by Laurence King Publishing.

The moral right of the author has been asserted.

Thanks to Gordon Rookledge and Sarema Press (Publishers) Ltd for permission to draw on *Rookledge's International Handbook of Type Designers*.

Library of Congress Control Number: 2005936143

ISBN: 0-300-11151-7

Book design and additional picture research by Phil Baines & Catherine Dixon. Cover/titlepage photography Tim Marshall, art directed by the designers (after Alan Spain & Nelson Christmas, Pelican A43, 1966).

Printed in Hong Kong.